Limited Classical Reprint Library

COMMENTARY ON THE EPISTLES

TO THE

SEVEN CHURCHES IN ASIA

REVELATION II. III.

BY

RICHARD CHENEVIX TRENCH, D.D.

ARCHBISHOP

SIXTH EDITION

REVISED AND IMPROVED

Klock & Klock Christian Publishers
2527 GIRARD AVE. N.
MINNEAPOLIS, MINNESOTA 55411

Originally Published by
Kegan Paul, Trench, Trubner and Co. Ltd.
1897

Printed by Klock and Klock in the U.S.A.
1978 reprint

FOREWORD

Most Bible students are familiar with Trench's famous *Notes on the Parables of Our Lord* and its companion volume dealing with Christ's miracles. Others have derived great benefit from his book on *New Testament Synonyms,* and some of an older generation can still remember when his *Studies in the Gospels* could be purchased in Christian bookstores. Few, however, are aware of the rich insights contained in his *Commentary on the Epistles to the Seven Churches of Asia.*

In this treatment of Revelation 2 and 3 (chapter 1 is covered in the Introduction), R. C. Trench exhibits the judicious scholarship for which he earned renown in the three principal cities of the British Isles in which he worked (viz., Oxford, Cambridge, and Dublin). His handling of the text is conservative and his painstaking exegesis helps readers probe the meaning and message of each letter.

It may validly be said that, because Dr. Trench wrote his commentary before Sir William Ramsay published his *Letters to the Seven Churches,* his work lacks much of the historical data for which the work by Ramsay was justly famous. Dr. Trench's strength lies in his exemplary treatment of the Greek text, and in this respect his work on this portion of Scripture is well deserving of serious consideration. It should also be remembered that as a result of his extensive exposure to classical literature, Dr. Trench had developed an intuitive awareness of the milieu of Asiatic Turkey in the first century of the Christian era. Many of his early beliefs were corroborated by Ramsay years later.

Readers will be blessed by Dr. Trench's delightful style and enriching devotional thoughts. Furthermore, as a result of their study of his *Commentary on the Epistles to the Seven Churches,* they will be better prepared to interpret these letters and apply their message to their lives.

Cyril J. Barber

PREFACE

IN PUBLISHING this volume I at length accomplish, however imperfectly, a wish which I have cherished for many years. During the time that I fulfilled my pleasant labours at King's College, I lectured three times to the theological students there on these seven Epistles; and the lectures to them delivered constitute the groundwork of the present volume, though much has been added, and some little changed, in the final revision which I have given to my work before venturing to challenge a larger audience for it. I confess that each time I have gone over these Epistles I have become more conscious of the manifold difficulties which they present; and more than once have been half disposed not to offer to others, in the way of interpretation of them, what has so little satisfied myself. I have not, however, held my hand. There has ever seemed to me a very useful warning contained in that German proverb which says, 'The best is oftentimes the enemy of the good;' and, without claiming for an instant that title of *good* for *my* book, I do not doubt that many a good book has remained unwritten, or, perhaps, being written, has remained unpublished, because there floated before the mind's eye of the author, or possible author, the ideal of a better or a best, which has put him out of all conceit with his good; meanwhile some other, having no ideal at all before him, either to stimulate or to repress, steps in and poorly fills the place which the other would have filled, if not excellently, yet reasonably, well.

But indeed, if there is much in the difficulties with which these Epistles abound to repel and deter, there is much also in these same difficulties to allure and attract. And not in these only. The number of aspects in which they present themselves to us as full of interest is extraordinary.

For example, the points of peculiar attraction which they offer to the student of ecclesiastical history are many. Who are these Angels of the Churches? What do we learn from their evident preëminence in their several Churches, about the government and constitution of the Church in the later apostolic times? or is it lawful to draw any conclusions? Again, was there a body of heretics actually bearing the name of Nicolaitans in the times of St. John? And those that had the doctrine of Balaam, and the followers of the woman Jezebel, with what heretics mentioned elsewhere shall we identify these? Or, once more, what is the worth of that historico-prophetical scheme of interpretation adopted by

our own Joseph Mede and Henry More, and many others
down even to the present day; who see in these seven
Epistles the mystery of the whole evolution of the Church
from the days of the Apostles to the close of the present
dispensation? Was this so intended by the Spirit? or
is it only a dream and fancy of men?

Nor less is there a strong attraction in these Epistles
for those who occupy themselves with questions of pure
exegesis, from the fact of so many unsolved, or imperfectly solved, problems of interpretation being found in
them. It is seldom within so small a compass that so
many questions to which no answer with perfect confidence can be given, occur. What, for instance, is the
exact meaning, and what the etymology, of χαλκολίβανος
(i. 15; ii. 18)? what the interpretation of the 'white
stone' with the new name written upon it (ii. 17)? why
is Pergamum called 'Satan's seat' (ii. 13)? with many
other questions of the same kind.

Nor can any one, I think, attentively studying, fail to
be struck with what one might venture to call the entire
originality of these seven Epistles, their entire unlikeness,
in some points at least, to anything else in Scripture.
Contemplate, for instance, the titles of Christ here, 'the
Amen,' 'the Faithful and True Witness,' 'the Beginning
of the Creation of God,' 'He that hath the seven Spirits
of God,' and others which I might name. While the
analogy of faith is perfectly preserved, while there is no

difficulty in harmonizing what is here taught of Christ's
person and offices with that which is taught elsewhere,
yet how wholly new a series of titles are these. It is the
same with the promises; some, it is true, as 'the tree of
life,' 'the crown of life,' 'the new name,' have been
anticipated in other parts of Scripture, yet how many
appear here for the first time; and set forth what
Augustine so grandly calls, 'beatæ vitæ magna secreta,'
under aspects as novel as they are animating and allur-
ing; such are the 'hidden manna,' the 'white stone,'
the 'white raiment,' the 'pillar in the temple of God,'
'the morning star.' And very striking, as combined
with this originality, with this free movement of the
Spirit here, is the strict and rigid symmetrical arrangement of these Epistles, the way in which they are all
laid out upon the same plan, distributed according to
exactly the same ever-recurring laws. The surprise which
we feel on tracing this for the first time, is similar to
that which overtakes one who, attempting any thing like
a critical study of the Psalms, discovers the rigorous laws
to which, so far as concerns the form, they are for the
most part submitted, or rather, which they have imposed
on themselves, and to which they delight to conform.

Then, once more, the purely theological interest of
these Epistles is great. I have already referred to the
titles of Christ, the entirely novel aspects under which
the glory of the Son of God is here set forth. But they

have another and profounder interest. Assuredly there is enough in these two chapters alone to render Arianism entirely untenable by any one who, admitting their authority, should consent to be bound in their interpretation by the ordinary rules of fairness and truth. On this matter I have several times dwelt in the course of my interpretation.

And, finally, the practical interest of these Epistles in their bearing on the whole pastoral and ministerial work is extreme. It is recorded of the admirable Bengel that it was his wont above all things to recommend the study of these Epistles to youthful ministers of Christ's Word and Sacraments. And indeed to them they are full of teaching, of the most solemn warning, of the strongest encouragement. We learn from these Epistles the extent to which the spiritual condition of a Church is dependent upon that of its pastors; the guilt, not merely of teaching, but of allowing, error; how there may be united much and real zeal for the form of sound words with a lamentable decay of the spirit of love; or, on the other hand, many works and active ministries of love, with only too languid a zeal for the truth once delivered; with innumerable lessons more. For one who has undertaken the awful ministry of souls, I know almost nothing in Scripture so searching, no threatenings so alarming, no promises so comfortable, as are some which these Epistles contain.

Surely, if all this be so, it is very much to be re-
gretted that, while every chapter of every other book of
the New Testament is set forth to be read in the Church,
and, wherever there is daily service, is read in the Church,
three times in the year, and some, or portions of some,
are read oftener there, while even of the Apocalypse
itself two chapters and portions of others have been
admitted into the calendar, under no circumstances whatever can the second and third chapter ever be heard in
the congregation. Any one who knows, or at all guesses,
how small the amount of the private reading of the Scriptures among our people, and the extent, therefore, to
which the stated public reading in the congregation is
the source of whatever knowledge of it the great mass of
our people possess, the means by which they are at all
leavened by it, must deeply regret that chapters so rich
in doctrine, in exhortation, in reproofs, in promises, should
thus be withheld from them. Certainly, if at any time a
reconsideration of the portions of Scripture appointed to
be read in the Church should find place, the slight cast
on these chapters, and in them on the Apocalypse itself,
with the injury inflicted on the people by their total
omission, ought not to be allowed to continue.[1]

Whether the attempt here made to draw out some of

---

[1] It need hardly be observed, that what I complain of here has
for several years ceased to be the fact.—*Note to the fourth edition*,
1883.

the riches contained in this portion of God's Word may
have any interest for others, I know not: but for myself
this volume must ever retain a very solemn interest.
Besides the serious solemnity of giving any work that
professes to be a work for God into the hands of men, I
can never disconnect this book from two great sorrows
which fell on me, while it was preparing for, and passing
through, the press; sorrows which have left me far
poorer than before; and yet, I would humbly hope, richer
too, if better able to speak to others of truths whose price
and value has been brought home with new power to
myself; if theology has been thus more closely connected
for me with life, and with life's toil and burden, from
which it is ever in danger of being dissociated and
divorced. It is my earnest hope that so it may prove;
and in this hope I humbly commend my book, with all
its shortcomings, to Him who can alone make it profit-
able to any.

DEANERY, WESTMINSTER:
    July 31, 1861.

CONTENTS

COMMENTARY

ON THE

EPISTLES TO THE SEVEN CHURCHES IN ASIA.

REVELATION II. III.

INTRODUCTION, REV. i. 4–20.

THE QUESTION, *Why* we enter the wondrous temple of this
Book by the vestibule of these seven Epistles, what the
exact relation in which they stand to the other parts of
the Apocalypse, or again, the question of its parts to the
whole, has not, within my knowledge, been ever very
satisfactorily answered. So far from receiving an answer, to most interpreters the question is one which
hardly seems to have so much as presented itself at all.
And yet a thoughtful student of God's Word might here
fitly pause, and reverently inquire *why* this Book should
have this introduction. We are sure that Scripture, as it
has every other perfection, so it must have the perfection
of *form* and *proportion*; while yet it does not seem very
easy to trace what is the relation here between these
two :—the Book prophetic, the introduction for the most
part historic; the Book universal in its character, including the whole Church in the range of its vision, the

B

introductory Epistles having to do with separate and
single Churches, and with the details of their inner
spiritual condition. I will not affirm that Bengel's explanation exhausts the whole matter, but it appears to me
the best which has been offered: 'Gravissima vii. harum
Epistolarum causa est. Populus legem in Sinai suscep-
turus, prius sanctificabatur : idem operâ Johannis Baptistæ'
cum immineret regnum Dei, per pœnitentiam præpara-
batur ; nunc Ecclesia Christiana ad tantam Revelationem
digne suscipiendam his instruitur epistolis. Id enim
agitur ut malos, prius admonitos, et mala ex medio sui
exterminans, ipsa cum suâ posteritate ad hoc pretiosissimum
depositum, hanc tanti momenti revelationem recte amplec-
tendam asservandamque, ad eventus maximos spectandos,
et fructus uberrimos percipiendos, plagasque effugiendas
præparetur, inspersis in ipsas epistolas revelationis reliquæ
stricturis fulgidissimis, ad attentionem excitandam, et
viam intelligentiæ muniendam aptissimis : ecclesiæque per
pœnitentiam renovatio, ut par est, conspectui iridis præ-
mittitur' (iv. 3).

Ver. 4.   '*John to the seven Churches*[1] *in Asia.*'—So
far as the Apocalypse is allowed to witness for its own
authorship, we find in these words a strong internal evidence that we possess in it an authentic work of St. John.
The writer avouches himself as '*John*;' but, though there
may have been Johns many in the Church at this time,
John the Presbyter and others, still it is well-nigh impossible to conceive any other but John *the Apostle* who
would have named himself by this single name, with no

---

[1] The words, '*which are,*' finding here a place in most modern
editions of our Authorized Version, have no place in the exemplar
edition of 1611.

further style or addition. We instinctively feel that for any other there would have been here an affectation of humility, veiling a most real arrogance, in the very plainness of this title. Who else, without arrogance, could have taken for granted that the bare mention of his name was sufficient to ensure his recognition, or that he had a right to appropriate this name in so absolute a manner as his own? The unique position in the Church of St. John, the beloved Apostle, and now the sole surviving Apostle, the one remaining link between the faithful of that time and of the human lifetime of their Lord, abundantly justified in him what would have ill become any other; just as a king or queen, as representative persons in a nation, fitly sign by their Christian names only, but none beside them. Thus there are many at this day who bear the name of Victoria, but only one who signs herself by this and no other name. Despite of all which has been urged to avoid this conclusion, it is assuredly either John Apostle and Evangelist, who writes the Apocalypse; or one who, assuming his title and style, desires to pass himself off as John—in other words a *falsarius*. Are the opposers of St. John's authorship of this Book prepared for the alternative?

Of the seven Churches which St. John addresses here there will be better opportunity of speaking in particular when we reach the nominal enumeration of them (ver. 11); but as only here they are described as Churches '*in Asia*,' it may be well worth while to say something of the '*Asia*' which is intended. We may trace two opposite movements going on in the names of countries, analogous to like move-ments which are continually finding place in other words. Sometimes they grow more and more inclusive, are applied in their later use to far wider tracts of the world than

they were in their earlier. It is thus with the name
'Italy.' Designating at one time only the extreme
southern point of the central peninsula of Europe, the
name crept on and up, till in the time of Augustus it
obtained the meaning which it has ever since retained,
including all within the Alps. So too 'Germany' was once
no more than a little corner on the left bank of the lower
Rhine (Grimm, *Gesch. der Deutschen Sprache*, p. 785).
'France,' 'Burgundy,' 'Switzerland,' 'Holland' are all later
examples of the same gradual extension of meaning which
names of countries have undergone. Other names, on the
contrary, once of the widest reach, gradually contract their
meaning, till in the end they designate no more than a
minute fraction of all that which they designated at the beginning. 'Asia' furnishes a good example of this. In the
New Testament, as generally in the language of men when
the New Testament was written, 'Asia' meant not what
it now means for us, and had once meant for the Greeks,
one namely of the three great continents of the old world
(Æschylus, *Prom. Vinct.* 412 ; Pindar, *Olymp.* vii. 18 ;
Herodotus, iv. 38), nor yet even that region which geo-
graphers about the fourth century of our era began to call
'Asia Minor ;' but a strip of the western sea-board containing hardly a third portion of this (cf. 1 Pet. i. 1 ; Acts ii. 9 ;
vi. 9). 'Asia vestra,' says Cicero (*Pro Flacc.* 27), addressing
some Asiatics, 'constat ex Phrygiâ, Mysiâ, Cariâ, Lydiâ ;'
its limits being nearly identical with those of the kingdom
which Attalus III. bequeathed (B.C. 133) to the Roman
people (see Wieseler, *Chronol.* p. 31–35). Take 'Asia' in
this sense, and there may be little or no exaggeration in the
words of the Ephesian silversmith, that 'almost throughout all Asia' Paul had turned away much people from the
service of idols (Acts xix. 26 ; cf. ver. 10) ; words which must

seem to exceed even the limits of an angry hyperbole to
those not acquainted with this restricted use of the term.
On the history of the word 'Asia' and what at different
times it was taken to include or exclude, see an excellent
note in Archdeacon Lee on Rev. i. 4, in the *Speaker's
Commentary*.

'*Grace be unto you, and peace, from Him which is
and which was, and which is to come.*'—This opening
salutation may fitly remind us (for in reading the Apocalypse we are often in danger of forgetting it), that the
Book is an Epistle, that, besides containing within its bosom those seven briefer Epistles addressed severally to the
seven Churches in particular, it is itself an Epistle addressed
to them as a whole, and as representing in their mystic
unity all the Churches, or the whole Church (ii. 7, 11, 23, &c.).
Of this larger Epistle, namely the Apocalypse itself, these
seven Churches are the original receivers; not as having
a nearer or greater interest in it than any other portion of
the Universal Church; though as members of that Church
they have an interest in it as near and great as can be
conceived (i. 3; xxii. 18, 19); but on account of this their
representative character, of which there will be occasion
presently to speak.   And being such an Epistle, it opens
with the most frequently recurring apostolic salutation:
'*Grace and peace.*'   This is the constant salutation of St.
Paul (Rom. i. 7; 1 Cor. i. 3, &c.), with only the exception
of his two Epistles to Timothy, where 'mercy' finds place
between 'grace and peace' (cf. 2 John 3); the salutation
also of St. Peter in both his Epistles; while St. James
employs the less distinctively Christian 'greeting' (χαίρειν,
i. 1; cf. Acts xxiii. 26).—On the departure from the ordinary rules of grammar, and apparent violation of them
in the words, ἀπὸ ὁ ὤν, καὶ ὁ ἦν, καὶ ὁ ἐρχόμενος, there

will presently be something more to say. Doubtless
the immutability of God, 'the same yesterday, and
to-day, and for ever' (Heb. xiii. 8), is intended to be
expressed in this immutability of the name of God, in this
absolute resistance to change or even modification which
that name here presents. ' I am the Lord ; I change not'
(Mal. iii. 6), this is what is here declared; and there could
be no stronger consolation for the faithful than thus to be
reminded that He who is from everlasting to everlasting,
'with whom is no variableness, neither shadow of turning'
(Jam. i. 17), was on their side; how then should they 'be
afraid of a man that shall die, and the son of man which
shall be made as grass' (Isai. li. 12, 13)?

And yet we must not understand the words, ' *and which
is to come*,' as though they declared the 'æternitas a parte
post' in the same way as ' *which was*' expresses the 'æternitas a parte *ante*.' It is difficult to understand how so
many should assume without further question that ὁ ἐρχόμενος here is = ὁ ἐσόμενος, and that thus we have the eternity of God expressed here, so far as it can be expressed,
in forms of time : ' He who was, and is, *and shall be*.' On
the inadequacy and imperfection of all such language
see Plato, *Timæus*, 38 A. But how ὁ ἐρχόνενος should
ever have this significance it is hard to perceive. There is
a certain ambiguity about our translation ; it cannot be
accused of incorrectness ; yet, on the other hand, one does
not feel sure that when our Translators rendered, ' *which
is to come*,' they did not mean ' *which is to be*.' The
Rheims, which is here kept right by the Vulgate ('et qui
venturus est'), so renders the words as to exclude ambiguity, ' *and which shall come*.' If any urge that ' *which
is, and which was*,' present and past, require to be completed with a future, ' *and which shall* be,' to this it may

be replied, that plainly they do not require to be so completed, seeing that at xi. 17, no such complement finds
place; for the words καὶ ὁ ἐρχόμενος have no right to a
place there in the text; and in strong confirmation of the
other interpretation, they are left out exactly because,
according to it, they would now be inappropriate; for He
is there contemplated as actually *having come* (εἴληφας τὴν
δύναμίν σου). And then, on the other hand, there is every
thing to recommend the grammatical interpretation. What
is the key-note to this whole Book? Surely it is, 'Mara-
natha,' 'Our Lord cometh.' The world seems to have all
things its own way, to kill my servants; but I come
quickly.' With this announcement the Book begins, i. 7;
with this it ends, xxii. 7, 12, 20; and this is a constantly
recurring note through it all, ii. 5, 16; iii. 11; vi. 17;
xi. 18; xiv. 7; xvi. 15; xviii. 20. It is Christ's word of
comfort, or, where they need it, of warning, to his friends;
of terror to his foes. We may say, indeed, that in some
sort ὁ ἐρχόμενος is a proper name of our Lord (Matt. xi. 3;
Luke vii. 19, 20; Heb. x. 37; John i. 15, 27; cf. Mal. iii.
1; Hab. ii. 3). Delitzsch: 'Es heisst ὁ ἐρχόμενος, nicht
ἐλευσόμενος, denn seit seiner Auffahrt ist Er und sein
Tag fort und fort im Kommen begriffen, so dass immer
von seiner Nähe die Rede seyn kann, und seine Erscheinung
jederzeit zu erwarten ist.' Origen further notes the evidence which this language, rightly interpreted, yields for
the equal divinity of the Son with the Father (*De Princ.*
§ 10): 'Ut autem unam et eandem omnipotentiam Patris
ac Filii esse cognoscas, audi hoc modo Joannem in Apocalypsi dicentem, Hæc dicit Dominus Deus, qui est, et qui
erat, et qui venturus est, Omnipotens. Qui enim venturus
est, quis est alius nisi Christus?' Compare Hengstenberg,
Authentie des Pentateuches, vol. i. pp. 236–250.—There

should be no comma dividing ' *which is* ' from the clause
following, ' *and which was.*' These rather form one sentence, which is to be balanced with the other, ' *and which
is to come.*' How the Seer himself interprets the last
clause of this description is clear from Rev. ii. 17, where
they find no place in the text (they are omitted rightly in
the R. V.) ; and why omitted ? because they belong to a
time when Christ had already come.

' *And from the seven Spirits which are before his throne.*'
—-Compare iii. 1 ; iv. 5 ; v. 6. Some have understood
by ' *the seven Spirits,*' the seven principal Angels, the
heavenly realities of which ' the seven princes of Persia
and Media, which saw the king's face, and which sat the
first in the kingdom ' (Esth. i. 14), the ' seven counsellors '
(Ezra vii. 14), were a kind of earthly copy. Room for
these seven Angels had been found in the later Jewish
angelology (Tob. xii. 15), and the seal of allowance set on
the number seven in this very Book (Rev. viii. 2). And
these have not been merely Roman Catholic expositors,
such as Bossuet and Ribera, tempted to this interpretation
by their zeal to find some support somewhere for the
worshipping of Angels; but others with no such temptations, as Beza, Hammond, Mede (in a sermon on Zech. iv.
10, *Works*, 1672, p. 40. cf. pp. 833, 908) ; and Ewald.
They claim some of the Fathers for predecessors in the
same line of interpretation; as Hilary, for example (*Tract.
in Ps.* 118, *Lit.* 21, § 5). Clement of Alexandria is also
claimed by Hammond ; but neither in the passage cited,
nor in the context (*Strom.* vi. 16), can I find that he affirms
anything of the kind. But this interpretation, which after
all is that of a small minority either of ancients or moderns,
must be rejected without hesitation. Angels, often as they
are mentioned in this Book, are never called ' Spirits.' So

also, in testimony of their ministering condition, their
creaturely state, they always *stand* (Rev. viii. 2; Luke i. 19;
1 Kin. xxii. 19, 21), but the Spirits '*are*' (ἐστίν) before
the throne. Again, how is it possible to conceive the Apostle
desiring ' *grace and peace* ' to the Church from the Angels,
let them be the chiefest Angels which are, or from any but
from God alone, who is the God of *all* grace? Or how can
we imagine Angels, created beings, interposed here between
the Father and the Son, and thus set as upon an equal
level with Them; the Holy Ghost meanwhile being passed
by, as according to this interpretation He must be, in this
solemn salutation of the Churches? Where, again, would
be the singular glory claimed for Himself by the Son in
those words, ' *He that hath the seven Spirits of God* ' (iii. 1)?
what transcendent prerogative in the fact that these
Angels, with all other created things, were within his
dominion?

There can then be no serious controversy on this point.
By ' *the seven Spirits* ' we must understand, not indeed the
sevenfold operations of the Holy Ghost, but the Holy
Ghost sevenfold in his operations; ' that doth his sevenfold gifts impart.' Neither need there be any difficulty in
reconciling this interpretation, as Mede urges, with the
doctrine of his personality. It is only that He is regarded
here not so much in his personal unity as in his manifold
energies; just as light, being one, does yet in the prism
separate itself into its seven colours; for ' there are diver-
sities of gifts, but the same Spirit ' (1 Cor. xii. 4). The
matter could not be put better than by Richard of St.
Victor: ' Et a septem Spiritibus, id est, a septiformi
Spiritu, qui simplex quidem est per naturam, septiformis
per gratiam; ' and compare Delitzsch, *Bibl. Psychologie*,
pp. 34, 147. The manifold gifts, operations, energies of

the Holy Ghost are here represented under the number
seven, being, as it is, the number of completeness in the
Church. We have anticipations of this in the Old Testament. When the prophet Isaiah would describe how the
Spirit should be given not by measure to Him whose name
is ' The Branch,' the enumeration of the gifts is sevenfold
(xi. 2); and the seven eyes which rest upon the stone
which the Lord has laid can mean nothing else but this
(Zech. iii. 9. cf. iv. 10; Rev. v. 6). On the number ' seven,'
and its significance in Scripture and elsewhere, above all
in this Book, there will be something to be said presently.

Ver. 5. '*And from Jesus Christ, who is the faithful
Witness.*'—In the last of these seven Epistles He calls
Himself ' the faithful and true Witness' (iii. 14); as,
therefore, we shall meet these words again, and they will
be there more conveniently dealt with, I shall content myself now with quoting Richard of St. Victor's noble comment
upon them : ' Testis fidelis, quia de omnibus quæ per Eum
testificanda erant in mundo testimonium fidele perhibuit.
Testis fidelis, quia quæcunque audivit a Patre fideliter dis-
cipulis suis nota fecit. Testis fidelis, quia viam Dei in
veritate docuit, nec Ei cura de aliquo fuit, nec personas
hominum respexit. Testis fidelis, quia reprobis damna-
tionem, et electis salvationem nunciavit. Testis fidelis, quia
veritatem quam verbis docuit, miraculis confirmavit. Testis
fidelis, quia testimonium Sibi a Patre nec in morte negavit.
Testis fidelis, quia de operibus malorum et bonorum in die
judicii testimonium verum dabit.'—A reference to the
original, where the nominative ὁ μάρτυς ὁ πιστός is in
apposition to the genitive Ἰησοῦ Χριστοῦ, will show that
we have here one of the many departures from the
ordinary grammatical construction, with which this Book
abounds. The officious emendations of transcribers have

caused very many of these, though not this one, to disappear from our received text; but in any critical edition of the Greek original the multitude of such is one of the most remarkable of the external features of the Book. To regard them, which some have done, as evidences of St. John's helplessness in the management of Greek, his ' Unbeholfenheit' therein, as Ewald terms it, is to regard them altogether from a wrong point of view. Thus, to take the case immediately before us, it is not this which is to explain anything anomalous and unusual here, but rather that the doctrinal interest here overbears the grammatical. Düsterdieck very well : ' Das Gewicht der Vorstellungen selbst durchbricht die Schranken der regelrechten Form ; die abrupte Redeweise hebt die gewaltige Selbstständigkeit aller drei Prädicate.' At all costs that all-important ὁ μάρτυς ὁ πιστός, with the other two titles of the Lord which follow, shall be maintained in the dignity and emphasis of the *casus rectus*. Compare xiv. 12 ; and xx. 2, where ὁ ὄφις ὁ ἀρχαῖος (changed in the received text into τὸν ὄφιν τὸν ἀρχαῖον), is in like manner in apposition to τὸν δράκοντα ; but above all, and as making quite clear that St. John adopted these constructions with his eyes open, and for a distinct purpose, the remarkable ἀπὸ ὁ ὢν κ. τ. λ. of the verse preceding that now under consideration.[1]

' *And the first begotten of the dead.*'—Cf. Col. i. 18, where very nearly the same language occurs, and the same title is given to the Lord : ὁ πρωτότοκος τῶν νεκρῶν here, πρωτότοκος ἐκ τῶν νεκρῶν there. The phrases are not precisely identical in meaning ; and even were they so,

---

[1] There is a good discussion on these grammatical anomalies in the Apocalypse in Lücke's *Einleitung zur Offenb.* 2d edit. pp. 458–464. For an exactly parallel case in English, and from the same motives, see *Paradise Lost*, vi. 900.

the suggestion of Hengstenberg, that St. John here builds upon St. Paul, setting his seal to the prior Apostle's word, seems to me highly unnatural. Glorious as this language is, who does not feel how easily two Apostles, quite independent of one another, might have arrived at it to express the same blessed truth? Christ is indeed ' *the first begotten of the dead*,' notwithstanding that such raisings from the grave as that of the widow's son, and Jairus's daughter, and Lazarus, and his who revived at the touch of Elisha's bones (2 Kin. xiii. 21), went before. ' None of them could be truly said to be " begotten from the dead," but rather begotten to die again; for to be born and begotten from the dead includes an everlasting freedom from the power and approach of death' (Jackson): There was for them no repeal of the sentence of death, but a respite only; not to say that even during their period of respite they carried about with them a body of death. Christ first so rose from the dead, that He left death for ever behind Him; did not, and could not, die any more (Rom. vi. 9); in this respect was ' the first-fruits of them that slept ' (1 Cor. xv. 20, 23), ' the Prince of life ' (Acts iii. 15). Alcuin: ' Primogenitus ideo dicitur quia nullus ante Ipsum non moriturus surrexit.' In this ' *first begotten of the dead*' (or ' first born *from* the dead,' as it is at Col. i. 18), I do not see the image of the grave as the womb that bare Him (λύσας τὰς ὠδῖνας τοῦ θανάτου, Acts ii. 24); but, remembering how often τίκτειν = γεννᾶν, I should rather put this passage in connexion with Ps. ii. 7, ' Thou art my Son; this day have I begotten thee.' It will doubtless be remembered that St. Paul (Acts xiii. 33; cf. Heb. i. 5) claims the fulfilment of these words not in the eternal generation before all time of the Son; still less in his human conception in the Blessed Virgin's womb; but

rather in his resurrection from the dead; 'declared to
be the Son of God with power by the resurrection from
the dead' (Rom. i. 4). On that verse in Ps. ii., and with
reference to Acts xiii. 32, Hilary (the depth and theological value of whose commentaries on Scripture seem to me
at this day very imperfectly recognized), has these words :
' Filius meus es Tu, Ego hodie genui Te ; non ad Virginis
partum, neque ad eam quæ ante tempora est generationem,
sed ad primogenitum ex mortuis pertinere apostolica auc-
toritas est.' To Him first, to Him above all others, God
said on that day when He raised Him from the dead,
and gave Him glory, ' Thou art my Son ; this day have I
begotten Thee.'

'*And the Prince of the kings of the earth.*'—A manifest reference to Ps. ii. 2, where the 'kings of the earth '
(cf. Rev. vi. 15, for the same phrase used in the same
sense) appear in open rebellion against the Christ of God;
cf. Acts iv. 26 ; Ps. cx. 5 ; lxxxix. 27 ; Isai. lii. 15 ; Matt.
xxviii. 18. Such a ' *Prince of the kings of the earth* ' He
becomes in the exaltation which follows on his humiliation,
and which is directly connected with it (Phil. ii. 9 ; Ps.
lxxxix. 27); and shows Himself such at his glorious coming, as set forth in the later parts of this Book, ' Lord of
lords, and King of kings' (xvii. 14 ; xix. 16) ; breaking in
pieces all of those ' *kings of the earth* ' who set themselves
in battle array against Him, receiving the homage of all
who are wise in time (Ps. ii. 10-12), and bring their glory
and honour to lay them at his feet, and to receive them
back at his hands (Rev. xxi. 24).

' *Unto Him that hath loved us, and washed us from our
sins in his own blood.*'—The words are richer still in comfort, when we read, as we ought, ἀγαπῶντι and not
ἀγαπήσαντι : ' *Unto Him that loveth us,*' whose love rests

evermore on his redeemed. There is in the theology of
the Greek Church an old and often-recurring play on the
words λύτρον and λουτρόν, words so nearly allied in sound,
and both expressing so well, though under images entirely
diverse, the central benefits which redound to us through
the sacrifice of the death of Christ. It is indeed older
than this, and is implicitly involved in the etymology of
Apollo, which Plato, in jest or in earnest, puts into the
mouth of Socrates (*Cratylus*, 405 B) : ὁ ἀπολούων τε καὶ
ἀπολύων τῶν κακῶν, these κακά being impurities of the
body and of the soul. This near resemblance between
λύειν and λούειν has given rise to a very interesting variety
of readings here. Whichever reading we adopt, λύσαντι
or λούσαντι, '*who hath released us*,' or '*who hath washed
us*,' the words yield a beautiful meaning, as in either case
they link themselves on to a whole circle of imagery already
hallowed and consecrated by Scripture use. If we adopt
λύσαντι, as does the R. V., the passage connects itself
then with all those which speak of Christ having given
Himself as a λύτρον (Matt. xx. 28), as an ἀντίλυτρον for
us (I Tim. ii. 6. cf. I Pet. i. 18 ; Heb. ix. 12); as redeem-
ing or purchasing us (Gal. iii. 13 ; iv. 5 ; Rev. v. 9 ; xiv.
3, 4); and somewhat more remotely with as many as
describe the condition of sin as a condition of bondage,
sinners as servants of sin (John vi. 17, 20 ; viii. 34 ;
2 Pet. ii. 19), and Christ as having obtained freedom for
us (John viii. 33, 36 ; Rom. viii. 21 ; Gal. v. 1). If on
the other hand we read λούσαντι, then the passage connects itself with such other as Ps. li. 4 ; Isai. i. 16, 18 ;
Ezek. xxxvi. 25 ; Rev. vii. 14 ; as Acts xxii. 16 ; Ephes.
v. 26 ; Tit. iii. 5 ; so, too, with all those which describe the
καθαρίζειν as the object (Eph. v. 26 ; Tit. ii. 14 ; Heb.
ix. 14), the καθαρισμός as the fruit, of Christ's death

(Heb. i. 3; 2 Pet. i. 9); and somewhat more remotely
with as many as under types of the Levitical law set
forth the benefits of this heavenly washing (Num. xix.
17-21). The weight of *external* evidence is so nearly
balanced that it is very difficult to say on which side it
predominates. The œquilibrium of the scale is clearly
marked by the way in which the critical editions are
divided here. The R. V. which, as we have seen, has
adopted λύσαντι, has yet thought it right to append
these words, 'Many authorities, some ancient, read λούσαντι.' Keeping in view the poetic character of this
Book, λούσαντι certainly seems preferable to the comparatively prosaic λύσαντι. Then, too, while it is quite true
that redemption may be contemplated as a λύειν ἐν τῷ
αἵματι, by better right, and with imagery livelier still, it
may be set forth as a λούειν ἐν τῷ αἵματι. Nor can it be
denied, if we interpret this Book, as clearly we ought,
from itself rather than from any other part even of Scripture itself, that Rev. vii. 14 points strongly this way.

Ver. 6. '*And hath made us kings and priests unto
God and his Father.*'—Or rather, and according to the
reading which must be preferred, '*And hath made us a
kingdom* [ἐποίησεν ἡμᾶς βασιλείαν], *priests unto God
and his Father*' ('Et fecit nos *regnum*, [et] sacerdotes
Deo,' Vulgate). There is a certain apparent inconcinnity
in the abstract βασιλείαν joined with the concrete ἱερεῖς,
but there can be no question about the reading, and the
meaning remains exactly the same; except, indeed, that
instead of the emphasis being equally distributed between
the two words, the larger portion of it now falls on the
first; and this agrees with the prominence given to the
reigning of the saints in this Book (v. 10; xx. 4, 6; xxii.
5. cf. Dan. vii. 18, 22).—The royal priesthood of the re-

deemed (see Exod. xix. 6; 1 Pet. ii. 9) flows out of the
royal priesthood of the Redeemer, a Priest for ever after
the order of Melchizedek (Ps. cx. 4; Zech. vi. 13; Heb. v.
10; vii. 17). That the whole number of the redeemed
shall in the world of glory have been made '*priests unto
God*' is the analogue as regards persons to the new Jerusalem being without temple, or, in other words, being all
temple, which is declared further on (xxi. 22; cf. Isai. iv.
5, 6). It is the abolition of every distinction between
holy and profane (Zech. xiv. 20, 21), nearer and more
remote from God, not through all being henceforward profane, which will be Antichrist's reconciliation of the con-
tradictions between the flesh and the spirit, but through
all being henceforth holy, all being brought the nearest
whereof it is capable, to God.

'*To Him be glory and dominion for ever and ever.
Amen.*'—A few words on the doxologies, or ascriptions of
glory to God, which are found in the New Testament, and
in which the Book of Revelation is pre-eminently rich, may
here fitly find place. Great variety reigns in these. Some
are much fuller than others; nor is this the only way in
which they assert their liberty, and make plain that they
are not restricted to any fixed words or order of words.
Not seldom the doxology is single; thus at Rom. xi. 36;
xvi. 27; at both which places δόξα by itself comprehends
all of glorious which is ascribed to God; while at Rev. vii.
10, σωτηρία stands single in the same way. Sometimes it
is twofold: thus, at 1 Tim. i. 17, τιμή and δόξα: at 1 Pet.
iv. 11, δόξα and κράτος: at v. 11 and at Rev. v. 13, the
same; at 1 Tim. vi. 16, τιμή and κράτος. We have next
the threefold ascription. Of this we have an example at
Rev. xix. 1, σωτηρία, δόξα and δύναμις, and another at
Rev. iv. 11. Sometimes the doxology is fourfold: thus

at Rev. v. 13, εὐλογία, τιμή, δόξα, κράτος : and again at Jude 25, δόξα, μεγαλωσύνη, κράτος, ἐξουσία. Sometimes the ascription is sevenfold. It is so at Rev. v. 12 : δύναμις, πλοῦτος, σοφία, εὐχαριστία, τιμή, δόξα, εὐλογία ; and again at vii. 12 ; with a noticeable change in the succession of the words, as well as the introduction of a new word in each : εὐλογία, δόξα, σοφία, εὐχαριστία, τιμή, δύναμις, ἰσχύς. When we count up these, and the frequency of their several recurrence, δόξα, which St. Basil does but poorly define as ὁ ἀπὸ πολλῶν ἔπαινος, appears, as might be expected, the oftenest—no less than ten times : τιμή, six times ; κράτος, as many ; δύναμις, three times ; εὐλογία, as often ; σοφία, twice ; εὐχαριστία, as often ; σωτηρία, μεγαλωσύνη, ἐξουσία, πλοῦτος, ἰσχύς, each of these but once.[1] A study of doxological words, or of words doxologically used, with an accurate comparison of them one with the other, would very amply repay the pains bestowed upon it ; above all as it served to remind us of the prominence which the doxological element assumes in the highest worship of the Church, the very subordinate place which it oftentimes takes in ours. We can perhaps make our requests known unto God ; and this is well, for it is prayer ; but to give glory to God, quite apart from anything to be directly gotten by ourselves in return, to give thanks to Him for his great glory, this is better, for it is adoration ; but if better, it is rarer too.

Ver. 7. '*Behold, He cometh with clouds*,' or '*with the clouds*.'—The constant recurrence of this language in all descriptions of our Lord's second advent is very remarkable (Dan. vii. 13 ; Matt. xxiv. 30 ; xxvi. 64 ; Mark xiv.

---

[1] In the doxology at 1 Chron. xxix. 11, 12, the only one which I know of with a fivefold ascription, three terms, καύχημα, νίκη, δυναστεία, not found in any of those of the N. T., occur.

C

62), and all the meaning of the announcement will scarcely
be attained till that great day of the Lord shall have
itself arrived. This much seems certain, namely, that
this *accompaniment of clouds* (it is μ ε τ ὰ τῶν νεφελῶν)
belongs not to the glory and gladness, but to the terror
and anguish, of that day; as indeed the context of the
present passage would indicate. These clouds have
nothing in common with the light-cloud, the νεφέλη
φωτεινή (Matt. xvii. 5), 'the glorious privacy of light'
into which the Lord was withdrawn for a while from the
eyes of his disciples at the Transfiguration, but are rather
the symbols of wrath, fit accompaniments of judgment:
'Clouds and darkness are round about Him; righteousness
and judgment are the habitation of his throne' (Ps. xcvii.
2; cf. xviii. 11; Nah. i. 3; Isai. xix. 1; cf. Rev. xi. 12).

'*And every eye shall see Him, and they also which
pierced Him, and all kindreds of the earth shall wail
because of Him. Even so, Amen.*' The R. V. has here
for '*kindreds*' '*tribes*,' and for '*wail*' '*mourn*.'—It will
sometimes happen that a prophecy, severe in the Old
Testament, by some gracious turn will be transformed from
a threat to a promise in the New; thus, the 'day of visitation' of the Apostle (1 Pet. ii. 12), and of his Lord (Luke
xix. 44), is another from the 'day of visitation' of the
prophets (Isai. x. 3; Jer. viii. 12; Hos. ix. 7),—the one
a day to be hoped for, the other to be feared. But it
is not so here. There is indeed a turn, yet not from the
severe to the gracious, but the contrary. The words of
the prophet Zechariah (xii. 10), on which this passage and
John xix. 37 in common rest, are words of grace: 'They
shall look upon Me, whom they have pierced, and they
shall mourn for Him.' They express the profound repentance of the Jews, when the veil shall be at length taken

from their hearts, and they shall behold in Jesus of Nazareth, whom they crucified, the Son of God, the King of
Israel. But it cannot be denied that in their adaptation
here they speak quite another language. They set forth
the despair of the sinful world, of 'all the tribes of the
earth' (cf. Matt. xxiv. 30), when Christ the Judge shall
come to execute judgment on all that obeyed not his
gospel, who pierced Him with their sins; they describe
their remorse and despair; but give no hint of their repentance. The closing words, '*Even so, Amen,*' are not
to be taken as the prophet's devout acquiescence in the
terribleness of that judgment-day,—a comparison with
xxii. 20 might easily lead an English reader into this mis-
understanding of them,—but as God's own seal and ratifi-
cation of his own word.

Ver. 8. '*I am Alpha and Omega, the beginning and
the ending, saith the Lord.*'—Cf. xxi. 6, where the words
'*the beginning and the ending*' have a right to a place
in the text; but not here; having been transferred from
thence, without any authority at all. He who is '*Alpha
and Omega*' (or better, '*Alpha and* Ω'), and thus indeed
'*the beginning and the ending,*' and 'the first and the
last' (i. 17; ii. 8), leaves no room for any other; is indeed
the only I AM; and beside Him there is no God (Isai.
xli. 4; xliii. 10; xliv. 6; xlviii. 12). Thus Clement of
Alexandria (*Strom.* iv. 25): κύκλος γὰρ ὁ Υἱὸς πασῶν τῶν
δυνάμεων εἰς ἓν εἰλουμένων καὶ ἐνουμένων· διὰ τοῦτο Ἄλφα
καὶ Ὦ εἴρηται: and Tertullian, bringing out the unity of
the Old and New Testaments, and the manner in which
the glorious consummations of the latter attach themselves
to the glorious commencements of the former (*De Monog.*
5): 'Sic et duas Græciæ litteras summam et ultimam sibi
induit Dominus, initii et finis concurrentium in se figuras;

uti quemadmodum *a* ad *ω* usque volvitur, et rursus *ω* ad
a explicatur, ita ostenderet in se esse et initii decursum
ad finem, et finis recursum ad initium; ut omnis dispositio
in Eum desinens, per quem cœpta est, per Sermonem
scilicet Dei qui caro factus est, proinde desit quemadmodum et cœpit.'

'*Which is, and which was, and which is to come, the
Almighty.*'—Cf. ver. 4. Παντοκράτωρ occurs several
times in this Book (as at iv. 8; xi. 17; xxi. 22); elsewhere only once in the New Testament, and then as a
quotation from the Old (2 Cor. vi. 18). We have always
translated it ' Almighty,' except at Rev. xix. 6, where with
a very sublime effect our Saxon ' Almighty' is exchanged
for the Latin 'Omnipotent.' In the Septuagint παντοκράτωρ does duty for two Hebrew words. In the Book of
Job, but in that exclusively (v. 17; xv. 25; xxvii. 2, and
often), it stands for שַׁדַּי, in which word is expressed the
strength, force, or power by which God is able to do all
things. Elsewhere it is used by the Septuagint Translators as one, the most frequent, but by no means the only,
rendering of יְהֹוָה צְבָאוֹת (as at Jer. iii. 19; Amos iii. 13;
Hab. ii. 13), which at other times they have rendered by
κύριος δυνάμεων, or στρατιῶν, or σαβαώθ, this last preferred by St. Paul (Rom. ix. 29) and St. James (v. 4), a
title expressing the rule and dominion which God has over
all. If it be asked, which of these divine titles Christ is
claiming here, which of these attributes He is here challenging for his own, omnipotence, or universal dominion,
—of course they run into one another, but still are capable
of being distinguished—a comparison of Rev. iv. 8 with
Isai. vi. 3 leaves no doubt that it is the last; ' dominion
over all, and the rule and government of all ' (see Pearson,
On the Creed, Art. 1; Suicer, *Thes.* s. v.). In the Arian

controversy the word was frequently appealed to and urged by the Catholics in proof of the equal divinity of the Son, who did not count it robbery to claim it for his own; thus see Gregory of Nyssa, *Con. Eunom.* i. 2.

Ver. 9. '*I John, who also am your brother, and companion in tribulation, and in the kingdom and patience of Jesus Christ, was in the isle that is called Patmos, for the word of God, and for the testimony of Jesus Christ.*'—Daniel alone among the prophets of the Old Testament uses this style—'I Daniel' (vii. 28; ix. 2; x. 2); it is one of the many points of resemblance, small and great, between this Book and that of Daniel. The καί, represented by '*who also am*' in our Version, and modifying this whole clause, should have no place in the text. It may have been suggested by 1 Pet. v. 1; and was probably inserted by some who esteemed ὁ ἀδελφὸς ὑμῶν too humble a title for one of the chief 'pillars' of the Church; and by that καί would make him to say, 'who, being an Apostle, am *also* a brother.'—It has been sometimes asked, *When* was that prophecy and promise fulfilled concerning John, that he should drink of his Lord's cup, and be baptized with his Lord's baptism (Matt. xx. 22)? The fulfilment, so far as his brother James was concerned, is plain; when the sword of Herod was dyed with his blood (Acts xii. 2). But for John it may not be so plain. Origen, however, no doubt gave the right answer long ago (*in Matt* tom. xvi. § 6, *in fine*): that threat or that promise, for we may call it either, found its fulfilment in this his banishment to Patmos; not thereby denying that there must have been a life-long θλῖψις for such an one as the Apostle John, but only affirming that the words obtained their most emphatic and crowning fulfilment now. Let us not fail to observe the connexion and the sequence—'*tribu-*

lation' first, and '*the kingdom*' afterwards; on which Richard of St. Victor well: 'Recte præmisit, *in tribulatione*, et post addit, *in regno*, quia si compatimur, et corregnabimus' (2 Tim. ii. 12. cf. Rom. viii. 17; 1 Pet. iv. 13). As yet, however, while the tribulation is present, the kingdom is only in hope; therefore he adds to these, as that which is the link between them, ' *and patience of Jesus Christ*;' compare Acts xiv. 22, where exactly these same three, the '*tribulation*,' the '*patience*,' and the '*kingdom*' occur. 'Υπομονή, which we have rendered '*patience*,' being exactly opposed to ὑποστολή (Heb. x. 36, 39), is not so much the '*patientia*' as the '*perseverantia*' of the Latin; which last word Cicero (*De Invent.* ii. 54) thus defines: 'In ratione bene considerata stabilis et perpetua mansio;' and Augustine (*Quæst.* lxxxiii. qu. 31): 'Honestatis aut utilitatis causâ rerum arduarum ac difficilium voluntaria ac diuturna perpessio.' It is indeed a beautiful word, expressing the brave and persistent endurance of the Christian—βασιλὶς τῶν ἀρετῶν, Chrysostom does not fear to call it (see my *Synonyms of the New Testament*, § 53).—Patmos, now Patmo or Palmosa, one of the Sporades, a rocky island in the Icarian Sea, S.-W. of Ephesus, might have remained through all the ages with faintest notice or with none, if its mention here had not drawn it from its insignificance and given to it a name and a fame in the Church for ever. This its entire previous insignificance is slightly, yet unmistakably, indicated in the words '*that is called Patmos*.' St. John does not assume his readers to be familiar with it, any more than St. Mark, writing for those living at a distance from Palestine, with the Jordan (cf. Mark i. 5 with Matt. iii. 5). It is otherwise that a well-known island, Crete or Cyprus, is introduced (Acts xiii. 4). The deportation of criminals,

or those accounted as such, to rocky and remote islands
was, as is well known, a common punishment among the
Romans. Titus, according to Suetonius, banished some
delators ' in asperrimas insularum' (*Tit.* 8; cf. Juvenal,
i. 73; Philo, *in Flacc.* § 18, 19). There is a description
of this island written up to the present date, and not
without a certain idyllic grace of its own, in Renan's
L'Antéchrist, pp. 372–379. At the same time very characteristic of the man are his regrets that some ' delicious
romance,' such as Longus might have written, had not
here been composed, so far preferable as this would have
been to the work of the gloomy enthusiast (' *visionnaire
ténébreux* '), which we actually possess.

The unprejudiced reader will hardly be persuaded that
St. John sets himself forth here as any other than one of
those *constrained* dwellers in Patmos, one dwelling there
not by his own choice, but who had been *banished* thither
' *for the word of God, and for the testimony of Jesus
Christ*;' thus compare vi. 9; xx. 4; and a possible reference to what he himself was undergoing, at xiii. 10.
Some modern interpreters find in these words no reference to any such suffering for the truth's sake, but only
a statement on the writer's part that he was in the isle
of Patmos for the sake of preaching the Word of God,
or, as others, for the sake of receiving a communication of the Word of God, that is, of the Book of this
prophecy; so Bleek, Lücke (*Offenbarung d. Johannes*, pp.
510–514), and others; but these refuse the obvious meaning, which moreover a comparison with vi. 9; xx. 4,
seems to render imperative, in favour of one which, if it
also may possibly lie in them, has nothing but this bare
possibility to plead. These expositors, it is difficult not
to think, have been unconsciously influenced by a desire

to get rid of the strong testimony to St. John's authorship
of the Book which lies in the consent of this declaration
with that which early ecclesiastical history tells us about
him, namely, that for his steadfastness in the faith of
Christ he was by Domitian banished to Patmos, and only
allowed to return to his beloved flock at Ephesus on the
accession of Nerva (Tertullian, *De Præsc. Hæret.* 36;
Clement of Alexandria, *Quis Div. Salv.* 42; Eusebius,
H. E. iii. 23; Jerome, *De Vir. Illus.*). The Apocalypse,
it is worth observing by the way, has all internal evidence
of having been thus written in time of persecution and by
a confessor of the truth. It breathes throughout the very
air of martyrdom. Oftentimes slighted by the Church in
times of prosperity, it is made much of, and its preciousness, as it were, instinctively discovered, in times of adver-
sity and fiery trial. This Bengel has noted well: 'In
tribulatione fidelibus maxime hic liber sapit. Asiatica
Ecclesia, præsertim a floridissimo Constantini tempore,
minus magni æstimavit hunc librum. Africana Ecclesia,
cruci magis obnoxia, semper hunc librum plurimi fecit.'
Tertullian may be quoted in proof of this assertion. How
often does he seek, now to strengthen the faithful with
the promises, and now to terrify the fearful, the δειλοί of
Rev. xxi. 8, those who out of fear of man go back from
Christ, with the threatenings, of this Book (*Scorp.* 12;
De Cor. 15; cf. Cyprian, *De Exhort. Mart.* passim).

Ver. 10. '*I was in the Spirit on the Lord's day.*'—In
one sense the faithful are always '*in the Spirit*;' they
are 'spiritual' (1 Cor. iii. 1. 15); are 'led by the Spirit'
(Rom. viii. 14); 'walk in the Spirit' (Gal. v. 16, 25).
But here, and at iv. 2; xxi. 10 (cf. Ezek. xl. 2, 'in the
visions of God'), the words are used in an eminent and
peculiar sense; they describe not the habitual condition

of faithful men, but an exceptional state, differing from
the other not in degree only, but in kind ; a condition in
which there is a suspension of all the motions and faculties
of the natural life ; that a higher life may be called, during
and through this suspension, into a preternatural activity.
It is the state of trance or ecstasy, that is, of standing out
of oneself, θεία ἐξαλλαγὴ τῶν εἰωθότων νομίμων Plato
(*Phædrus*, 265 A) calls it, and on its positive side, ἐνθου-
σιάζειν (*Apol.* 22 c), the man being ἔκφρων that he may
be ἔνθεος (*Ion*, 533 E) ; constantly described in Scripture as
the condition of those to whom God would speak more
directly (Acts x. 10 ; cf. xi. 5 ; xxii. 17) ; the antithesis to
it, or the return out of it, being a γενόμενος ἐν ἑαυτῷ (Acts
xii. 11), or ἐν τῷ νοΐ (1 Cor. xiv. 15).[1]   St. Paul exactly
describes the experience of one who has passed through this
state, 2 Cor. xii. 2–4.   That world of spiritual realities is
one from which man is comparatively estranged so long as
he dwells in this house of clay ; he has need to be trans-
ported out of himself, before he can find himself in the
midst of it, and come into direct contact with it.   Here we
have the explanation of the fact that the Lord never was
' in the Spirit,' namely, because He was *always* ' in the
Spirit,' because he always moved in that region as his
proper haunt and home.

Separated in body from the fellowship of the faithful,
the beloved Apostle was yet keeping with them the weekly

---

[1] Augustine (*Enarr. in Ps.* ciii. 11): ' Illo orante [Acts x. 10]
facta est illi mentis alienatio, quam Græci ecstasin dicunt ; id est,
aversa est mens ejus a consuetudine corporali ad visum quendam con-
templandum, alienata a præsentibus ; ' cf. *in Ps.* lxvii. 28 ; *Quæst. in
Gen.* l. 1, qu. 80 ; and *De Div. Quæst.* l. 2, qu. 1 : ' Mentis alienatio
a sensibus corporis, ut spiritus hominis divino Spiritu assumptus
capiendis atque intuendis imaginibus vacet.' Cf. Aquinas, *Sum.
Theol.* 2ᵃ 2ᵐ, qu. 175.

feast of the Resurrection on the day which the Lord,
giving to it his own name, had made peculiarly his own.   It
was, as St. John is careful to declare to us, '*on the Lord's
Day*,' which occupied for the Church the place occupied by
the Sabbath for the Jews, that he thus passed out of himself, and was brought within the veil, and heard unspeak-
able words, and beheld things which, unless shown by God,
must have remained for ever hidden from mortal gaze.
Some have assumed from this passage that ἡμέρα κυριακή
was a designation of Sunday already familiar among
Christians.   This, however, seems a mistake.   The name
had probably its origin here.   See generally on the subject the article 'Lord's Day' in Smith's *Dictionary of
Christian Antiquities*.   A little later we find κυριακη
employed by Ignatius to designate Sunday (*ad Magnes.*
§ 9), and by Melito of Sardis (Routh, *Reliq. Sac.* vol. i.
pp. 114, 129), as 'Dominica solemnia' (*De Animâ*, c. 9),
'dies Dominicus' (*De Idol.* 14) by Tertullian; cf. Dionysius of Corinth, quoted by Eusebius, *H. E.* iv. 23, 8;
Clement of Alexandria, *Strom.* vii. 12; Origen, *Con. Cels.*
viii. 22.   But though the name, '*the Lord's Day*,' will
very probably have had here its rise (the actual form of
the phrase may have been suggested by κυριακὸν δεῖπνον,
1 Cor. xi. 20),—the thing, the celebration of the first day
of the week as that on which the Lord brake the bands
of death, and became the head of a new creation, called
therefore sometimes ἀναστάσιμος ἡμέρα, this was as old
as Christianity itself (John xx. 24-29; 1 Cor. xvi. 2; Acts
xx. 7; *Ep. of Barnabas*, c. 15: ἄγομεν τὴν ἡμέραν τὴν
ὀγδόην εἰς εὐφροσύνην; cf. Suicer, *Thes.* s. v. κυριακή).
The strange fancy of some that ἡμέρα κυριακή means
here 'the day of the Lord,' in the sense of 'the day of
judgment' (as at Joel i. 15; iii. 14), intended as it is to

subserve a scheme of Apocalyptic interpretation which certainly needs all support which it can anywhere find, has been abundantly refuted by Alford.

'*And I heard behind me a great voice, as of a trumpet.*'—The wondrous vision which the Seer shall behold does not break upon him all at once; he first hears behind him (cf. Ezek. i. 12) '*a voice, great as of a trumpet,*' summoning his attention, and preparing him for the still greater sight which he shall see. It is a '*great voice,*' as the voice of the Lord must ever be (Ps. xxix. 3–9; lxviii. 33; Dan. x. 6; Matt. xxiv. 31; 1 Thess. iv. 16) : a voice penetrating and clear, '*as of a trumpet;*' cf. Sophocles, *Ajax*, 17, where Ulysses compares in like manner the voice of Athênè to the sound of a trumpet. In the comparison there *may be* allusion, as Hengstenberg is sure there is, to the divinely-instituted rule of calling together by a trumpet the congregation of the Lord, when He had anything to impart to them (Num. x. 2; Exod. xix. 16, 19; Joel ii. 1, 15; Matt. xxiv. 31; 1 Thess. iv. 16); although this to me does not seem very probable.

Ver. 11. '*Saying, I am Alpha and Omega, the first and the last : and, What thou seest, write in a book, and send it to the seven Churches which are in Asia; unto Ephesus, and unto Smyrna, and unto Pergamos, and unto Thyatira, and unto Sardis, and unto Philadelphia and unto Laodicea.*'—Omit '*I am Alpha and Omega, the first and the last,*' which has no right whatever to stand in the text. Over-busy transcribers have transferred the first of these clauses from ver. 8, the second from ver. 17. Omit also '*which are in Asia,*' as the R. V. has done. Of the several cities I will say something when we come to treat of them one by one. It is disputed whether the '*book*' which St. John is to write, and having written, to

send to the seven Churches, is this whole Book of the
Apocalypse, or only the seven shorter Epistles contained
in chapters ii. and iii. Hengstenberg affirms the last; but
I am persuaded wrongly, and he has against him the great
body of interpreters. ' *What thou seest* ' must in that case be
restrained to ver. 12–16 of this present chapter. All the
rest, to the end of chapter iii., he will have *heard*; but will
have seen nothing; and moreover ver. 19 is decisive that
what he is to write of is more than that which he has
then seen: ' *Write the things which thou hast seen, and the
things which are, and the things which shall be hereafter.*'

Doubtless it is not for nothing that *seven* Churches,
neither more nor fewer, are here named. The reason of
this lies deeper than some suggest, who will have these
seven to include and exhaust all the principal Churches of
Asia; whatever other Churches there were being merely
annexed and subordinate to these. But taking into account the rapid spread of the Gospel in the regions of
Asia Minor, as recorded in Scripture (Acts xix. 9; 1 Cor.
xvi. 9), and in other historical documents of a date very
little later, we cannot doubt that towards the end of the
life of St. John there were flourishing and important
Churches in many other cities of that region besides
these seven; that if the first purpose of the great ascended Bishop of the Church had been to bring under
spiritual review the whole Church of Asia, in this case
Colosse, to which St. Paul addressed an Epistle, and
Hierapolis, where was already the nucleus of a Church
in the same Apostle's time (Col. iv. 13), and where a little
later Papias was bishop, and Miletus, the scene of apostolic
labours (Acts xx. 17), and Tralles, called by Cicero ' gravis,
ornata et locuples civitas,' to the Church in which city
Ignatius wrote an epistle some twenty years later, as he

did to that in Magnesia as well, these with others would
scarcely have been passed by.[1] But what we may call the
mystical or symbolic interest overbears and predominates
over the actual. No doubt this actual was sufficiently
provided for in another way, and these seven words of
warning and encouragement so penetrated to the heart of
things that, meeting the needs of these seven Churches,
they also met the needs of all others subsisting in similar,
or nearly similar conditions. Typical and representative
Churches, these embodied, one or another of them, I will
not say *all* the great leading aspects of the Church in her
faithfulness or her unfaithfulness; but they embodied a great
many, the broadest and the oftenest recurring. Grotius :
' Sub earum nomine tacite comprehendit et alias Ecclesias,
quia earum status et qualitates ad septem quasi genera pos-
sunt revocari, quorum exemplum præbent illæ Asiaticæ.'
The seven must in this point of view be regarded as consti-
tuting a complex whole, as possessing an ideal completeness.
Christ, we feel sure, could not have placed Himself in the
relation which He does to them, as holding in his hand

---

[1] An instructive chapter in the Annals of Tacitus (iv. 55), throws
much light on the relative dignity and position, at a period a little
earlier than this, of the chief cities in proconsular Asia. He is describing a contention which found place among eleven of them,
which should have the honour of erecting a statue and temple to
Tiberius. Among the eleven contending for this glorious privilege,
which involved as well the maintaining as the founding of this cult,
five out of our seven appear. Two, namely Philadelphia and Thyatira, do not enter the lists. Laodicea, with others not included in our
seven, is set aside, as unequal in wealth and dignity to the task; Pergamum as having already a temple to Augustus, Ephesus as devoted
to Diana, and other cities for various causes ; till at length Smyrna
and Sardis are the only competitors which remain. Of these Smyrna
is preferred, mainly on account of its greater devotedness to the interests of Rome in times when as yet the fortunes of the Imperial
City were not so completely in the ascendant as now they were.

the seven stars, walking among the seven golden candlesticks, these stars being the Angels of the Churches, and
the candlesticks the Churches themselves, unless they
ideally represented and set forth, in some way or other,
the universal Church, militant here upon earth.

But this, which I have here rather assumed than
proved, together with another question, namely, whether
besides possessing this typical and representative character,
these seven Epistles are not also historico-prophetical, do
not unfold the future of the Church's fortunes to the end
of time, seven *successive* stages and periods of its growth
and history, has been so eagerly discussed, has, strangely
enough, roused so much theological passion, that I am
unwilling to treat the subject with the brevity which a
place in this *Exposition* would require. I must therefore
refer the reader to an Excursus at the end of the volume,
in which I have traced, rapidly indeed, but with some
attempt at completeness, a sketch of the controversy, and
have stated, and sought to justify, the conclusions on the
points in debate at which I have myself arrived.

Ver. 12. '*And I turned to see the voice that spake with
me. And being turned, I saw seven golden candlesticks.*'
—Λυχνία is a word condemned by the Greek purists, who
prefer λύχνιον (Lobeck, *Phrynichus*, p. 313). The '*seven
candlesticks*'—the rendering is not a very happy one,
though it is not easy, perhaps impossible, to better it—
send us back, and are intended to send us back, to the
seven-branched candlestick, or candelabrum, which bears
ever the same name of λυχνία in the Septuagint (Exod.
xxv. 31 ; cf. Heb. ix. 2 ; Philo, *Quis Rer. Div. Hær.* 44 ;
Josephus, *B. J.* v. 5. 5) ; or λυχνία τοῦ φωτός (1 Macc. i.
21) ; the six arms of which with the central shaft (καλα-
μίσκοι, Exod. xxv. 31 ; κλάδοι, Philo, *Vit. Mos.* iii. 9)

made up the mystical seven, each with its several lamp
(λύχνος, Zech. iv. 2). Nor is this the first occasion when
that portion of the furniture of the tabernacle has had a
higher mystical meaning ascribed to it. Already in the
candlestick all of gold, which Zechariah saw (iv. 2), there
was an anticipation of this image; being one of the many
remarkable points of contact between his prophecies and the
Apocalypse. Here, however, it is not one candlestick with
seven branches which St. John beholds : but rather seven
separate candlesticks. Nor is it without a meaning that the
seven thus take the place of the one. The Jewish Church
was one; for it was the Church of a single people; the
Christian Church, that too is one, but it is also many; at
once the 'Church' and the 'Churches.' These may be
quite independent of one another, the only bond of union
with one another which they absolutely require being that
of common dependence on the same Head, and derivation
of life from the same Spirit; and are fitly represented by
seven, the number of mystical completeness.

In the image itself by which the Churches are sym-
bolized there is an eminent fitness. The candlestick, or
lamp-stand, as we must rather conceive it here, is not
light, but it is the bearer of light, that which diffuses it,
that which holds it forth and causes it to shine throughout
the house; being the appointed instrument for this. It
is thus with the Church. God's word, God's truth, including in this all which He has declared of Himself in
revealed religion, is its light (Ps. cxix. 105; Prov. vi. 23);
the Church is the light-bearer, light in the Lord (Ephes.
v. 8), not having light of its own, but diffusing that which
it receives of Him. Each too of the faithful in particular,
after he has been illuminated (Heb. vi. 4), is a bearer of
the light; 'ye are the light of the world' (Matt. v. 14–

16); 'lights in the world, holding forth the word of life'
(Phil. ii. 15). In agreement with this aspect of the
matter, in the Levitical tabernacle the seven-branched
candlestick stood in the Holy Place (Exod. xxvi. 35; xl.
4), which was the pattern of the Church upon earth, as
the Holy of Holies was the pattern of the Church in
heaven; and the only light which the Holy Place received
was derived from the candlestick; the light of common
day being quite excluded from it, in sign that the Lord
God was the light thereof, that the light of the Church was
not the light of nature, but of grace. Compare *Irenæus*,
v. 20. 1 : 'Ubique enim Ecclesia prædicat veritatem, et
hæc est ἑπτάμυξος lucerna, Christi bajulans lumen.'[1]

These candlesticks are of gold (cf. Exod. xxv. 31 ;
Zech. iv. 2), as so much else in this Book ; the '*golden*
girdle' (i. 13); '*golden* crowns' (iv. 4) ; '*golden* vials'
(v. 8); '*golden* censer' (viii. 3); '*golden* altar' (ibid.);
golden reed' (xxi. 15); 'the city of pure *gold*' (xxi.
18); 'the street of the city of pure *gold*' (xxi. 21). No
doubt the preciousness of all belonging to the Church of
God is indicated by the predominant employment of this
the costliest and most perfect metal of all.   A hint no doubt
we have here of this, exactly as in the Ark and furniture
of the Ark so much in like manner is of pure gold, the
mercy-seat, the cherubim, the dishes, spoons, covers,
tongs, snuff-dishes (Exod. xxv. 17, 18, 29, 38), the pot
which had manna (Exod. xvi. 33),[2] everything in short

---

[1] 'Ἐπτάμυξος is a rare Church word; but 'myxa' is in Martial,
and the following quotation from him is apt, and tells its own story :

'Illustrem cum tota meis convivia flammis,
Totque geram myxas, una lucerna vocor.'

[2] So much is not here said, but that this was a *golden* pot we learn
from Heb. ix. 4; cf. LXX. in loc., and Philo, *Cong. Erud. Gent.* § 18·

which did not by its bulk and consequent weight absolutely preclude this, and even that was for the most part
overlaid with gold (Exod. xxv. 10, 11, 23, 24).[1] But the
mere costliness of gold, that it was of all metals the rarest,
and therefore the dearest, this was not the only motive
for the predominant employment of it. Throughout all
the ancient East there was a sense of sacredness attached
to this metal, such as still to a great extent survives.
Thus 'golden' in the Zend-Avesta is throughout synony-
mous with heavenly or divine. So also in many Eastern
lands while silver might be degraded to profane and every-
day uses of common life, might as money pass from hand
to hand, 'the pale and common drudge 'twixt man and
man,' it was not permitted to employ gold in any services
except only royal and divine (see Bähr, *Symbolik*, vol. i.
pp. 273, 282, 292). The permission to drink out of gold
was a special favour vouchsafed to few (1 Macc. xi. 58); so
too the permission to wear gold (1 Macc. xiv. 43) is re-
ported as a peculiar honour and privilege.

Ver. 13. '*And in the midst of the seven candlesticks
One like unto the Son of man, clothed with a garment
down to the foot.*'—Some translate '*like unto a son of
man,*' that is to say, 'like unto a man,' the words merely
for them expressing that He who was seen was in human
shape, and, so far as the appearance warranted the conclusion, the sharer of a human nature (Ezek. xxxvii. 3, 16 ;

---

[1] Cocceius : ' Aurum in figuris et symbolicis locutionibus significat id quod est omnium optimum, quod omnia perficit, et a nullo
perficitur ; sed in se est perfectissimum et purissimum, nullique mu-
tationi obnoxium ; quemadmodum aurum omnium metallorum perfectissimum est, et ab aliis non perficitur ; sed quibus accedit ea
perficit, et nec temporis, nec ignis, omnium destructoris, violentiam
injuriamque sentit.'

xxxix. 1). The absence of the articles, however, does not require this either here or at xiv. 14; any more than υἱὸς Θεοῦ (Matt. xxvii. 54) demands to be translated, 'a son of God,' or πνεῦμα Θεοῦ, 'a Spirit of God.' The beloved Apostle by this 'like unto the Son of man' would imply that in this sublime apparition he recognized Him whom he had once known on earth, the born of the Virgin Mary; who even in those days of his flesh had claimed to be executor of all judgment, because He was the Son of man (John v. 27; cf. Dan. vii. 13, where this title first appears).—We are again reminded of Daniel's vision, where in like manner He whom the prophet saw on the banks of Hiddekei was 'clothed in linen' (x. 5; xii. 6, 7), or, as it would be more rightly translated, 'in a long linen garment.' Ποδήρης, from πούς and ἄρειν, the 'poderis' of ecclesiastical Latin, is properly an adjective here, with χιτών or στολή or other such word understood; thus ποδῆρες ἔνδυμα, Wisd. xviii. 24, ἀσπὶς ποδήρης, Xenophon, Cyrop. vi. 2. 10, a shield reaching down to the feet, such as the θυρεός (Ephes. vi. 16), and covering the whole person; see my Synonyms of the New Testament, § 50. The long robe or stole is everywhere in the East the garment of dignity and honour (Gen. xxxvii. 3 ; Mark xii. 38 ; Luke xv. 22)—the association of dignity with it probably resting originally on the absence of the necessity of labour, and thus of loins girt up, which it seemed to imply : see, on the other hand, 2 Sam. x. 4. The word nowhere else occurs in the New Testament, but several times in the Old ; and designates there sometimes the long linen garment common to all the priests, the chetoneth, or 'holy linen coat' (Lev. xvi. 4 ; Exod. xxxix. 27), sometimes the High Priest's 'robe of the ephod' (Exod. xxviii. 31 ; Zech. iii. 4 ; Wisd. xviii. 24); στολὴ δόξης, as it is called, Ecclus. xlviii.; 7.

Yet these passages must not lead us, as they have led some,
to regard this as a manifestation of Christ in his *priestly*
character alone. The Rheims Version, indeed, renders
ποδήρης here 'a *priestly* garment,' but has no warrant
for this. *Any* stately garment, *any* 'vestis talaris,' may
be indicated by the word (Ecclus. xxvii. 8), as for instance,
that worn by the Angel of the covenant (Ezek. ix. 2, 3).
So too in Isaiah's magnificent vision (vi. 1), *He* whom the
prophet beheld was clothed with a ποδήρης, though the
word does not there occur, sitting as a King upon his
throne, and *whose train filled the temple.* The ποδήρης,
in fact, is quite as much a kingly garment as a priestly,
even as Christ presents Himself here not only as the Priest,
but the King, and so far as there is any superiority of
the one over the other, more the King than the Priest,
ruling in the midst of his Church.

'*And girt about the paps with a golden girdle.*'—We
read in like manner of the Angels who carry out the
judgments of God, as 'having *their breasts* girded with
golden girdles' (xv. 6; cf. Ovid: 'cinctæque *ad pectora*
vestes'). The ordinary girding for one actively engaged
was *at the loins* (1 Kin. ii. 5; xviii. 46; Isai. xlv. 1; Jer.
i. 17; xiii. 11; cf. Luke xii. 35; Ephes. vi. 14; 1 Pet. i.
13); but Josephus (*Antt.* iii. 7. 2) expressly tells us that
the Levitical priests were girt higher up, about the breast,
or as it is here '*about the paps*' (ἐπιζώννυνται κατὰ
στῆθος)—favouring, as this higher cincture did, a calmer,
more majestic movement (see Braun, *De Vest. Hebr.* p.
402). The girdle, as knitting up into a compact unity
all the scattered forces of a man, is often contemplated as
the symbol of strength and activity (Isai. xxii. 21 ; xlv.
5 ; Jer. xiii. 11 ; Job xii. 18); and as nothing is so strong
as righteousness and truth, therefore the prophet foretells

of Messiah, 'Righteousness shall be the girdle of his loins,
and faithfulness the girdle of his reins' (Isai. xi. 5; cf.
Ephes. vi. 14). The girdle here is '*golden*;' not merely
with a golden clasp or buckle, as Hengstenberg, relying
on I Macc. x. 89; xi. 58; xiv. 44, where such appears as
the ensign of royalty, would have it; but all of gold; cf.
xv. 7; and Dan. x. 5 : 'His loins were girded with fine
gold of Uphaz.' It is quite true that the 'curious girdle'
of the High Priest was not golden, but only wrought and
interwoven with gold (Exod. xxviii. 8; xxxix. 5); but this,
with other departures in this appearance of the Lord from
the investiture of the High Priest, only helps to confirm
what was just asserted, namely, that we have to do with
Him here not as the Priest only, but as also the King, in
his Church; for it is in this direction that all the variations tend.

Ver. 14. '*His head and his hairs were white like wool*'
[or '*as white wool*,' so the R. V.], '*as white as snow*.'—Cf.
Dan. vii. 9 : 'The hair of his head was like the pure wool;'
wool and snow being joined together on the score of their
common whiteness both there and at Isai. i. 18. Those
interpreters are altogether astray who see in this whiteness
of the Lord's hairs the symbol of age, the hoary head as
of the Ancient of Days, which should inspire honour and
respect. Clement of Alexandria has not escaped this error
(*Pædag.* 1. iii. p. 262); nor Augustine (*Exp. ad Gal.* iv.
21): 'Dominus non nisi ob antiquitatem veritatis in
Apocalypsi albo capite apparuit;' nor Vitringa, who gives
a reference to Lev. xix. 32. That it is an error a moment's
consideration must convince. The white hairs of old age
are at once the sign and the consequence of the decay of
natural strength, in other words, of death commencing;
the hair blanching because the blood refuses to circulate

any longer in these extremities, as it will one day refuse to circulate in any part of the frame. Being then this token of decay, how can the white hairs, the hoary head which is the sign of weakness and of the approach of death, be ascribed to Him who, as He is *from* everlasting, so also is He *to* everlasting? Even the Angel at the sepulchre appears as a *νεανίσκος*, 'a *young* man' (Mark xvi. 5; cf. Zech. ii. 4); so in *Paradise Lost* (iv. 845) the cherub is 'severe in *youthful* beauty;' what then the Angel's Lord (cf. 2 Esdr. ii. 43, 47)? But this being so, how shall we explain this hair '*white like white wool*'? It is a part of the transfiguration in light of the glorified person of the Redeemer; a transfiguration so complete that it reaches to the extremities, to the very hairs of the head. A comparison with the passage in Daniel, already referred to (vii. 9), will leave no doubt of this. Fire at its highest intensity is *white*; the *red* in fire is of the earth earthy, implies something which the fire has not yet thoroughly mastered and transmuted, while the pure flame is absolutely white. 'Das Weiss ohne alle Beimischung von Finsterniss den reinen absoluten Triumph des Lichtes darstellt' (Delitzsch, on Isai. i. 18). This must be kept in mind whenever we read of white as the colour and livery of heaven.

'*And his eyes were as a flame of fire.*'—Cf. Dan. x. 6: 'His eyes [were] as lamps of fire.' This too has been understood by some, of the clearsightedness of Christ, all things being open and manifest to the eyes of Him with whom we have to do; thus Vitringa: 'Significant perspicaciam divinæ et puræ mentis omnia arcana pervadentis.' The explanation is insufficient; and Cocceius much better: 'Significat hoc iram *ἀπαραίτητον* in adversarios.' The words do not say merely that nothing can escape his searching penetrative glance; that 'his eyes behold and his eyelids try the children of men' (Ps. xi. 4); they express much more than this—the indignation of the Holy One at the discoveries of evil which He thus makes.   These '*eyes of fire*' do not merely *look through* the hypocrite and the sinner, but *consume* him, him and his sins together,— unless indeed he will suffer them to consume his sins, that so *he* may live.   For indeed in the symbolism of Scripture fire is everywhere the expression of the divine anger; and, seeing that nothing moves that anger but sin, of the divine anger against sin (Gen. xix. 24; Lev. x. 2; Num. xi. 1; xvi. 35; Deut. xxxii. 22; Ps. xi. 6; xxi. 9; l. 3; xcvii. 3; 2 Kin. i. 10, 12; Isai. ix. 18, 19; x. 17; xxx. 27; xxxi. 9; xxxiii. 14; xlvii. 14; lxvi. 15, 16, 24; Ezek. xxxviii. 19, 22; xxxix. 6; Dan. vii. 9, 10; Zeph. i. 18; Mal. iv. 1; Luke ix. 54; xvi. 24; 2 Thess. i. 8; Heb. x. 27; xii. 29; Jude 7; Rev. xi. 5; xx. 9).   It need hardly be observed, as confirming this interpretation, that the eyes flashing fire are evermore the utterance, the outward tokens of indignation and wrath; thus Homer (*Il.* xiii. 474): ὀφθαλμὼ δ' ἄρα οἱ πυρὶ λάμπετον: cf. Lucretius, iii. 290; Virgil, *Æn.* ii. 172; xii. 101, 102; Ovid, *Met.* iii. 33.   If any hesitation existed in ascribing this meaning to the symbol here, it must be removed by a comparison with xix. 11, 12.   The whole imagery there is of Christ as a man of war coming forth in his anger to fight against and destroy his enemies, and the '*eyes as a flame of fire*' are again ascribed to Him there.   In Plato (*Legg.* v. 739 c), we have φωσφόρα ὄμματα.

Ver. 15. '*And his feet like unto fine brass, as if they burned in a furnace.*'—For '*fine*' the R. V. has '*burnished,*' and for '*as if they burned,*' '*as if it had been refined.*'   The ποδήρης, reaching, as the name indicates, *to the feet*, yet did not fall so low but that it permitted these to be seen. They were no doubt bare; as were the feet of the Levitical priesthood ministering in the sanctuary. We are nowhere indeed expressly told of these that they ministered barefoot, but everything leads to this conclusion. Thus, while all other parts of the priestly investiture are described with the utmost minuteness, and Moses is accurately instructed how they should be made, there is no allusion to any covering for the feet. Then again the analogy of such passages as Exod. iii. 5; Josh. v. 15; Acts vii. 33, and the fact that the *moral* idea of the shoe or sandal is that of a protection against the *defilements* of the earth, of which defilements there could be none in the Holy Place, all this irresistibly points to the same conclusion. Plutarch's assertion to the contrary (*Symp.* iv. 6. 2), who ascribes, to the High Priest at least, buskins (κοθόρνους), cannot be regarded as of the slightest weight on the other side. It is only one little error more, added to the heap of other errors which he makes about the worship of the Jews; and over against this we may set the testimony of Juvenal (*Sat.* vi. 158): 'Observant ubi festa *mero pede* sabbata reges.' Uncovered at all events the feet on the present occasion were; for St. John seeing, is able to compare them to '*fine brass*'—so we have rendered the word.

Χαλκολίβανος—for there is no reason why we should assume a neuter, χαλκολίβανον, for the nominative, as very commonly is done—occurs only here and at ii. 18; being, in all probability, a word of St. John's own compounding. It has much perplexed, one might say has hitherto defied, interpreters to give any certain account of it—to do more than guess at its etymology and its meaning. Some have suggested, and the suggestion is as

old as Arethas,—it is indeed older, for the Syriac and the
Ethiopic Versions assume it,—that we are to find Λίβανος,
or Lebanon, in the latter part of the word, and that χαλκολίβανος, means 'brass *of Mount Lebanon*,' such as was
there found ; or more generally ' mountain-brass,' ' auri-
chalcum,' as it is in the Vulgate ; in the first syllable of
which, as need hardly be observed, we are not to find
' aurum,' as though this mixed metal were of *gold* and
brass, and the word designating it a hybrid, partly Latin,
partly Greek, but ὄρος, ' *ori*chalcum ' (Virgil, *Æn.* xii. 87)
= ὀρείχαλκος. So one quoted by Wolf : ' Libanus pro
monte quolibet, fortasse quod Libanus dederit ejusmodi
genus metalli ; ' which it has been further sought to prove
by putting together the promise to Asher, 'Thy shoes
shall be iron and brass ' (Deut. xxxiii. 25), and the fact
that Lebanon was within the borders of this tribe. It is
hardly fair to urge against this etymology the objection
that it violates the law which holds good in Greek com-
posite words, namely, that the more important word should
come last, and the merely qualitative first (see Donaldson,
Gr. Gram. §§ 370, 372) ; an objection holding good
quite as much in our own language, in which ' brass-
mountain ' would signify something very different from
' mountain-brass,' and ' rose-tree ' from ' tree-rose.' It is, I
say, hardly fair to urge this, that the word should be rather
λιβανόχαλκος than χαλκολίβανος, because the same objection may be urged against every other attempted
explanation, including that which seems to me the most
probable of all. Another suggestion, first made by Sal-
masius, and which Ludolf (*Lex. Æthiop.* p. 234) has
adopted, to the effect that this mysterious word is a somewhat euphonic form of χαλκοκλίβανος, brass *of the fur-*
nace (κλίβανος), is scarcely likely to find favour, and is

not worthy of any serious notice. As little, I confess, does the solution of the riddle of this word, which Bishop Wordsworth has allowed (see too Ewald, *Johan. Script.* vol. ii. p. 118), commend itself to me, namely, that the second part of the word is λίβavos, frankincense, brass *of the colour of frankincense,* that is, brass of a dark copper hue; for, to say nothing of the extreme unlikelihood of frankincense being sought out to suggest what the colour was, this part of the description is thus put in direct opposition with all the rest. Everything else is light, fire, of a white shining brightness; the feet must be so as well.

The explanation which satisfies this, as well as other conditions, and commends itself above any other, is one first proposed by Bochart (in a learned disquisition, *De Animal. S. Script.* pars ii. c. xvi. p. 883); and since adopted by Grotius, Vitringa, Hengstenberg, Bleek, and others. Bochart sees in χαλκολίβavos, a hybrid formation, the combination of a Greek word and a Hebrew, χαλκός, and לבן='albare,' to make white; brass which in the furnace has attained what we call *'white* heat.' In this word on a small scale, as in the Apocalypse itself on a larger, the two sacred tongues, Greek and Hebrew, will thus be wonderfully married. If this be the key of the word, it will then exactly correspond to, and the seer will have intended to express by it, the *'burnished* brass' of the feet of the four living creatures (Ezek. i. 7; cf. ver. 27; viii. 2; xl. 3); the *'polished* brass' of the feet of Him whom Daniel saw on the banks of Hiddekel (Dan. x. 6), neither 'burnished' nor 'polished' in those passages of our Translation exactly expressing the force of the original; which the LXX by ἐξαστράπτων in the first passage, στίλβων in the second (the Vulgate has well 'candens' in both), had

more precisely seized.   If this be correct, the χαλκολίβανος
will not be the '*fine brass*,' of our A. V., nor yet the ' *burnished* ' of the R. V., but the ' glowing brass.' [1]   This
conclusion is very much strengthened by the epexegesis,
' *as if they burned in a furnace*; ' words of explanation
immediately added by St. John, as probably knowing the
difficulty which his readers would find in this unusual
term.   A further confirmation we may draw from a comparison with x. 1, where feet as ' pillars *of fire*,' which can
only be feet as glowing or burning brass, are ascribed to
the mighty Angel who there appears.   This grand and
terrible image sets forth to us Christ in his power to tread
down his enemies ; at once to tread down and to consume them—' ut potentissimum in conculcandis hostibus'
(Marckius).

' *And his voice as the sound of many waters.*'—
Hitherto St. John has trodden closely on the footsteps of
Daniel in his delineation of Him whom his eyes beheld ;
but grand as is the imagery which Daniel offers (' the
voice of his words [was] like the voice of a multitude,'
Dan. x. 6), the Seer of the New Testament, leaving this,
draws now his comparison from another quarter, from Ezek.
xliii. 2 : ' his voice was like a noise of many waters ; ' cf.
xiv. 2 ; xix. 6 ; Ezek. i. 24 ; Jer. l. 42 ; Isai. xvii. 12.   We
may note herein a special characteristic of this wonderful
Book.   Were it not that the term ' mosaic ' always seems
to imply, or to suggest, something artificial, we might in
many parts liken the Apocalypse to such a costly mosaic ;
the stones of which, polished and wrought into novel combinations of beauty, have been gathered from all the

---

[1] Of an athlete in perfect health and highest training, Dio
Chrysostom says (*Orat.* 28), εἶχε δὲ τὸ χρῶμα ὅμοιον χαλκῷ κεκραμένῳ :
but something more is intended here.

richest mines of the Old Testament and the New.—By
this comparison of the voice of the Lord to '*the sound of
many waters*,' is not to be understood the 'prædicatio
Evangelii' (Vitringa), but the terribleness of the voice
with which He will rebuke his foes within the Church and
without.

Ver. 16. '*And He had in his right hand seven stars.*'
—Cf. ver. 20; ii. 1 ; iii. 1.   How and in what combination we are to conceive that the Lord thus ' *had in his right
hand*' these '*seven stars*,' has been often asked, and the
question variously answered.   Was it as so many jewelled
rings on the fingers?   The threatened rejection of the
Laodicean Angel (iii. 16) would then find a remarkable
parallel in Jer. xxii. 24 : ' Though Coniah, king of Judah,
were the signet upon my right hand, yet would I pluck
thee thence.'   But, not to mention other objections, the
seven stars would ill distribute themselves on *four* fingers.
Better therefore to represent them to our mind's eye as a
wreath or garland which He grasped in his right hand.
' *The mystery of the seven stars* ' we shall return to before
long (ver. 20); and on two occasions shall have need to
consider what is the spiritual signification of his having
or holding these stars in his right hand (ii. 1 ; iii. 1); all
which may therefore for the present be passed over.

   ' *And out of his mouth went a sharp two-edged
sword.*'—Cf. ii. 12; xix. 15 ; Isai. xlix. 2.   Ῥομφαία,
sometimes ῥομβαία, in artificial Greek-Latin ' rhom-
phæa,' but in Latin proper, ' rumpia ' (Ennius, *Annal.* 14
[the passage has not reached us]; Valerius Flaccus, vi. 96),
is a Thracian word for a Thracian weapon (A. Gellius, x. 25 ;
cf. Diefenbach, *Origines Europææ*, p. 409).   It is properly
the ' framea,' the long and heavy broadsword (ῥομφαία
βαρυσίδηρος, Plutarch, *Æmil. Paul.* 18; cf. Livy, xxxi.

39), with which the Thracians and other barbarous nations
were armed; very much resembling the Gaelic claymore;
and as such distinguished from the μάχαιρα, the sacrificial
knife, or short stabbing sword; though the Septuagint does
not recognize any such distinction (Judg. i. 8, 25). The
word, occurring six times in the Apocalypse, only occurs
once besides in the New Testament (Luke ii. 35). This
sword is 'two-edged' here (δίστομος, cf. Heb. iv. 12,
μάχαιρα δίστομος = ἀμφίστομος = ἀμφήκης, Homer, Il. x.
256; Sophocles, Antig. 1212); the sharpness of it being
reckoned as its mouth; cf. Heb. xi. 34, στόματα μαχαίρας,
and Judg. iii. 16; Ps. cxlix. 6; Prov. v. 4; Ecclus. xxi.
4; πρόσωπον μαχαίρας, Isai. xxxi. 8. The phrase 'the
devouring sword' (2 Sam. xviii. 8; Isai. i. 20; xxxi. 8;
Jer. ii. 30), rests on the same image. Yet it is not a mere
Hebraism; but may be met in classical Greek poetry, and
indeed in Greek prose as well; thus δίστομα φάσγανα
(Euripides), πέλεκυς δίστομος. As it is from the mouth
that man's word proceeds, so this sword, not wielded in
the hand, but proceeding from the mouth, of the Son of
God, is his Word (cf. Isai. xlix. 2: 'He hath made my
mouth like a sharp sword'); but his Word as it is also
Spirit; 'the sword of the Spirit, which is the Word of
God' (Ephes. vi. 17; cf. Heb. iv. 12; Isai. xi. 4). They
fall short of the full meaning of this emblem, who press
mainly as the *tertium comparationis* here the penetrative searching power of the Word of God, amputating
our vices, convincing us of our sins; as does Tertullian
(*Adv. Marc.* iii. 14); Cocceius: 'Notatur vis verbi in
conscientiam;' and Henry More (*Mystery of Iniquity*,
ii. xiv. 6): 'A prophetic symbol of that wonderful con-
trition of heart that the powerful Word of God makes
when sincerely and seasonably evibrated against the

enemies of his kingdom.' The whole feeling and sense of
this passage requires that we should regard this sword from
the mouth as expressing rather the *punishing* than the
convincing power of God's Word; as Delitzsch, on Heb. iv.
12, says well: 'Ein Bild des sichtenden, richtenden, vernich-
tenden Werkes des Wortes der Worte.' With this sword
from his mouth He *fights* against his enemies and destroys
them (cf. ii. 12, 16; xix. 15, 21); for the Word of the Lord
is no empty threat, but having in readiness to avenge all
disobedience (cf. Hos. vi. 5; Isai. xi. 4; 2 Thess. ii. 8;
Wisd. xviii. 15, 16).—Shall we give any spiritual significance to the *two-edgedness* of this sword? Of course it indicates the power which it has to pierce and to penetrate;
but many have seen in it more than this; Tertullian for
instance (*Adv. Jud.*): 'Bis acutus duobus Testamentis,
legis antiquæ, et legis novæ;' cf. Augustine, *Enarr. in Ps.*
cxlix. 6; *De Civ. Dei*, xx. 21. 2; and Richard of St. Victor:
'Qui gladius utrâque parte dicitur acutus, quia in Veteri
Testamento amputavit vitia carnalia, in Novo etiam spiri-
tualia. Utrâque parte acutus est, quia qui foris in nobis
amputat luxuriam carnis, intus resecat malitiam cordis.
Utrâque parte acutus est, quia in his qui contemnunt quæ
præcepit, corpus et animam punit. Utrâque parte acutus
est, quia malos et a bonis discernit, et singulis quod
merentur reddit.' Philo (*De Cher.* 9) likens the Λόγος,
thus quick and piercing, to the φλογίνη ρομφαία (Gen. iii.
24) with which the Cherubim kept the way of the tree of
life. Compare Prov. x. 13 (LXX).

'*And his countenance was as the sun shineth in his
strength.*'—Of the Angel who stood by the vacant tomb on
the Resurrection morn it is said, 'His countenance was like
lightning' (Matt. xxviii. 3; cf. Judg. xiii. 6; Dan. x. 6);
here the countenance of the Lord is compared to the sun

'*in his strength*' (cf. x. 1), at his brightest and clearest, in the splendour of his highest noon, no veil, no mist, no cloud obscuring his brightness (Judg. v. 31). When He shall appear, they that are his shall be like Him, for they shall see Him as He is ; therefore of them too it can be said that in that day 'they shall shine forth *as the sun* in the kingdom of their Father' (Matt. xiii. 43 ; cf. Wisd. iii. 7). No doubt if there had been aught in nature brighter than the sun, the Seer would have chosen it to set forth the transcendant and intolerable brightness of that countenance which he now beheld.

This description of the glorified Lord, which has now been brought to a conclusion, sublime as a purely mental conception, but intolerable, if we give it an outward form and expression, and picture Him to ourselves or to others with this sword proceeding from his mouth, these feet as glowing brass, this hair white as wool, and the rest, may suggest a few reflections on the apocalyptic, and generally the Hebrew symbolism, and on the very significant relations of difference and opposition in which it stands to the Greek. Religion and Art for the Greek ran into one another with no very signal preponderance of the claims of the former over the latter. Even in his religious symbolism the sense of beauty, of form, of proportion, overrules every other, and must at all costs find its satisfaction ; so that the first necessity of the symbol is that it shall not affront, that it shall satisfy rather, the æsthetic sense. Rather than it should offend this, it would be moulded and modified even to the serious injury of the idea of which it was intended to be the exponent (Renan, *Antéchrist*, p. 378). But with the Hebrew symbolism it is altogether different. The first necessity there is that the symbol should set forth truly and fully the religious idea of which

it is intended to be the vehicle. Thus the New Jerusalem 'lieth foursquare; the length and the breadth and
the height of it are equal' (Rev. xxi. 16). A city, con-
stituting thus a perfect cube, is simply inconceivable to
us; but the divine Seer did not care that we should conceive it; he was only careful to express the fact that this
was a City which should never be moved; and of this
fact the tetragon was the aptest symbol. In the present,
as in so many other cases, how the idea would appear
when it clothed itself in an outward form and shape,
whether it could clothe itself in this at all, and, if it
could, whether it would find favour and allowance at
the bar of taste, as satisfying the conditions of beauty,
this all was a secondary consideration. Nay, we may
affirm that this was not a consideration at all; for indeed, with the one exception of the Cherubim, there was
no intention that the symbol should embody itself outwardly, but rather that it should remain ever and only
a purely mental conception, the unembodied sign of an
idea;—I may observe, by the way, that no skill of delineation can make the Cherubim themselves other than un-
sightly objects to the eye. Thus in this present description
of Christ, sublime and majestic as it is beyond all conception of ours, it is only such so long as we keep it wholly
apart from any external embodiment. Produce it outwardly, the sword going forth from the mouth, the eyes as
a flame of fire, the hair white as wool, the feet as molten
brass; and each and all of these images in one way or
another violate and offend our sense of dignity and beauty.
Bengel, missing this important distinction, has ventured
to give a picture of the Lord Jesus according to this description, prefixing it to his German *Commentary on the
Apocalypse*; a picture which is almost degrading, and

only not deeply offensive to every sentiment of reverence and religious awe, because we are sure that it could not have been so intended by this admirable man.[1]

The explanation of the difference does not lie altogether in the fact that the Greek created his symbol, and therefore could do what he pleased with his own; while the Hebrew received his from God, and could not therefore venture to touch it. It would have existed more or less without this distinction between the given and the invented, the inspired and uninspired. The unsightliness, often the repulsiveness, of the symbol so long as it is judged merely by the laws of æsthetic beauty, is common to all the religions of the East. What an ugly sight is the 'Artemis multimammia,' the Artemis with many breasts, of Ephesus,—an Oriental deity, it need hardly be said, and not a Greek; what monstrous forms the Indian idols, with their many heads and their hundred arms, present; expressing as these many heads do, thought, and these hundred arms, power to embody that thought in act. With all this we should altogether err if we accepted this as the mark of an inferiority of these nations to the Greeks. Inferiority in one aspect no doubt it does indicate, a slighter perception of the beauty of form; but superiority in other and more important matters, a deeper religious earnestness, a feeling upon their part that the essence was above the form, a conviction that *truth*, such

---

[1] Others have done the same, though with quite a different object and aim. I can perfectly remember seeing exposed in Carlile's shop-window a blasphemous picture with the title, 'The God of the Bible,' or, 'The God of the Old Testament,' constructed according to a similar scheme. Two or three days after, a Jew was brought before the magistrates, a 'zealot,' who in a righteous indignation had dashed his hand through the window, seized and destroyed it; and I do not think it appeared again.

as they conceived it, was more than *beauty*, and that everything else, as of inferior moment, was to be sacrificed to this.

Ver. 17. '*And when I saw Him, I fell at his feet as dead.*' On this second aorist (ἔπεσα) with a termination of the first, an Alexandrian, and afterwards a Byzantine, form, see Lobeck, *Phrynichus*, p. 724, and Sturz, *De Dialecto Alexandrinâ*, p. 61. See also Westcott's *New Testament*, p. 164.—This falling, as is evident, is no voluntary act of homage on the part of St. John, but an involuntary expression of the effect produced upon him by that awful vision which he saw. Finding, as it does, its parallel in almost all manifestations of a divine, or even an angelic, presence, it must be owned to contain a mighty, because an instinctive witness for the sinfulness of man's nature ; out of which it comes to pass that any very near revelation from the heavenly world fills the children of men, even the holiest among them, with terror and amazement, yea, sometimes with the expectation of death itself. Examples innumerable make evident that this holds true of good men quite as much as of bad (Gen. iii. 8 ; xvii. 3 ; Exod. iii. 6 ; Num. xvi. 22 ; xxii. 31 ; Josh. v. 14 ; Judg. vi. 22 ; xiii. 6, 20, 22 ; 1 Chron. xxi. 20 ; 2 Chron. vii. 3 ; Job iv. 12–15 ; xlii. 5, 6 ; Isai. vi. 5 ; Ezek. i. 28 ; iii. 23 ; xliii. 3 ; xliv. 4 ; Dan. vii. 15 ; viii. 17 ; x. 7–9, 15 ; Tob. xii. 16 ; Matt. xvii. 6 ; xxviii. 4, 5 ; Mark xvi. 5, 8 ; Luke i. 12, 29 ; ii. 9 ; v. 8 ; xxiv. 5 ; John xviii. 6 ; Acts ix. 4 ; x. 4). The unholy, and all flesh is such, cannot endure immediate contact with the holy, the human with the divine. Heathen legend, so far as the homage of its testimony may be accepted, consents here with Christian truth. Semele must perish, if Jupiter reveals himself to her in his glory, being consumed in the

E

brightness of that glory; cf. Exod. xxxiii. 18, 20 : 'Thou
canst not see my face; for there shall no man see Me,
and live.' And for examples in art of this overwhelming
terror as an accompaniment of all very near revelations of
the higher world, see such passages as these in Virgil, Æn.
ii. 774; iii. 29, 30; 47, 48; 175; iv. 279, 280; vii. 458,
459; xii. 867. For *every* man it is a dreadful thing to
stand face to face with God; and they have missed the true
facts of the case who have missed this. The beloved disciple, who looked upon, and whose hands had handled, the
Word of life (1 John i. 1), who had lain in his Lord's bosom
in the days of his flesh, could as little as any other endure
the revelation of his majesty, or do without that '*Fear not*,'
with which that Lord at once reassures him.

'*And He laid his right hand upon me, saying unto
me, Fear not.*'—'*Unto me*' should be omitted. This
same '*Fear not*' is uttered on similar occasions to Daniel
(x. 12), to Peter (Luke v. 1), to the Three at the Transfiguration, of whom John himself was one (Matt. xvii. 7);
to the holy women at the sepulchre (Matt. xxviii. 5 ; Mark
xvi. 6). Nor is this reassurance confined to words only;
the Lord at the same time lays his hand upon him,—
something parallel to which goes along with more than
one '*Fear not*' of those referred to just now (cf. Jer. i. 9;
Isai. vi. 7); and from the touch of that hand the Seer
receives strength again, and is set, no doubt, upon his
feet once more (Ezek. i. 28; ii. 1, 2; Acts xxvi. 16). The
right hand being ever contemplated in Scripture as the
hand of power alike for God (Deut. xxxiii. 2; Isai. xlviii.
13; Acts vii. 55) and for man (Gen. xlviii. 14; Zech. iii.
1 ; Matt. v. 30), it is only fit that with the *right* hand of
the Lord he should be thus strengthened and revived (cf.
Isai. xli. 10).

'*I am the first and the last.*'—This prerogative is three times claimed for the Lord Jehovah in Isaiah (xli. 4; xliv. 6; xlviii. 12); and in like manner three times in this Book (here, and ii. 8; xxii. 13). It is the expression of absolute Godhead: 'I am the first and the last, and beside Me there is no God' (Isai. xliv. 6). He is from eternity to eternity, so that there is no room for any other. All creation comes forth from Him (John i. 1–3), all creation returns to Him again, as from whom and by whom and to whom are all things. Not the semi-Socinian expositors alone, as Grotius and Wetstein, but others who lie under no such suspicion, Cocceius for instance, and Vitringa, have here gone astray, making '*first*' to mean the first in glory, and '*last*' the last in humiliation; 'I am He who, being the foremost and first in all honour, became the lowest and last in dishonour, sounding the lowest depths of ignominy and shame.' This, which itself is true (Phil. ii. 7, 8), is yet not the truth of this place. That truth is nobly expressed in the comment of a medieval theologian, Richard of St. Victor, more than once quoted already; ' Ego sum primus et novissimus. Primus per creationem, novissimus per retributionem. Primus, quia ante Me non est formatus Deus; novissimus, quia post Me alius non erit. Primus, quia a Me sunt omnia; novissimus, quia ad Me sunt omnia; a Me principio, ad Me finem. Primus, quia Ego sum causa originis; novissimus, quia Ego judex et finis.'

Ver. 18. '*I am He that liveth and was dead, and behold, I am alive for evermore. Amen.*'—Translate rather '*And the living One, and I became dead, and behold, I am living for evermore.*' Gain, as it appears to me, will thus accrue to every clause of the sentence. In the first place, καί, connecting this verse so closely with the one

preceding, will have its rights, which are wholly overlooked
in our Version. Then ὁ ζῶν expresses not so much that
He, the speaker, ' lived,' as that He was 'the Living One,'
the Life (John i. 4; xiv. 6), αὐτοζωή, having life in Himself, and being the fountain and source of life to others;
ὁ τῆς ἀπείρου πρύτανις ζωῆς, as Clement · of Alexandria
grandly calls Him (Quis Div. Salv. 25). It is true
that in one sense it is the exclusive prerogative of the
Father to have life in Himself, but a prerogative which
He has communicated with the Son (John v. 26); of Him
too it may be said, in the words of the Psalmist, παρὰ Σοὶ
πηγὴ ζωῆς (Ps. xxxvi. 10, LXX). To Him belongs absolute being (ὄντως εἶναι), as contrasted with the relative
being of the creature, with the life which may be no life,
seeing that it inevitably falls under the dominion of corruption and death, so soon as it is separated from Him,
the source from which it was derived; for others may
share, but He only hath, immortality (1 Tim. vi. 16), being
οὐσία ἀθάνατος, οὐ μετουσίᾳ (Theodoret). All this is
included in Christ's assertion here of Himself as ὁ ζῶν.
Being thus The Living One, He goes on to say, 'I yet
became (ἐγενόμην) dead; I the source of all life stooped
even to taste of death.' Such is the second clause, and
then follows the glorious third. 'This state of death endured for Me but for an instant. I laid down my life that
I might take it again. I drank of the brook in the way,
and therefore have I lifted up my head (Ps. cx. 7); death
has now in Me been so swallowed up in life, that behold,
I am living for evermore.'

'And have the keys of hell and of death.'—We should
read rather ' of death and of hell,' for so all the best
MSS. and Versions have it, while the reading of our
Translation inverts the natural and logical order; for it is

death which peoples hell or Hades; it is a king Death who
makes possible a kingdom of the dead (vi. 8; xx. 13, 14);
for by '*hell*,' or Hades, this invisible kingdom or dominion
of the dead is intended, and that in all its extent, not
merely in one dark province of it, the region assigned to
the lost.   Hengstenberg indeed affirms in his own confident way that '*death*' here means the second death, and
as a consequence that '*hell*,' or Hades, can mean only
gehenna; observing that in the New Testament this
second death is alone set forth as an object of fear.   But
why is it that the other death, itself the outward sign and
seal of God's extreme indignation against sin, has ceased
to be an object of terror, has been robbed for the faithful
of its sting?   Why, except for that fact which we find
proclaimed in these words, namely, that the Son of God
has gone down into the dark realm of shadows and returned from it again—and not this only, but returned
from it a conqueror, having overcome death, and burst,
like another Samson (Judg. xvi. 3), the gates of the city
of the grave which shut Him in; and in pledge of this
having the keys of both, the absolute Lord who opens and
shuts them at his will for all the children of men.   For
myself I cannot doubt, above all when I look at the words
which immediately go before, that Christ sets Himself forth
here as the overcomer of death natural; which it must
always be remembered is rather death *unnatural*; for
man was made for immortality (Gen. ii. 17), and death
is the denial and reversal of the true law of his creation
(Rom. v. 12; Wisd. i. 13–16).   He who is the Prince of
life is indeed but saying here what already He had been
bold to say, while the victory was yet unwon: 'I am the
Resurrection, and the Life' (John xi. 25); life, that is, in
conflict with death, and overcoming it.   The keys are the

emblems of authority (cf. iii. 7); to have the keys is to
have the power of Himself going in and out as He pleases,
of admitting and excluding, shutting up and delivering
others : cf. Deut. xxxii. 39, 'I kill and I make alive;'
and 1 Sam. ii. 6.   The metaphor rests on the conception of
Hades as a city with walls and gates; Christ had spoken
in his earthly life of the 'gates of hell' (Matt. xvi. 18;
cf. Isai. xxxviii. 10; Job xxxviii. 17 ; Ps. cvii. 18).

Let me express here, before leaving this subject, the
regret which all who have thoughtfully compared our Version with the original must feel that the one word 'hell'
covers in it two words so different in meaning as ᾅδης and
γέεννα, the first 'Sheol,' the gathering-place of all departed souls (Prov. xxvii. 20), the second the λίμνη τοῦ
πυρός of this Book (xix. 20; xx. 10), the final abode of
the lost.   All must lament the manifold confusions which
out of this have arisen ; the practical loss, indeed, among
our people of any doctrine about Hades at all.   In the
R. V. the error is corrected ; but who can measure the
years which must pass before the correction of the error
makes itself popularly felt among us, if ever it does this?
The relations of ᾅδης to γέεννα, and also to παράδεισος,
are well put in this extract from a funeral sermon of
Jeremy Taylor: 'The word Ἅιδης signifies indefinitely
the state of separation, whether blessed or accursed; it
means only " the invisible place," or the region of darkness, whither whoso descends shall be no more seen.   For
as among the heathens the Elysian fields and Tartara are
both ἐν Ἅιδου,[1] so among the Jews and Christians para-

---

[1] As witness the lines of the comic poet :

καὶ γὰρ καθ' Ἅιδην δύο τρίβους νομίζομεν,
μίαν δικαίων, χατέραν ἀσεβῶν ὁδόν.

disus and *gehenna* are the distinct states of *Hades.'*
Compare König, *Die Lehre von Christi Höllenfahrt*, 1842,
a very complete monograph on its subject; and an article
Niedergefahren zur Hölle, by Laible, in the *Zeitschrift
für Luth. Theol.* 1863, pp. 22–92.

Ver. 19. ' *Write the things which thou hast seen, and
the things which are, and the things which shall be hereafter.'*—It was certainly a piece of carelessness on the part
of our Translators to have omitted, which none of the previous translators had done, the οὖν ('Write *therefore'*),
about the right of which to a place in the text no question
has been ever made. With what intention the illative
particle is used, is not so easy to determine ; perhaps it is
best referred to what goes immediately before : 'Seeing
that I am this mighty One, the first and last, who was
dead and am alive, do thou therefore write ; for the things
declared by Me are all steadfast and sure.'

Ver. 20. ' *The mystery of the seven stars which thou
sawest in my right hand, and of the seven golden candlesticks. The seven stars are the Angels of the seven Churches,
and the seven candlesticks which thou sawest are the seven
Churches.'*—We may either regard the first sentence as
governed by the ' *Write'* of the verse preceding ; so no
doubt our Translators, who place only a comma at the
conclusion of that verse ; or else, placing a full-stop there,
regard these words as a sort of nominative absolute, the
statement of the ' *mystery,'* or spiritual riddle, of which
the solution follows in the latter half of the verse—a
distribution which to my mind seems preferable to the
other.—A ' mystery ' in the constant language of Scripture
is something which man is capable of knowing, but only
when it has been revealed to him by God (Matt. xiii. 11 ;
Rom. xi. 25 ; Ephes. vi. 19 ; 1 Cor. xiii. 2), and not through

any searching of his own. Thus 'mystery' and 'revelation,' μυστήριον and ἀποκάλυψις, are correlative terms (Rom. xvi. 25); and as in the former clauses of the present verse there is the μυστήριον, so in the latter the ἀποκάλυψις μυστηρίου. From this, the revelation of the mystery, we learn that '*the seven stars are the Angels of the seven Churches.*' In all the typical language of Scripture stars are symbols of lordship and authority, ecclesiastical or civil. Thus a star is the symbol of the highest dominion of all: 'There shall come a *Star* out of Jacob' (Num. xxiv. 7); and the actual birth of Him whom Balaam prophesied of here, is announced by a star (Matt. ii. 2; cf. Isai. xiv. 12). Faithful teachers are stars that shall shine for ever (Dan. xii. 3); false teachers are wandering stars (Jude 13), or stars which fall from heaven (Rev. viii. 10; vi. 13; xii. 4). But only when we know exactly what '*the Angels of the seven Churches*' mean, shall we feel perfectly sure that we have interpreted the '*stars*' aright; or rather that we have apprehended aright the interpretation of them given here by the Spirit.

These '*Angels*' have given rise to much discussion and debate. Some have understood by them the *heavenly* messengers who bear this name. They urge that, often elsewhere in this Book as the word 'Angel' recurs, it is never employed in any other sense; therefore that in these we are to recognize the guardian Angels over the several Churches, 'their Angels;' that if single persons had thus their Angels (Matt. xviii. 10; cf. Acts xii. 15), much more the same might be predicated of Churches (Dan. xii. 1). Thus Origen (*Hom*. xiii. *in Luc*.): 'Si audacter expedit loqui Scripturarum sensum sequenti, per singulas Ecclesias bini sunt Episcopi, alius visibilis, alius invisibilis; ille visui carnis, hic sensui patens. Et quomodo homo, si

commissam sibi dispensationem bene egerit, laudatur a
Domino, si male, culpæ et vitio subjacet, sic et Angelus.'
And again (*Hom.* xx. *in Num.*): 'Secundum ea quæ Johannes in Apocalypsi scribit, unicuique Ecclesiæ generaliter
Angelus præest, qui vel collaudatur pro bene gestis populi,
vel etiam pro delictis ejus culpatur. In quo etiam stu-
pendi mysterii admiratione permoveor, quod intantum Deo
cura de nobis sit, ut etiam Angelos suos culpari pro nobis
et confutari patiatur. Sic enim cum pædagogo traditur
puer, si forte minus dignis, nec secundum paternam nobi-
litatem imbutus appareat disciplinis, continuo culpa ad
pædagogum refertur, nec ita puer a patre ut pædagogus
arguitur.' Cf. Jerome (*In Mich.* vi. 1, 2), who here follows close in the footsteps of Origen.

The preoccupation of an obvious objection is in the
words just quoted ingeniously attempted, but not success-
fully accomplished. Indeed the objection is one which it
is impossible to surmount: this, namely, How could *holy*
Angels be charged with such delinquencies as are laid to
the charge of some of the Angels here (ii. 4; iii. 1, 15)?
There are some good observations on this point in Augustine (*Ep.* 43, § 22): 'Angelo Ecclesiæ Ephesi scribe;
Quod si de Angelo superiorum cœlorum, et non de præ-
positis Ecclesiæ vellet intelligi, non consequenter diceret:
Sed habeo adversum te, quod caritatem primam reliquisti.
Hoc de superioribus Angelis dici non potest, qui perpetuam
retinent caritatem, unde qui defecerunt et lapsi sunt, dia-
bolus est et angeli ejus.' Moreover, as Röthe well asks,
if these Angels are *heavenly* ones, what meaning would
the injunction '*Write*' in this case possess (*Anfänge der
Kirche*, p. 423)?

This then of the '*Angels*' meaning *heavenly* Angels
may certainly be dismissed. All which Alford has urged

in its favour will fail to produce any wide acceptance for
it. The Angel must be some person or persons in the
Church on earth, not one overlooking it from heaven. I
say some person *or persons*, not as myself thinking it
possible that he can represent a plurality, but having in
view explanations which by some have been offered, and
on which something will need to be said.

But if some human person in the Church, who but the
chief shepherd, in other words, the bishop? To whom
else would all which we here in these Epistles find ascribed
to the Angel apply? For myself, I cannot but think that
the argument for the existence of the episcopate in the
later apostolic times, and that as a divinely recognized
institution, which may be drawn from the position of the
Angels in the several Churches, and from the language
in which they are addressed, is exceedingly strong. The
Angel in each Church is one; but surely none can suppose for an instant that there was only one presbyter, or
other minister serving in holy things, for the whole flourishing Church of Ephesus, or of Smyrna; and that we are
in this way to account for the single Angel of the several
Churches. Thirty years before this time St. Paul had
uttered his parting words at Miletus to the elders of the
Ephesian Church (Acts xx. 17), and certainly addressed
them even then as many (ver. 25). Taking into account
what we know of the spread of the Christian faith in these
parts during the intermediate time, it is probable that
their number was at this time largely increased. And
yet, numerous as by this time the presbyters must have
been, there is only one Angel in each of these Churches.
What can he be but a bishop?—a bishop too with the
prerogatives which we ascribe to one. His preëminence
cannot be explained away, as though he had been merely

a ruling elder, *primus inter pares*, with only such authority and jurisdiction as the others, his peers, may have agreed to lend him. For the great Bishop of souls who is here on his spiritual visitation, everywhere holds the Angel responsible for the spiritual condition of his Church; for the false teaching which he has not put down, for the false teachers whom he has not separated off from the communion of the faithful,—in short, for every disorder in doctrine or discipline which has remained unrepressed. But Christ could not so deal with them, could not charge them personally with these negligences and omissions, unless upon the ground that they had been clothed with power and authority sufficient to prevent them, so that these evils could only exist through their neglect or connivance.

I am very far from affirming that bishops were commonly called Angels in the primitive Church; or called so at all, except with a more or less conscious reference to this use of the word in the Apocalypse. There is a certain mysteriousness, and remoteness from the common language of men, in the adoption of this term, and such there is intended to be. It belongs to the enigmatic symbolic character of the Book, elevated in its language throughout above the level of daily life. Those to whom this title is ascribed are herein presented to the Church as clothed with a peculiar dignity, and are herein themselves reminded that they stand before One, whose ministries of grace and love they should be swift to fulfil on earth, even as those whose names they bear are swift to fulfil them in heaven. There is then a certain, though very partial right in what Origen taught; and 'Angel' *is* a heavenly title here; but a heavenly title which has been borrowed by earth, which has been transferred and applied to men; a transfer

not without its analogies in the Old Testament (Eccles.
v. 6; Hagg. i. 13; Mal. ii. 7; iii. 1); and rendered more
easy by the fact that Angel is a name not designating the
personality, but only the *office*, of those heavenly beings
by whom it properly is borne. Thus the author of the
Commentary once ascribed to Augustine : 'Nam quia etiam
Angelus nuntius interpretatur, quicumque aut episcopus,
aut presbyter, aut etiam laicus frequenter de Deo loquitur,
et quomodo ad vitam æternam perveniatur annunciat,
merito angelus Dei dicitur.'

It is nothing wonderful that those who maintain the
government of the Church to have been presbyterian at
the first, and who see in the episcopate a result of declension from apostolic purity, and of the springing up of a
sinful φιλοπρωτεύειν (3 John 9) in the Church, should
refuse to accept these conclusions. At the same time
they are far from being at one in the method whereby
they have sought to escape the argument for primitive
episcopacy which we believe that we are here justified in
finding.

Thus some affirm that the Angel is not any one person,
but stands for and represents the whole body of the
προεστῶτες, the collective presbytery, contemplated and
addressed as this single person   So for the most part the
early anti-episcopal Protestants, Brightman for example.
That such commentators as Hengstenberg have been able
to satisfy themselves with such an explanation, has always
filled me with wonder. The mere statement that the
Angel means 'das gesammte Kirchenregiment' (his own
words), seems to involve its own condemnation. Vitringa
(*De Synag. Vet.* p. 911) with more candour mentions this
explanation only to reject it, and finds a clear testimony
here for the superior dignity of one in these several

Churches; though naturally the episcopate which he thus recognizes is of the mildest form, of the Ussherian type; and Beza in like manner glosses τῷ ἀγγέλῳ, i. e. προεστῶτι; though, curiously enough, he considers that the upgrowth of the tyrannous hierarchy of Rome is evidence sufficient that, however there were these προεστῶτες in the apostolic Churches, it was never intended of God that such should always continue.

But those who are determined that at any rate there shall be no bishop here, are not all agreed among themselves how they shall get rid of him; and this resolving of the Angel into a presbyterian board has appeared to some, to Ebrard for instance, so poor an escape from the embarrassment, that they have devised another, but if possible a poorer still. The explanation they offer rests on the entirely gratuitous assumption that the seven Churches had sent *their* messengers to St. John at Patmos, therefore called the '*Angels* (cf. Luke ix. 15) *of the Churches,*' as having been sent by them. These in these Epistles are now successively addressed, that they may carry back his word, or rather the word of Christ, to the congregations from which they had been deputed. But in answering a letter by a messenger, men write *by* him, they do not usually write *to* him; nor is it easy to see where is the correspondency between such messengers, subordinate officials of the Churches, and stars; or what the '*mystery*' of the relation between them then would be; or how the Lord should set forth as an eminent prerogative of his, that He held the seven stars, that is, the seven messengers, in his right hand (ii. 1). The scheme breaks down at every point, and among many lame and impotent explanations must needs be regarded as the lamest and most impotent of all. On this subject compare what

Jeremy Taylor has affirmed in his *Episcopacy Asserted*, sect. 9.

I will take the opportunity of a pause between this, the Introduction to the seven Epistles, and the seven Epistles themselves, to say a few needful words on the mystery of the number seven; which only I have left unsaid so long, because unwilling to interrupt the exposition by any thing in the shape of a dissertation; not to say that I found it difficult to attach particularly to any one of those important sevens which have already occurred, considerations which properly belonged to them all.

Even the most careless reader of the Apocalypse must be struck with the manner in which almost every thing there is ordered by sevens. Thus, besides the seven Churches, and their seven Angels, we have already in this first chapter the seven Spirits (ver. 4), the seven candlesticks (ver. 12), the seven stars (ver. 16); and further on, seven lamps of fire (iv. 4), seven seals (v. 1), seven horns and seven eyes of the Lamb (v. 6), seven heavenly Angels with their seven trumpets (viii. 2), seven thunders (x. 3) seven heads of the dragon, and seven crowns upon these heads (xii. 3), the same of the beast rising out of the sea (xiii. 1), seven last plagues (xv. 1), seven vials (xv. 7), seven mountains (xvii. 9), seven kings (xvii. 10); not to speak of other recurrences, not so obvious, of this number seven as the signature of the Book; as, for instance, the distribution of the entire Book into seven visions, the sevenfold ascription of glory to the Lamb (v. 12), and to God (vii. 12).

But indeed the recurrence, and, I shall seek to show, the symbolic dignity of the number seven runs through the whole of Scripture from first to last,—to say nothing of the echoes of this sense of its significance which abound in every religion of heathendom;[1] and if this is more strongly marked in the Apocalypse than in any other book of Scripture, it is only that this, like so much else, has culminated here. Should it be asked, What is the special significance, and what the sacredness and peculiar dignity of seven, and of what is it the signature? the answer is not very hard to give. A careful induction from all the passages where this number cannot be regarded as fortuitous, but is evidently of Divine ordinance and appointment (I call fortuitous such sevens as occur, Acts xix. 14; xx. 6), will leave no doubt that it claims throughout Scripture to be considered as the covenant number, the sign and signature of God's covenant relation to mankind, and above all to that portion of mankind with which this relation is not potential merely, but actual, namely, the Church.

The evidences of this reach back to the very beginning. We meet them first in the hallowing of the seventh day, in pledge and token of the covenant of God with man (Gen. ii. 3; cf. Ezek. xx. 12).[2] So too circumcision, being the sign of a covenant, is accomplished on the eighth, or after seven days (Gen. xvii. 12; Lev. xii. 3). And as seven is the signature of God's covenant with man, so of all man's covenants with his fellows, resting as these do,

---

[1] 'Die allgemeine Heiligkeit der Siebenzahl haben die Alten schon in allen Beziehungen bemerkt' (Creuzer, *Symbolik*, vol. ii. p. 161, where see a large collection of the literature on the subject).

[2] It was therefore a true instinct of hatred against a divine institution which led those who in the first French Revolution proclaimed the abolition of the Christian religion, to make war also on the Christian week, the distribution of time by sevens, and to substitute that by decades in its stead. They felt that here was a witness for God in the world, a witness that He was the measurer out of our times to us, and of our duty to sanctify to Him the times that He had thus measured out, which must not be allowed to continue.

and must, on the anterior covenant with God; thus of treaties of peace (Gen. xx. 20), of marriages (Judg. xiv. 12). Nor should it be left unnoticed that the word seven is bound up in the Hebrew word signifying an oath, or a covenant confirmed with an oath. Seven is the number of sacrifice, by aid of which the covenant, once established, is continually maintained in its first vigour and strength, and the relations between God and man, which sin is evermore disturbing, and threatening to bring to an end, are restored (1 Kin. viii. 65; 2 Chron. xxix. 21; Job xlii. 8; cf. Num. xxiii. 1, 14, 29). It is the number of purification and consecration, as the fruit of the sacrifice (Lev. iv. 6, 17; viii. 11, 33; xiv. 9, 51; xvi. 14, 19; Num. xix. 12, 19), of forgiveness (Matt. xviii. 21, 22; Luke xvii. 4). Then, again, seven is the number of every grace and benefit bestowed upon Israel; these being thus marked as flowing out of the covenant and resulting from it (2 Kin. iv. 35). The priests compass Jericho seven days, and on the seventh day seven times, that all Israel may know that the city is given into their hands by their God; and that its conquest is a direct and immediate result of their covenant relation to Him (Josh. vi. 4, 15, 16; Heb. xi. 30). It is the number of reward to those that are faithful in the covenant (Deut. xxviii. 7; 1 Sam. ii. 5; Prov. xxiv. 16; Ecclus. xxxii. 13); of punishment to those who are froward in the covenant (Lev. xxvi. 21, 24, 28; Num. xii. 14, 15; Deut. xxviii. 25; 2 Sam. xii. 18; xxi. 6; xxiv. 13), or to those who injure the people in it (Gen. iv. 15, 24; Ps. lxxix. 12; Exod. vii. 25); or again of punishment, regarded in the light of a making of amends, a readjusting of the disturbed balances of justice, and so a restoring of harmony between the sinner and the outraged law of God (Prov. vi. 31; Ecclus. vii. 3; xl. 8). All the feasts, as is obvious, are ordered by seven, or else by seven multiplied into seven (7×7), and so made intenser still. Thus, not to recur again to the Sabbath, the mother of all feasts, it is with the Passover (Exod. xii. 15, 16), the feast of weeks (Deut. xvi. 9), of tabernacles (Deut. xvi. 13, 15), the sabbath-year (Lev. xxv. 2, 3; Deut. xv. 1), and the jubilee (Lev. xxv. 8);[1] thus also with Solomon's feast of dedication (1 Kin. viii. 65; cf. 2 Chron. xxx. 22, 23).

Further we may observe that wherever God is at work in the history of other nations outside of the covenant, while yet He would make it plainly to appear that it is for Israel's sake, and having respect to the covenant, that He is so working, this signature of seven in his dealing with those nations is never wanting. Thus it is the number of the years of plenty and of the years of famine, in sign that these were sent not so much for Egypt's sake, as for Israel's, and as conducing to the divine preparation through which the chosen people were to pass (Gen. xli. 26, 27). Naaman is to wash in Jordan seven times, that he may acknowledge in the God of Israel the author of his cure (2 Kin. v. 10). Seven times pass over Nebuchadnezzar, that he may learn in his abasement that the God of his Jewish captives is indeed the King over all the earth (Dan. iv. 16, 23, 25). But the subject is inexhaustible, the significance of the number seven meeting us at every turn in Scripture. When St. Jude reminds us that Enoch, in whom the patriarchal piety reached its highest bloom, was 'the seventh from Adam' (ver. 14), it is surely something more than a mere genealogical notice which he is

---

[1] See Philo, *De Septenario, De Abrah.* § 5; and again *Legg. Alleg.* § 4, the passage beginning χαίρει ἡ φύσις ἑβδομάδι, and indeed his works, throughout, on the ἱερὰ ἑβδομάς, as he constantly calls it. Compare Gfrörer, *Alexandr. Theosoph.* vol. ii. pp. 98 sqq.

giving;[1] as certainly it is not by accident that in Lamech, he too the seventh from Adam, the impiety of the apostate race of Cain reached its highest height (Gen. iv. 23). Who again will venture to affirm it an accident that there are seven beatitudes, seven petitions in the Lord's Prayer, that the parables in Matthew xiii. are seven, that the woes denounced in twenty-third chapter of St. Matthew against the Pharisees are seven,[2] that the Lord spake seven words from his cross, that by seven words He brought his discourse with the Samaritan woman to its glorious termination (John iv. 7, 10, 13, 16, 18, 21, 26)? St. Matthew ascribes such a virtue to the number, that, as might almost seem, he employs a certain violence that he may distribute our Lord's genealogy into three groups of fourteen, that is, of double sevens (i. 17).

Leaving then the *fact*, which is sufficiently evident, let us inquire into the *reason* of the fact. To the question, *Why* does seven take this place, what are the grounds of its adoption to this high dignity and honour, the answer is not very difficult to give. It is true that in all speculations upon numbers we may very profitably lay to heart the wise caution of Fuller,[3] clothed, as is ever the case with his wisdom, in witty words: 'For matter of numbers fancy is never at a loss, like a beggar never out of his way, but hath some haunts where to repose itself. But such as in expounding of Scripture reap more than God did sow there,

---

[1] **Gregory** of Nyssa (*In Verb. Faciam Hom. Orat.* 2): Ἕβδομος ἀπὸ γενέσεως οὐκ εἶδε θάνατον Ἐνώχ, μυστήριον ἐκκλησίας. He has much of interest on the mystery of seven.

[2] In our Authorized Version they are eight; but the woe of verse 14 has been brought here by transcribers, who have transferred it from Mark xii. 40 and Luke xx. 47. It has here no proper place.

[3] *A Pisgah Sight of Palestine*, b. iii. c. 6.

never eat what they reap thence, because such grainless husks, when seriously threshed out, vanish all into chaff.' And yet I feel very sure that in this matter which is now before us, we need not fear lest we should be threshing barren ears, with only chaff for our pains.

To the question then asked above it may be replied by first calling attention to the fact that the number seven results from the combination of three and four; for we may observe that whenever this sacred seven falls of itself, or is divided, into two groups, it is never into five and two, or six and one; but always into three and four, or four and three; thus the Lord's Prayer (Matt. vi. 9–15) contains three εὐχαί, having to do with the glory of God, and four αἰτήματα, relating to the needs of men; while on the other hand the seven parables of Matthew xiii. are divided into groups; first of four, spoken on the sea-side and to the multitude (ver. 1), and then of three, spoken after a considerable pause in the house and to the disciples (ver. 36). It is the same in this Book with the trumpets (viii. 13), and the vials (xvi. 3–7). But can it be shown that this three and four in Scripture have severally any symbolic significance of their own? Assuredly yes: three, the signature of God; four, that of the world; and thus seven, or these numbers brought into contact and relation, the token and signature of the covenant between the two.

That three is the number of God, of the ever-blessed Trinity, this of itself needs no proof. And it is so recognized in Scripture. There are vestiges of this in the Old Testament; in the three mysterious angel-visitors who appear to Abraham in the plains of Mamre (Gen. xviii. 1) in the blessing as from three distinct persons, Num. vi. 24–26; in the *Trisagion* of Isai. vi. 3; in the prominent

position assumed throughout by the Angel of the Covenant,
hereafter to be acknowledged as the second Person of the
Trinity; in the often mention not of God, but of *the Spirit*
of God, hereafter to be acknowledged as the third Person
therein (Gen. i. 2; Ps. li. 11). These footprints of the
Trinity are purposely more or less obscure, and only clear
when they are traced in the light of a later revelation;
for the office of the Church of the Old Testament was to
guard the truth of the unity of the Godhead, not to
declare the Trinity; which, indeed, so long as polytheism
was not overcome, but still had its roots even in the
minds and hearts of the chosen people itself, could not yet
have been safely declared. Here is explanation amply
sufficient of the reserve with which the number three is
employed in the Old Testament as the signature of Deity;
the reason why this is only perfectly plain and clear in the
New (Matt. xxviii. 19; 1 John v. 7).

Four, the next number to three, and growing immediately out of it, is the signature of the world—of the
world, not indeed as a rude undigested mass, but as a
κόσμος, as the revelation, so far as nature can be the revelation, of God. Four is stamped everywhere on this
organized world. Thus, not to speak of the four elements,
the four seasons, neither of which are recognized in Scripture, but are rather taken for granted, we have there the
four winds (Ezek. xxxvii. 9; Dan. vii. 2; Matt. xxiv. 31;
Rev. vii. 1); the four corners of the earth (Isai. xi. 12;
Ps. cvii. 3; Rev. vii. 1; xx. 8); the four living creatures,
emblems of all creaturely life (Rev. iv. 6), and each of
these with four faces and four wings (Ezek. i. 5, 6); the
four beasts coming up from the sea, and representing the
four great world-empires which in the providence of God
should succeed one another (Dan. vii. 3); the four metals

composing the image which sets forth the same phases of
empire (Dan. ii. 32, 33); the four forms of the judgments
of God, namely the sword, the famine, the pestilence, the
wild beasts (Rev. vi. 8; Jer. xv. 3); the four Gospels, or
the four-sided Gospel (εὐαγγέλιον τετράγωνον, as one
called it of old), in sign of its destination for all the world;
the sheet tied at the four corners (Acts x. 11; xi. 5); [1]
the four carpenters, and the four horns, the sum total of
the forces of the world as arrayed against the Church
(Zech. i. 18, 20); the enumeration, wherever this is wished
to be exhaustive, of the inhabitants of the world by four,
kindreds, tongues, peoples, and nations (Rev. v. 9; cf. vii.
9; x. 11; xi. 9; xiv. 6; xvii. 15). For other significant
enumerations by four, see Ezek. xiv. 21; Matt. xv. 31;
Rev. vi. 8; John v. 3. Of the number twelve, which is
also obtained by aid of three and four, but by these in
another combination (not as $3+4$, but as $3\times4=12$)
there is no need here to speak. It is only in later parts
of the Book that its full significance appears (vii. 5; xxi.
12; xxii. 2, and elsewhere).

There are reasons then amply sufficient why seven, being thus, as it is, made up of three and four, should be
itself the signature of the covenant. No mere accident or
caprice dictated the selection of it. And if this be the
number of the covenant, then we can account for its constant recurrence in this Book; for admitting, as few would
refuse to do, that the idea of God's covenant with his
Church as the key to all history, comes to its head in the

---

[1] Augustine (*Enarr. in Ps.* ci. *Serm.* iii.): 'Discus qui quatuor
lineis continebatur orbis terrarum erat in quatuor partibus. Has
quatuor partes sæpe Scriptura commemorat, orientem et occidentem,
aquilonem et meridiem. Ideo quia totus orbis per Evangelium
vocabatur, quatuor Evangelia conscripta sunt.'

Apocalypse, it is nothing wonderful that this Book should be more markedly ordered by seven, and have this number stamped upon it even more strongly, than any other portion of Scripture.[1]

---

[1] On this whole subject of the symbolic worth and dignity of numbers in Scripture, see Bähr, *Symbolik des Mos. Cultus*, vol. i. pp. 128-209; Züllig, *Offenb. Johannis Erklärt*, vol. i. pp. 115-127; Delitzsch, *Genesis*, 2nd edit. p. 225; in Herzog, *Encyclopädie*, art. Zahlen; and Kurtz, *Theol. Stud. u. Krit.* 1844, pp. 315-370.

THE SEVEN EPISTLES.

REV. ii. iii.

BEFORE proceeding to consider these seven Epistles in de-
tail, it may be well worth while to invite the reader's attention to the symmetry, to what we should call in any human
composition the remarkable art, to be traced in the construction of them all: quite justifying the words of
Henry More : ' There never was a book penned with that
artifice as this of the Apocalypse.' They are all constructed
precisely on the same model. They every one of them
contain—

a. A command in exactly the same terms to the Seer
that he should write to the Angel of the Church.

β. One or more glorious titles which Christ claims for
Himself, as exalting the dignity of his person, and thus
adding weight and authority to the message which He
sends ; these titles being in almost every case drawn more
or less evidently from the attributes ascribed to Him, or
claimed by Him, in the manifestation of Himself which
has just gone before (i. 4–20).

γ. The actual message from Christ to the Angel of the
Church, declaring his intimate knowledge of its condition,
good, or bad, or mixed, with a summons to steadfastness
in the good, to repentance from the evil—all this brought
home by the fact that He was walking up and down in

the midst of his Churches, having in readiness to punish, and also no less to reward.

δ. A promise to the faithful, to him that should ' *over-come* '—the heavenly blessedness being presented under the richest variety of the most attractive, and often the most original, images.

ε. Finally, the whole is summed up with an exhortation which shall give an universal character to these particular addresses, a summons to every one with a spiritual ear that he should give earnest heed to the things which were indeed spoken to all. In the addresses to the four last Churches the positions of δ and ε are reversed.

On comparing these Epistles one with another, we may observe that in two Churches, namely in Smyrna and Philadelphia, the great Shepherd and Bishop of souls finds matter only for praise; in two, Sardis and Laodicea, with very smallest exception in the former, matter only for rebuke. In three of the Churches, Ephesus, Pergamum, and Thyatira, the spiritual condition is a mixed one, so that with some things to praise, there are also some, more in one, fewer in another, to condemn. It will be perceived at once what far-looking provision is made in the selection of these particular Churches to be addressed, as in the scheme of the addresses to them, for the most varied instructions; for reproof, for praise, for reproof and praise mingled together and tempering one another; for promises and threatenings. The spiritual condition of the several Churches gives room and opportunity, nay, constitutes a necessity, for each and all of these.

I take this opportunity of mentioning that one who probably knew by experience how easily we lose sight of the fact that it is Christ Himself who speaks in these Epistles—Thomas Allen is his name—has written a book not further known to me, but with the following title: *The Christian's Sure Guide to Eternal Glory, or Living Oracles of the Lord Jesus Christ from Heaven in his Royal Embassy to the Seven Churches of Asia*, 8vo., London, 1733. Certainly the title promises well, and seems to invite a closer acquaintance with the body of the book.

I.

EPISTLE TO THE CHURCH OF EPHESUS.

Rev. ii. 1–7.

Ver. 1. '*Unto the Angel of the Church of Ephesus write.*'—Ephesus, the chief city of Ionia, πρώτη τῆς Ἀσίας, as the Ephesians themselves styled it, asserting in this style that primacy for Ephesus which Smyrna and Pergamum disputed with it, had now so far outstripped both its competitors that it was at once the civil and ecclesiastical centre of that 'Asia' with which we have to do. Wealthy, prosperous, and magnificent, 'Asiæ lumen,' as it was called, a meeting-place of oriental religions and Greek culture, and famous on many grounds in heathen antiquity, it was most famous of all for the celebrated temple of Diana, one of the seven wonders of the world, about which in Acts xix. we read so much (cf. Creuzer's *Symbolik*, vol. ii. p. 515; Wood's *Discoveries at Ephesus*; *Edinburgh Review*, Jan. 1877; Lewin's *St. Paul*, vol. i. p. 320 sqq.; Faulkener's *Ephesus and the Temple of Diana*; Renan's *St. Paul*, p. 333 sqq.).[1] But Ephesus had better

---

[1] For more about Ephesus, see Bishop Alexander's *Introduction to the First Epistle of John* (*Speaker's Bible*, vol. iv. p. 275).

titles of honour than these. It was a city greatly
favoured of God. St. Paul laboured there during three
years (Acts xx. 31); he ordained Timothy to be bishop
there (1 Tim. i. 3; cf. Eusebius, *H. E.* iii. 4); Aquila,
Priscilla, Apollos (Acts xviii. 19, 24, 26), Tychicus (Ephes.
vi. 21), all contributed to build up the Church in that
city. And if we may judge from St. Paul's Epistle to the
Ephesians, and from his parting address to the elders of
that Church (Acts xx. 17–38), nowhere did the word of
the Gospel find a kindlier soil, strike root more deeply, or
bear fairer fruits of faith and love. St. John too had
made it the chief seat of his ministry, his metropolitan
throne, during the closing years of his protracted life;
from whence he exercised a wide, though not wholly un-
questioned, jurisdiction (for see 3 Ep. 9, 10) over the
whole of ' *Asia.*' How early that ministry there began
it is impossible to say, the date of his withdrawal from
Jerusalem being itself uncertain, and uncertain also
whether he at once chose Ephesus for the middle point of
his spiritual activity. From a Church to which so much
was given, much would be required. How far it had
profited as it might by these signal advantages, how far
it had maintained itself at those spiritual heights to
which it had once attained, will presently be seen.

 ' *These things saith He that holdeth the seven stars in
his right hand.*'—Cf. i. 20, where ' *the mystery of the
seven stars* ' is unfolded. It is only when all the titles
furnished by chap. i. 4–20 are exhausted, that Christ
seeks them from any other quarter. At the same time
there is a significant alteration here. There He is ὁ ἔχων,
' *He that hath*'—here more emphatically ὁ κρατῶν, ' *He
that holdeth, the seven stars*'—this being stronger and
more emphatic than that, ' *He that holdeth*' (cf. ii. 25;

iii. 14) than ‘*He that hath.*’   Christ *holds* these stars in
his grasp,—an announcement full of comfort for them, if
only they are true to Him ; none shall pluck them out of
his hand (John x. 28) ; none shall harm them in the
delivery of their message (Matt. x. 30; Acts xviii. 9, 10);
or if the malice of their enemies is so far permitted that
they are able to kill the body, they shall only in this way
prepare for them an earlier and a speedier passage to
glory (Acts vii. 56, 60 ; Rev. xi. 7, 12) ; but an announcement full of fear for the unfaithful, for the idol shepherds
(Zech. xi. 17), who feed themselves and not the flock
(Exek. xxxiv. 1–10).   Them too He holds in his grasp,
and none can deliver them from his hand.

‘ *Who walketh in the midst of the seven golden candlesticks.*’—‘ *Who walketh* ’ is new.   The Seer had indeed
already beheld the Lord ‘ *in the midst of the seven candlesticks* ’ (i. 13), but not ‘ *walking* ’ in their midst.   The
word expresses the unwearied activity of Christ in his
Church, moving up and down in the midst of it ; beholding the evil and the good ; evermore trimming and
feeding with oil of grace the golden lamps of the sanctuary.   Marckius : ‘ Ad innuendam clarius perpetuitatem
actûs et curam Christi contra conatus oppositos Satanæ.’
It is impossible not to admire the appropriateness of these
titles, expressing as they do the broader and more general
relations of Christ to his Church, for the first Epistle in
this series; which constitutes, as this and a thousand
other tokens declare, not an accidental aggregate, but a
divinely-ordered complex, with all its parts mutually up-
holding and completing one another.

Ver. 2. ‘ *I know thy works.*’—In considering these
and all the 'following words of Christ, we must never leave
out of sight what an old interpreter has so well expressed,

'unam facit Angeli Ecclesiæque personam.' Any attempt
to distinguish between them is futile, and contrary to the
intention of the Lord. This formula, '*I know thy works*,'
is common to all the Epistles, serving as the introduction
to all ;—which being so, '*works*' are not, as some interpreters understand them, *good* works; for Christ uses
this language where there were no works which He could
count good (iii. 15); as little are they *bad* works (iii. 8);
but the word is used with the same freedom here as in
other parts of Scripture, now for good (John vii. 21 ; 1 Cor.
iii. 14), and now for evil (Isai. lxvi. 18; 1 Cor. iii. 15;
Tit. i. 16). '*I know thy works*,' therefore has another
intention than to express either praise or blame. It declares the omniscience of Him who walks up and down
among the candlesticks of gold, whom nothing escapes
(Amos iv. 13; Ps. xi. 4, 5; John ii. 24, 25; Heb. iv. 13;
Rev. ii. 23; Acts i. 24; xv. 8); an assurance of comfort
and strength for all them who, amid infinite weaknesses
and failures, are yet able to say, 'Search me, O Lord, and
know my heart; try me, and know my thoughts, and see if
there be any wicked way in me' (Ps. cxxxix. 23, 24), or with
St. Peter, 'Lord, Thou knowest all things, Thou knowest
that I love thee' (John xxi. 17); but words full of terror
and alarm for every one who would fain keep back anything in his outer or inner life from the Lord. All things
are naked and opened unto the eyes of Him with whom
we have to do (Heb. iv. 13); and this in these words He
declares.

'*And thy labour, and thy patience*.'—There was an
earlier Angel of this same Church of Ephesus, on whom
as on his son St. Paul had urged that he should not fail
in this '*labour and patience*' (2 Tim. ii. 24, 25); and
Christ's commendation here shows that the holy lesson

had been laid to heart by him who had now stept into his
place. The κόπος, occasioned probably by the earnest
resistance which it was necessary to oppose to the false
teachers in the Ephesian Church, would naturally fall
chiefly on the bishop and presbyters—above all, on the
first.—Κόπος and κοπιάω are frequently used in reference
both to apostolic and ministerial labours (Rom. xvi. 12;
1 Cor. xv. 10; Gal. iv. 11); κόπος often in connexion
with μόχθος (1 Thess. ii. 9; 2 Thess. iii. 8; 2 Cor. xi·
27); the latter perhaps marking the toil on the side of
the magnitude of the obstacles which it has to surmount,
as the derivation μόγις, and the possible connexion with
μέγας, seems to suggest (Ellicott); the former alluding to
the toil and suffering which in these labours strenuously
and faithfully performed is involved.   Thus see my
Synonyms of the New Testament, § 102.   For indeed
this word κόπος, signifying as it does not merely labour,
but labour *unto weariness*, may suggest some solemn
reflections to every one who at all affects to be working
for his Lord, and as under his great Taskmaster's eye,
and as looking for his ' Well done.'   This is what Christ
expects, this is what Christ praises, in his servants.   But
how often does labour, which esteems itself labour for
Him, stop very short of this, take care for itself that it
shall never arrive at this point; and perhaps in our days
none are more tempted continually to measure out to
themselves tasks too light and inadequate, than those to
whom an office and ministry in the Church has been committed.   Indeed, there is here to them an ever-recurring
temptation, derived from the fact that they do for the most
part measure out their own day's task to themselves.
Others in almost every other calling or profession have
this measured out to them; if not the zeal, earnestness,

sincerity which they are to put into the performance of it,
yet at any rate its form and frame, the amount of time
which they shall devote to it, and often the definite
amount of work which they shall accomplish. It is not
so with us. We give to it exactly the number of hours
which we please; we are for the most part responsible to
no man; and when toilers thus apportion their own
burdens, and do this day after day, how near the danger
lies that they should unduly spare themselves, and make
their burdens far lighter than they should have been.
We may well keep this word κόπος, and all that it signifies, namely labour unto weariness, in mind; and remember ever that it is this which the Lord praises and allows.
—For ὑπομονή see p. 22.

'*And how thou canst not bear them which are evil.*'—
Christ has good things to say of the Church of Ephesus,
and He who, as highest Love, συγχαίρει τῇ ἀληθείᾳ, has
pleasure in and *with* the truth (1 Cor. xiii. 6), dwells on
these good things first; He graciously puts in the foremost place all which He can find to approve; and only
after this has received its meed of praise, notes the shortcomings which He is also compelled to rebuke. Many
graces had decayed at Ephesus; of this we may be sure;
seeing that the grace of all graces, namely, love, had
decayed (ver. 4); but in the midst of this decay there
survived an earnest hatred of certain evil-doers and evil
deeds. The κακοί here are not exactly equivalent to the
κακοὶ ἐργάται of Phil. iii. 2. These last are the *prominent* workers of mischief in the Church, false apostles,
false prophets, and the like; but the κακοί will include
the whole rabble of evil-doers as well. It is not a little
remarkable that the grace or virtue here ascribed to the
Angel of the Ephesian Church, and still more strongly

at ver. 6, should have a name in later heathen Greek, μισοπονηρία (Plutarch, *Quom. Am. ab Adul.* 12), the person of whom the grace is predicated being μισοπόνηρος, while neither of these words, nor yet any equivalent to them, occurs in the N. T.   This is the stranger, as this hatred of evil purely as evil, however little thought of, or admired now, is eminently a *Christian* grace (Rom. xii. 9 : cf. Gen. xxxvii. 2 ; xlix. 6 ; Ps. cxxxix. 21 ; 2 Pet. ii. 7, 8).   The sphere in which the Angel of Ephesus had the chief opportunity of manifesting a holy intolerance of evil-doers was, no doubt, that of Church-discipline, separating off from fellowship with the faithful those who named the name of Christ, yet would not depart from iniquity (2 Tim. ii. 19).   The infirmities, even the sins, of *weak* brethren, are burdens which *may* be borne, nay, which those that are spiritual are commanded to bear (cf. Gal. vi. 2, where the same word βαστάζειν is used) ; but these offenders here are not *weak* brethren, but *false* ; and there must be no such toleration of them (Ps. ci. 7, 8 ; cxix. 115 ; 1 Cor. v. 11).

'*And thou hast tried them which say they are apostles and are not, and hast found them liars.*'—We translate by the same word the πειράζειν here and the δοκιμάζειν of 1 John iv. 1.   What this Angel at Ephesus had done, and effectually done, St. John there bids the faithful to do —namely, to prove the spirits of those who came to them claiming to teach as with authority, and to bring a direct message from God (cf. 1 Thess. v. 21 ; 1 Tim. iv. 1).   The touchstone which he there gives, the Ithuriel's spear which should compel each false teacher to start up and show himself in his proper shape, is the acknowledgment or denial of the true humanity of the Son of God, that Jesus Christ was come in the flesh (ver. 2, 3 ; 2 John 7 ;

and Ignatius, passim). At the same time we must not regard this as so absolutely *the* touchstone, that other times and other conditions of the Church might not demand other tests. Thus, in the fourth century and during the Arian conflict, the *Homoousion*, ' of one substance with the Father,' was that by which the spirits were to be tried; a little later, during the Nestorian controversy, it was the θεοτόκος. And when our Lord, warning against false prophets, lays down this rule, ' Ye shall know them by their fruits' (Matt. vii. 16), He adds another test by which all such, sooner or later, may be known. By what methods the Angel of this Church had tried these pretenders to the apostolate, and discovered the falsehood of their claims, we are not told; but probably by a union of both these tests. If these false prophets were, as is generally assumed, the chiefs and leaders of the Nicolaitan wickedness, which is presently named by its name (ver. 6), then *doctrinally* he will have tried them by the touchstone of Christ's true humanity, whether they would confess this or deny it;—we may be sure that they had that in common with all other Gnostics, which led them to the denial of it;—and *practically*, by the fruits which they bore; which, being works of shame and darkness, avouched that the workers of them were not, and could not be, sent of Him who is light, and in whom is no darkness at all. And even were they not precisely identical with the Nicolaitans, on which there will be something to say at ver. 6, these tests would not the less effectually have revealed of what spirit they were, and to what kingdom they belonged.

We must not press ' *apostles* ' here, as though it implied a claim on their parts to have seen and been immediately sent by the Lord Jesus Christ, which was

necessary for an Apostle in the highest sense of the word
(Acts i. 21, 22; 1 Cor. ix. 1), nor even by the mother
Church at Jerusalem. It was now too late for either. St.
John alone of living men could claim the first prerogative,
and Jerusalem had long ago been destroyed. As little are
these 'which say they are apostles' identical in the actual
form of their resistance to the truth with those 'false
apostles, deceitful workers,' who everywhere sought to
hinder the labours of St. Paul, and everywhere denied the
apostolic authority and commission which he claimed
(2 Cor. x. 11). Those and these had indeed this in common,
that they alike opposed the truth; but those were Ju-
daizers, seeking to bring back the ceremonial law and the
obligations of it (see Acts xv. 1; Phil. iii. 2; 1 Tim. i. 7;
Gal. ii. 12; iii. 2; v. 2, 6, and indeed passim); these, on the
other hand, do not judaize, but heathenize, seeking to
throw off every yoke, to rid themselves not of the ceremonial law only, but also of the moral; and to break
down every distinction separating the Church from a
world lying in the Wicked one.[1]

Ver. 3. 'And hast borne, and hast patience, and for
my name's sake hast laboured, and hast not fainted.'—

---

[1] This intolerance of error, this resolution to hold fast the
precious deposit of the truth, to suffer nothing to be added to it,
nothing to be taken from it, nothing to be altered in it, was still the
mark and glory of the Ephesian Church at a date somewhat later
than this. It is a remarkable testimony to this which Ignatius,
writing not many years after, bears, and it admirably agrees with
the testimony which the Lord Himself bears here to its zeal for
doctrinal purity (ad Ephes. vi.): αὐτὸς μὲν οὖν 'Ονήσιμος ὑπερεπαινεῖ
ὑμῶν τὴν ἐν Θεῷ εὐταξίαν, ὅτι ἐν ὑμῖν οὐδεμία αἵρεσις κατοικεῖ· ἀλλ' οὐδὲ
ἀκούετέ τινος πλέον ἤπερ 'Ιησοῦ Χριστοῦ λαλοῦντος ἐν ἀληθείᾳ. And
again, c. ix.: ἔγνων δὲ παροδεύσαντάς τινας ἐκεῖθεν, ἔχοντας κακὴν
διδαχήν· οὓς οὐκ εἰάσατε σπεῖραι εἰς ὑμᾶς, βύσαντες τὰ ὦτα, εἰς τὸ μὴ
παραδέξασθαι τὰ σπειρόμενα ὑπ' αὐτῶν.

There is a good deal of filling up by transcribers here, and
more than one phrase to be omitted. The following version will represent more truly the original as it stands in
the best critical editions: ' *And hast patience, and didst
bear for my name's sake, and hast not grown weary.*' It
is not hard to see the inducements which led transcribers
to meddle with the text, and in the last clause of the verse
to change καὶ οὐ κεκοπίακας into κεκοπίακας καὶ οὐ κέ-
κμηκας. They took the verb κοπιάω only in the sense of
'to labour;' but how could it be said in praise of the
Ephesian Angel that he had *not* laboured ; above all when
his κόπος had just before (ver. 2) been the especial object
of the Lord's commendation, as indeed it is throughout the
Epistle? so they changed the word to what we have in the
received text and in our Version; ' *thou hast laboured,
and hast not fainted.*' But κοπιάω is not only to labour,
but implying, as we have seen it does, strenuous and ex-
hausting labour, will often mean farther, to grow weary
with labour (thus John iv. 6; Matt. xi. 28: κοπιῶντες καὶ
πεφορτισμένοι); and it is this for which the Lord here
praises the Angel and in him the Church at Ephesus, that
he was φερέπονος (Marc. Antoninus, v. 5), that he and
the others had borne the burden and heat of a long day's
toil without fainting under it, or waxing weary of it (Gal.
vi. 9). This recurrence to the κόπος of the verse preceding is very instructive, though it is hard, if not
impossible, to reproduce it in English. 'Thou knowest,'
He would say, ' what κόπος is, without knowing what
κοπιᾶν is ;' and that this is not accidental seems evident
from the exactly similar recurrence of βαστάζειν in both
verses : 'There are things which thou *canst not* bear, and
things which thou *canst* bear ; thou *canst not* bear the
wicked, such false brethren as name the name of Christ

only to bring shame and disgrace upon it; thou hast
something of the spirit of him who declared, "He that
telleth lies shall not tarry in my sight" (Ps. ci. 10; cf.
2 John 10); but thou *canst* bear my reproach, my cross;'
cf. Luke xiv. 27, where the same word βαστάζειν is used
as here; so also John xix. 17. Wetstein: 'Eleganter
opponuntur: οὐ δύνῃ βαστάσαι et ἐβάστασας. Ferre
potes molestias propter Christum et vexationes; at *non
potes* ferre pseudapostolos.'

Ver. 4. '*Nevertheless I have somewhat against thee, because thou hast left thy first love.*'—Ἔχω κατὰ σοῦ: cf.
for the same phrase Matt. v. 23; Mark xi. 25; and for a
similar, Col. iii. 13. This is one of three occasions (see
ver. 14, 20) on which Christ has to make a like exception,
and to dash and qualify his praise with blame. In
neither, however, of the other cases is the blame so severe
as here, the '*somewhat*,' which appears in part to mitigate
the severity of this judgment, having nothing corresponding with it in the original. It is indeed not a '*somewhat*,' which the Lord has against the Ephesian Church;
it threatens to grow to be an 'everything;' for see the
verse following, and compare 1 Cor. xiii. 1–3. The great
passage on '*first love*' is Jer. ii. 2: 'I remember thee,
the kindness of thy youth, the love of thine espousals,
when thou wentest after Me in the wilderness, in a land
that was not sown,'—words which set forth the first
warmth of gratitude, the first devotion of heart on the
part of Israel to its Redeemer and Lord (Exod. xiv. 31;
xv. 1), when it seemed as if the high flood-tides of a
thankful love would never ebb, but would bear it triumphantly over every obstacle, that the heart of the people
was knit for ever, by bands which could never be broken,
to Him that had brought them out of the iron furnace of

Egypt. Such a '*first love*' of the Bride to the heavenly
Bridegroom, and in Him to all that were his, dwelt largely
in the Ephesian Church when St. Paul wrote his Epistle
to it; he gives God thanks for their love unto all the
saints (i. 15); he introduces them without a misgiving
into the deepest mysteries of human love and divine (v.
23-33). The suggestion that this leaving of the first
love can refer to the abating of any other love but that to
God and Christ, grows out of an entire ignorance of the
whole spiritual life, the ways by which it travels, and the
dangers to which it is inevitably exposed, and which,
alas! only too often prove fatal to it. See Maurice,
Lectures on the Apocalypse, pp. 62, 63.

On the question, *When* the Apocalypse was given, we
have a certain amount of implicit evidence here, in this
reproach with which the Lord reproaches the Ephesian
Angel; such as has its value in confirming the ecclesiastical tradition which places it in the reign of Domitian, as
against the more modern view which gives the reign of
Nero as the date of the composition of this Book. It has
been well observed that in St. Paul's Epistle to the Church
of Ephesus, there are no signs, nor even presentiments, of
this approaching spiritual declension with which the great
Searcher of hearts upbraids it here. Writing to no Church
does he treat of higher spiritual mysteries. There is no
word in the Epistle of blame, no word indicating dissatis-
faction with the spiritual condition of his Ephesian converts. He warns them, indeed, in his parting charge given
at Miletus, against dangers threatening them at once from
within and from without (Acts xx. 29, 30); but no word
indicates that they by any fault of theirs were laying themselves open to these. As many as place the Apocalypse in
the reign of Nero hardly allow ten years between that

condition and this—too brief a period for so vast and lamentable a change.   It is inconceivable that there should
have been such a letting go of first love in so brief a time.
No : what is here described marks, as Hengstenberg has
excellently urged, the rise of another generation—a condition analogous to that of the children of Israel, when
Joshua and the elders who had seen the great wonders of
Egypt and of the desert were gathered to their fathers
(Josh. xxiv. 31 : Judg. ii. 7, 10, 11).   With their disappearance from the scene another order of things commences.
A second generation rises up with the traditions rather of
earnest religion than with its living power.   The forms,
which were once instinct with life, still survive ; but the
life itself has, not indeed altogether, yet in good part, departed from them.   Place the Apocalypse under Domitian,
and thirty years will have elapsed since St. Paul wrote his
Epistle to Ephesus—exactly the interval which we require,
exactly the life of a generation.   The outlines of the truth
are still preserved ; but the truth itself is not for a second
generation what it was for the first.   The later has the same
watchwords as had the earlier, but they do not rouse as
they did once.   The virtue which they once had has gone
from them.   In appearance there is nothing changed ;
while in fact everything is changed.   How often has something of this kind repeated itself in the Church.[1] Thus,

---

[1] A passage in Bishop Burnet's *History of his own Times* has
always seemed to me to throw light on this picture of the Ephesian
Church, active, laborious, resolute to maintain in forms of sound
words the truth once delivered, and yet with its inner principle of
love so far decayed.   He is describing the state of the Protestant
communities of Switzerland, Germany, and Holland, and of the
French Protestant refugees who had found shelter among them from
the dragonnades, the 'mission bottée,' as it is so facetiously called
by some Roman Catholic writers, of Louis XIV.   His words, written

not to look nearer home, how remarkably was all this fulfilled in the great Pietist revival in Germany, which
Franck and Spener so gloriously commenced; and those
who succeeded them so feebly carried forward; offering
as they did the faintest and feeblest resistance to the
rationalism and infidelity which a little later invaded the
Church. Gerhard Groot was wont to say of the *Fratres
Communis Vitæ*, an Order which he founded, and which
wrought much and well in the matter of preparing the
way for the Reformation, 'The first generation will be
holy, the second learned, the third worldly.'

Ver. 5. '*Remember therefore from whence thou art
fallen, and repent, and do the first works.*'—There are ever
goads in the recollection of a better and a nobler past, goad-
ing him who has taken up with meaner things and lower,
and urging him to reclaim and recover what he has lost;
as, to take an extreme instance, it is the prodigal's recollection of the 'bread enough and to spare' in his father's
house, which makes the swine's husks and the famine even

in the year 1680, are as follows: 'I was indeed amazed at the
labours and learning of the ministers among the Reformed. They
understood the Scriptures well in the original tongues, they had all
the points of controversy very ready, and did thoroughly understand the whole body of divinity. In many places they preached
every day, and were almost constantly employed in visiting their
flock. But they performed their devotions but slightly, and read
their prayers, which were too long, with great precipitation and
little zeal. Their sermons were too long and too dry. And they
were so strict, even to jealousy, in the smallest points in which they
put orthodoxy, that one who could not go into all their notions, but
was resolved not to quarrel with them, could not converse much
with them with any freedom.' Speaking of the French refugees
from the dragonnades, he says: 'Even among them there did not
appear a spirit of piety and devotion suitable to their condition,
though persons who have willingly suffered the loss of all things
rather than sin against their consciences, must be believed to have
a deeper principle in them than can well be observed by others.'

among them so intolerable to him (Luke xv. 17; cf. Heb.
x. 32.) And therefore is it that this Ephesian Angel is
bidden to remember the glorious heights of grace, the
heavenly places, whereupon, though yet on earth, he once
walked with Christ during the fervency of his first love.
Perhaps the desire shall thus be kindled in him to scale
these heights again. In this *'from whence thou art
fallen'* an allusion may possibly lie to Isai. xiv. 12, ' How
art thou fallen from heaven, O Lucifer, son of the morning.'—' *And repent, and do the first works.'* Christ does
not say, ' Feel thy first feelings ; ' that perhaps would have
been impossible, and even if possible, might have had
but little value in it; but ' *Do the first works,'* such as
thou didst in the time of thy first devotedness and zeal.
Not so much the *quantity*, as the *quality*, of his works
was now other and worse than once it had been.

' *Or else I will come unto thee quickly, and will remove thy candlestick out of his place, except thou repent.'*
—The ' *quickly* ' is wanting in most MSS., and has probably found its way here from ver. 16; iii. 11; xxii. 7, 12,
20. The removing of the candlestick from a place implies the entire withdrawal of Christ's grace, of his Church
with all its blessings, from that spot, with the transfer of
it to another ; for it is *removal* of the candlestick, not
extinction of the candle, which is threatened here—judgment for some, but that very judgment the occasion of
mercy for others. And so it has proved. The Churches
of Asia Minor are now no more, or barely and hardly exist;
but the grace of God, withdrawn from them, has been
bestowed elsewhere. The seat of the Church has been
changed, but the Church itself still survives. The candlestick has been removed, but the candle has not been
quenched; and what the East has lost the West has

gained. How awful for Ephesus the fulfilment of the
threat has been every modern traveller who has visited
the ruins of that once famous city has borne witness. One
who did so not long ago found only three Christians there,
and these sunken in such ignorance and apathy as scarcely
to have heard the names of St. Paul or St. John. This
same transfer of the Church's privileges from some to
others more worthy of them is expressed elsewhere under
other images (Matt. xxi. 41 ; Rom. xi. 17) ; while sometimes the image expresses only the judgment, and not the
mercy as well which is behind the judgment (Isai. v. 5, 7 ;
Luke xiii. 6–10).

Ver. 6. ' *But this thou hast, that thou hatest the deeds
of the Nicolaitans, which I also hate.'*—Very beautiful is
the tenderness of the Lord in thus bringing forward a
second time some good thing which He had found at
Ephesus. Having been compelled to speak sharp severe
words, He yet will not leave off with these ; but having
wounded, He will, so far as it is safe to do so, also heal.[1]
It is no slight praise to love that which Christ loves, and
to hate that which Christ hates ; and this praise the Lord
will not withhold from the Angel of Ephesus.

---

[1] On this mingling of praise, so far as truth will allow, with the
necessary blame, and the leaving off not with blame, but with
praise, Plutarch has much to say in his delightful treatise, ' *How
to discern a Flatterer from a Friend,*' which is full of instruction
on the true spirit of Christian rebuke. On this, which the Lord so
notably practises here, namely the not leaving off with rebuke, but
if possible with praise, he beautifully says (c. xxxvii.) : Ἐπεὶ τοίνυν,
ὥσπερ εἴρηται, πολλάκις ἡ παῤῥησία τῷ θεραπευομένῳ λυπηρὰ ὑπάρχει, δεῖ
μιμεῖσθαι τοὺς ἰατρούς· οὔτε γὰρ ἐκεῖνοι τέμνοντες, ἐν τῷ πονεῖν καὶ
ἀλγεῖν καταλείπουσι τὸ πεπονθὸς, ἀλλ' ἐνέβρεξαν προσηνῶς καὶ κατηόνη-
σαν· οὔτε οἱ νουθετοῦντες ἀστείως, τὸ πικρὸν καὶ δηκτικὸν προσβαλόντες
ἀποτρέχουσιν, ἀλλ' ὁμιλίαις ἑτέραις καὶ λόγοις ἐπιεικέσιν ἐκπραΰνουσι
καὶ διαχέουσιν. Cf. c. xxxiii.

But the Nicolaitans, whose deeds were the object of the earnest hate of Christ's servants, as also of his own, who were they? It is not an easy question to answer. Was there, in the first place, any sect existing at the time when these words were uttered, which actually bore this name? I believe not. The other names of this Book, Egypt, Babylon, Sodom, Jezebel, in agreement with its apocalyptic character, are predominantly mystical and symbolic; and in all probability this is so as well; while the key to the right understanding of it is given us at ii. 14, 15; where those '*that hold the doctrine of Balaam*' (ver. 14) are evidently identical with those '*that hold the doctrine of the Nicolaitans*' (ver. 15). We are here set upon the right track. It is probable that we hardly rate highly as we ought the significance of Balaam as an Anti-Moses, and therefore as an Antichrist, in the Old Testament. But without entering more into this, it may be observed that his name, according to the best etymology, signifies 'Destroyer of the people' ('qui absorpsit populum,' from בָּלַע and עַם); and Νικόλαος (νικᾶν τὸν λαόν) is no more than a grecizing of this name (see Hengstenberg, *Die Gesch. Bileams*, pp. 20–25)—such alternation, or duplication, presenting a word, now in its Greek, now in its Hebrew aspect, being altogether in the character of the Book, Greek in language, but Hebrew in form and spirit, and several times recurring in it; thus, Ἀπολλύων and Ἀβαδδών (ix. 11); Διάβολος and Σατανᾶς (xii. 9; xx. 2); ναί and ἀμήν (i. 7). The genesis of the name, which, so understood, will almost exactly correspond to Armillus (= ἐρημόλαος), the name under which the final Antichrist, according to Jewish fables, shall seduce the followers of Christ to their ruin (see Eisenmenger, *Entd. Judenth.* vol. ii. p. 705, sqq.), may be accounted for in this way.

The Nicolaitans, as we have seen, are the Balaamites ; no
sect bearing the one name or the other ; but those who
in the New Dispensation repeated the sin of Balaam, and
sought to overcome or lay waste the people of God by the
same temptations whereby Balaam had sought to overcome
them in the Old.   But it was into the fleshly sins of
heathenism that he had sought to lead them, to introduce
such among the people of God, to draw them to eat idol
meats and to commit fornication (Num. xxv. 1–9; xxxi.
16); and this the leading character of his wickedness
must be the leading one also of theirs.

The Nicolaitans, then, or Balaamites, are those who,
after the pattern of Balaam's sin, sought to introduce a
false freedom, the freedom of the flesh, into the Church
of God.   These were the foremost tempters of the Church
in the later apostolic times when the Apocalpyse was
written, and in the times immediately succeeding.   The
first great battle which the Church had to fight was with
Jewish legalism.   This came to its head *historically*, and
found its condemnation, in the Council of Jerusalem (Acts
xv. 1–31), *dogmatically* in St. Paul's Epistle to the Galatians ;—those who refused to accept the Church's decisions
on the matter of the relations of the Christian man to the
law gradually forming themselves more and more into a
body at once schismatical and heretical, known by the
name of Ebionites; not any longer within, but henceforth
without, the Church's pale.   But this danger overcome,
St. Paul lived to see before the close of his ministry the
rise of another, and that exactly the opposite error—that,
namely, of heathen false freedom and libertinism; while
in the later writings of the New Covenant, in the Epistle
of St. Jude, in the second of St. Peter, and in the Apocalypse of St. John, we find these libertine errors already

full blown. These all speak of lawless ones (2 Pet. ii. 19), who abused St. Paul's doctrine of grace (iii. 16), who promised liberty to others, being themselves servants of corruption (ii. 19), who turned the grace of God into lasciviousness (Jude 4) ; or, as these Nicolaitans, would fain entice the servants of God to eat idol meats and commit fornication. It is not indeed a little remarkable, as attesting the identity of those whose works the Lord here declares that He hates with them whom his Apostles denounce, that Balaam, whose name, as we have seen, is the keyword to the title which these Nicolaitans bear, and to the works which they do, is set forth alike by St. Peter (ii. 15) and St. Jude (ver. 11) as the seducer in whose path of error these later seducers were themselves running and enticing others to run.

But it may be urged against this explanation of the matter that we find actual Nicolaitans in the second century. Doubtless we do so. That there existed in the second and third centuries a sect of antinomian Gnostics, who bore this name, has been denied by some; but on grounds quite insufficient. Irenæus (i. 26. 3; compare Hippolytus, *Con. Hær.* vii. 36) is probably in error when he makes the founder of this sect to have been Nicolas, the proselyte of Antioch, whom we find in such honourable company in the Acts (vi. 3, 5) ; and who, if this were true, must afterwards have miserably fallen away from the faith ;[1] while yet the fault of Irenæus is probably no more than that he too lightly admitted the claim which they

---

[1] At the same time it is certainly significant, as Ewald (*Gesch. des Volkes Israel,* vol. vii. p. 173) has observed, that he should occupy the *last* place in the enumeration of the Deacons (Acts vi. 5) ; compare the place invariably assigned in lists of the Apostles to Judas Iscariot (Matt. x. 4; Mark iii. 19).

made to Nicolas as the author of their heresy. It is
certainly difficult to see what authority any statement of
Irenæus would retain with us, if we felt at liberty to set
aside his distinct assertion of such a sect as existing in
his own time.   But still more explicit are the references
made to Nicolaitans by Tertullian (*De Præsc. Hær.* 46).
It cannot be urged of him, as it sometimes is of Irenæus,
that he knows nothing about them except what he has
drawn from these passages of Scripture; for he gives an
account of their doctrines, not merely libertine, but
Gnostic, at considerable length.   Clement of Alexandria
also (*Strom.* ii. 20) speaks without hesitation of claimants
to be followers of Nicolas (οἱ φάσκοντες ἑαυτοὺς Νικολάῳ
ἕπεσθαι) who existed as a body in his day; and elsewhere
(*ib.* iii. 4) records their unbridled and excessive lusts.
He, indeed, entirely acquits Nicolas the deacon of any
share in the authorship of this heresy, giving no credit to
this boasted genealogy of theirs.   The *Apostolic Constitutions* (vi. 8) do the same.   With such distinct notices of
Nicolaitans as existing in the second century, it seems a
piece of unwarrantable and excessive scepticism to deny
the historic existence of such a sect (see Neander, *Kirch.
Gesch.* i. 2, p. 774).   At the same time, there is no need
to suppose that they were the spiritual descendants of
actual Nicolaitans, of libertines I mean, bearing this name
in the times of St. John.   Rather, springing up at a later
day, one of the innumerable branches of the Gnostic heresy,
they assumed a designation which they found ready made
for them in the Apocalypse. [1]

It may seem indeed, at the first showing, almost in-

---

[1] The fullest collection of all passages of antiquity bearing on
the Nicolaitans which I know, is in Stern's *Commentar über die
Offenbarung*, 1854, pp. 141–145.

conceivable that a sect, professing to stand even in the remotest relation to Christianity, should appropriate to itself a name so branded with infamy as in Holy Scripture is this. But we must remember that with many of the Gnostics this was a relation of absolute and entire opposition to nearly all of the Scripture; and the history of these daring fighters against God would supply many parallel instances of blasphemous impiety. Thus, not to speak of the Ophites, there were the Cainites (Tertullian identifies them and the Nicolaitans, *De Præsc. Hær.* 33), all whose saints and heroes were selected from among those whom the Scripture had stamped with deepest reprobation, the list beginning with Cain and ending with Judas Iscariot (*ib.* 47). When too we keep in mind the intense antagonism of the antinomian Gnostics to St. John as a judaizing Apostle, contradistinguishing these from St. Paul, who with their own Marcion was to sit, Paul on the right hand, and Marcion on the left hand, of Christ in his kingdom, being those for whom this was reserved of the Father (Matt. xx. 23; Origen, *in Luc. Hom.* 25; cf. Irenæus, iii. 13); assuredly there is nothing strange that a name which St. John, or the Saviour by his lips, branded with worst dishonour, they, glorying in their shame, should assume as one of chiefest honour;—just as in an infidel publication of the present day which has sometimes come under my eye, there are letters signed in blasphemous earnest with the signature of 'Antichrist.'

One point still remains. Is the hating of the deeds of the Nicolaitans of this verse identical with the not being able to '*bear them which are evil*' of ver. 2? or, being a grace growing out of the same holy impatience of evil, is there for all this a certain difference between them, so that while that was rather a hatred of error *in doctrine,*

of departure from the faith once delivered, an unmasking
of them that said they were apostles and were not, this is
more a hatred of evil *done*, of *the deeds* of the Nicolaitans?
In other words, is the Lord here recurring to that good
thing which He has already found and praised in Ephesus?
or is this new praise, and the recognition of a further
grace? Most expositors take for granted that Christ here
reverts to and repeats his commendation already uttered,
that the Nicolaitans therefore of this are identical with
'*them that are evil*' of the former verse. I cannot think
it; but must see here not the repetition of praise bestowed
before, which would be somewhat flat, but a further·merit
which Christ is well pleased to find and to acknowledge in
his Church at Ephesus. The '*deeds of the Nicolaitans*'
were, no doubt, the crowning wickedness there, the bitter
fruit growing out of that evil root of false doctrine; but
whether in root, as He testified before, or in fruit, as He
testifies now, this evil was equally hated by the Angel and
Church of Ephesus.

Ver. 7. '*He that hath an ear, let him hear what the
Spirit saith unto the Churches.*'—These words recur in all
the Epistles; with only this difference, that in the earlier
three they occur *before*, in the later four *after*, the final
promise. Is there any meaning in this change of place?
It is difficult to believe that there is none. The Apocalypse is a work of such consummate art, a device of such
profound wisdom, so penetrated through and through with
what we might call a divine cabala, and fashioned according to its laws, that one is slow to assume anything accidental in it, or that any departure in it from a rule which
has been once admitted is without a purpose. Still I must
own that I have never seen any satisfactory explanation of
this transposition. That in every case the words usher

in, or commend, truths of the deepest concernment to all, there can be no doubt. This we might confidently argue from the very form of the exhortation; but we further gather it from a comparison of the passages, all of them of deepest significance, where the same summons to attention recurs (Matt. xi. 15; xiii. 9, 43; Mark vii. 16; Rev. xiii. 9); so that Irving (*Expos. of the Revelation*, vol. i. p. 354) has perfect right when he affirms, 'This form always is used of radical, and as it were generative, truths, great principles, most precious promises, most deep fetches from the secrets of God, being as it were eyes of truth, seeds and kernels of knowledge.' It is always a matter of weightiest concernment to the whole Church of God, which these words usher in or seal.

But let us look a little closer at them, and see what other lessons this summons, in the form which it here takes, is capable of yielding. And first the '*ear*' here is not a *natural* ear, neither is this a summons to every man, for every man has such a natural ear, to attend to the words now spoken; but rather the words are an equivalent to the ὁ δυνάμενος χωρεῖν χωρείτω of Matt. xix. 12, and imply that spiritual truth needing a spiritual organ for its reception, only he will be able to hear to whom God has given the hearing ear (Deut. xxix. 4), whose ear He has wakened (Isai. l. 4, 5); of others it is true, 'their ear is uncircumcised, and they *cannot* hearken' (Jer. vi. 10). And yet for all this the words are in another sense addressed to every one, inasmuch as he who has not this hearing ear, who discovers from the failure of these words of Christ to reach the depths of his spirit, that he has it not, is implicitly bidden to seek it of Him who can alone give it to any, and who would be well pleased to give it to all. But secondly we are taught by these words how ab-

solute is the identity between the workings of the Son and
of the Holy Ghost; how truly the Spirit is the Spirit of
speaking throughout; but now without a word of explanation, what *He* speaks is declared to be what the Spirit speaks.
It is the Spirit who declares these things to the Churches.
And in that phrase, ' *the Churches*,' we are further reminded
of the universal character which this Epistle and those that
follow it possess. It might seem that all which had hitherto
been uttered had been uttered only to one Church, to that
of Ephesus; nor would I in the least deny this primary destination, nor that all the reproofs, encouragements, warnings, promises which it contains were designed for Ephesus.
But they are not limited to it. He who utters these words
will allow of no such limitation. In a form somewhat
more solemn he virtually repeats what He once spoke in
the days of his flesh, ' What I say unto you, I say unto all ; '
for, standing as He does at the central heart of things, in
his particular there ever lies involved an universal; and
therefore is it that heaven and earth may pass away, but
his words can never pass away. This universal character
of these addresses, that, addressed to one they were at the
same time spoken to all, was recognised long ago. Thus
in the famous Muratori fragment we find it : ' Johannes in
Apocalypsi licet septem Ecclesiis scribat, tamen omnibus
dicit.'

' *To him that overcometh will I give to eat of the tree
of life, which is in the midst of the Paradise of God.*'—It
is deeply interesting and instructive to observe how in this,
and probably in every other case, the character of the promise corresponds to the character of the faithfulness displayed. They who have abstained from the idol-meats,
from the sinful dainties of the flesh and world, shall, in
return, ' *eat of the tree of life*;' or, as it is in the Epistle

to Pergamum, '*of the hidden manna*' (ii. 17); the same
law of correspondency and compensation reigning in most,
if not all the other promises as well. They who have not
feared those who can kill the body only, who have given,
where need was, their bodies to the flame, shall not be
hurt by the second death (ii. 11). They whom the world
has not vanquished, shall have dominion over the world
(ii. 26, 27). They who keep their garments here unde-
filed, shall be clad in the white and shining garments of
immortality there (iii. 4, 5). They who overcome Jewish
pretensions (and the earnest warnings of the Epistle to
the Hebrews show us that this for some was not done
without the hardest struggle), shall be made free, not of
an earthly, but of an heavenly, Jerusalem (iii. 12). The only
Church in which any difficulty occurs in tracing the cor-
relation between the form of the victory and the form of
the reward, is the last.

But this much said by way of general introduction to
all the promises, the promise here may well claim closer
attention. The image of the Christian as a conqueror, one
'*that overcometh*,' is frequent with St. Paul (2 Tim. ii. 5;
1 Cor. ix. 24, 25); even as on the other hand he contemplates sin as an ἥττημα, a being worsted or overcome (1 Cor.
vi. 7); but such phrases as νικᾶν τὸν κόσμον, νικᾶν τὸν
πονηρόν, or simply νικᾶν as here, nowhere occur in his
Epistles—the only passage in them which in the least
resembles these, or where the word is employed to express
the moral victory over sin and temptation, is Rom. xii. 21.
This use of νικᾶν, with that single and partial exception,
is exclusively St. John's; and the frequent recurrence of
it on the one side in his Gospel and Epistles, and on the
other in the Apocalypse (thus compare John xvi. 33; 1 Ep.
ii. 13, 14; v. 4, 5, with Rev. ii. 11, 17, 26; iii. 5, 12, 21;

xii. 11; xxi. 7), constitutes an interesting point of contact
between the language of this Book and of those others
whereof he is the author as well; and, for those who need
such evidence, an evidence for the identity of the author
of those and of this.   It occurs in the ethical terminology
of heathen philosophy at its best.   Thus Plato (*Legg*. i.
626 E): τὸ νικᾶν αὐτὸν πασῶν νικῶν πρώτη τε καὶ ἀρίστη.

It is very noteworthy,—and this '*I will give*,' reeurring
as it does so constantly in all these Epistles, bids us
to note,—how absolutely without reserve or qualification
Christ assumes for Himself throughout them all the distribution of rewards, as supreme and sole μισθαποδότης
(Heb. xi. 6) in the kingdom of glory (ii. 10, 17, 26, 28;
ii. 21: cf. xxi. 6; 2 Tim. iv. 8; Matt. xx. 8).   Elsewhere
St. Paul has said, 'The gift *of God* is eternal life' (Rom.
vi. 23); here it appears eminently as the gift *of Christ*.
And his '*I will give*,' though still in the future, is sure.
It has nothing in it of the δώσω of that ever promising but
never performing king of Macedon; who, having ever this
same δώσω on his lips, but never the δῶρον in his hands,
acquired the name of *Doson*, fastened as no honourable
distinction upon him who, being rich in promises, yet
never crowned the promise with the performance.

The use of ξύλον, the *dead* timber in classical Greek,
for δένδρον, the *living* tree, is Hellenistic; not indeed exclusively confined to the Septuagint and the N.T., being
found in the Alexandrian poets, Callimachus for instance,
as well; indeed, there is an anticipation of it in Herodotus, iii. 47.   In '*the tree of life*' there is manifest
allusion to Gen. ii. 9.   The tree which disappeared with
the disappearance of the earthly Paradise, reappears with
the reappearance of the heavenly, Christ's kingdom being
in the highest sense 'the restitution of all things' (Acts

iii. 21). Whatever had been lost through Adam's sin is won back, and that too in a higher shape, through Christ's obedience. That the memory of ' *the tree of life* ' had not in the mean time perished, we gather from such references or allusions to it as Prov. iii. 18; xi. 30; xiii. 12; xv. 4.[1] ' *To eat of the tree of life* ' is a figurative phrase to express participation in the life eternal; cf. Gen. iii. 22; Ezek. xlvii. 12;[2] Rev. xxii. 2, 14; 2 Esdr. ii. 12; vii. 53; and Ecclus. xix. 19: 'They that do things that please Him shall receive the fruit of the tree of immortality' (ἀθανασίας δένδρον καρποῦνται). Compare the words of the Christian Sibyl:

Οἱ δὲ Θεὸν τιμῶντες ἀληθινὸν ἀεναόντε
Ζωὴν κληρονομοῦσι τὸν αἰῶνος χρόνον, αὐτοὶ
Οἰκοῦντες Παραδείσου ὁμῶς ἐριθήλεα κῆπον,
Δαινύμενοι γλυκὺν ἄρτον ἀπ' οὐρανοῦ ἀστερόεντος.

We meet with echoes and reminiscences of this ' *tree of life* ' in the mythologies of many nations; or, if not actual reminiscences of it, yet reachings out after it, as in the Yggdrasil of our own northern mythology (Grimm, *Deutsche Mythol.* p. 756); and still more remarkable in the Persian Hom. This Hom is the king of trees, is called in the Zend-Avesta the Death-destroyer; it grows by the fountain of Arduisur, in other words, by the waters of life; while

---

[1] The Rabbis, of course, know a great deal about this ' *tree of life.*' Its boughs overshadow the whole of Paradise. It has five hundred thousand fragrant smells, and its fruit as many pleasant tastes, not one of them resembling any other (Eisenmenger, *Entdecktes Judenthum*, vol. ii. p. 311; which book also see, pp. 260-320, for much on the Upper and Under Paradise, as the Jews were wont to call them).

[2] Lucian's words (*Ver. Hist.* ii. 14), in his account of the Island of the Blest, sound very much like a scoff at this: αἱ μὲν ἄμπελοι δωδεκάφοροί εἰσι, καὶ κατὰ μῆνα ἕκαστον καρποφοροῦσι.

its sap drunken imparts immortality (Creuzer, *Symbolik*, vol. i. p. 187, and often).

For the words, '*which is in the midst of the Paradise of God*,' we should read, '*which is in the Paradise of God*—transcribers having brought their '*in the midst*' from Gen. ii. 9. Παράδεισος is a word whose history is well worth tracing. The word and the thing which it designated are both generally said to be Persian; though this is now earnestly denied by some, who claim for it a Semitic origin (see Tuch, *Genesis*, p. 68; Delitzsch, *Genesis*, p. 137, 2nd edit.). It was first naturalized in Greek by Xenophon, who designated by it the parks or pleasure-gardens of Persia, in which wild beasts were kept or stately trees grown (*Hell.* iv. 1. 15; *Œcon.* iv. 13; *Cyrop.* i. 4. 11), being at once the 'vivarium' and the 'viridarium' (Augustine, *Serm.* 343; 'leporarium' Varro calls it) of the Romans; for classical Latin, it may be observed by the way, did not know the word 'paradisus' (see A. Gellius, ii. 20. 4, and the long circumlocution by which Cicero, *De Senect.* 17, is compelled to express the thing). Where the Septuagint Translators employ παράδεισος, it is commonly to designate the garden of Eden (Gen. ii. 8; iii. 1; Ezek. xxviii. 13), though sometimes it stands there for any stately garden of delight whatever (Isai. i. 30; Jer. xxix. 5; Eccl. ii. 5: ἐποίησά μοι κήπους καὶ παραδείσους). Philo refers to it often as such, describing it in language which has an Homeric touch about it: χῶρον οὔτε ὄμβροις οὔτε νιφετοῖς, οὔτε κύμασι βαρυνόμενον, ἀλλ᾽ ὃν ἐξ Ὠκεανοῦ πραῢς ἀεὶ ζέφυρος ἐπιπνείων ἀναψύχει. The word, by the time that it appears in the N.T., has taken a great spring. The ideal beauty of that dwelling-place of our first parents, perhaps also the fact that it had now vanished from the earth, has caused the

name ' Paradise ' to be transferred to that region and pro-
vince in Hades, or the invisible world, where the souls of
the faithful are gathered, waiting for their perfect consummation and bliss. 'Their [the Jews'] meaning therefore was
this : that as paradise, or the garden of Eden, was a place
of great beauty, pleasure, and tranquillity, so the state of
separate souls was a state of peace and excellent delights'
(so Jeremy Taylor in his beautiful *Sermon at the Funeral
of Sir George Dalstone*).   It is in this sense, as a place of
rest after the storms of life, that Christ allowed and employed the term, when to the penitent malefactor He
said, 'This day shalt thou be with Me in Paradise'
(Luke xxii. 43).[1] But even this is not all. The word
takes a higher meaning yet ; for this inferior Paradise
is not to be confounded with the superior or heavenly,
' the Paradise *of God*,' as it is here called (the *phrase* has
already occurred in the Septuagint, Ezek. xxxi. 7, 8), ' the
third heaven,' where is the immediate presence and glory
of God (2 Cor. xii. 2, 4).   We may thus trace παράδεισος
passing through an ascending scale of meanings.   From
any garden of delight, which is its first meaning, it comes
to be predominantly applied to the garden of Eden ;
then to the resting-place of separate souls in joy and
felicity ; and lastly, to the very heaven itself ; and we
see eminently in it, what we see indeed in so many words,
how revealed religion assumes them into its service, and
makes them vehicles of far higher truth than any which
they knew at first, transforming and transfiguring them,
as in this case, from glory to glory.

---

[1] The two chief passages in the Fathers on Paradise contemplated as this middle state, are Tertullian, *De Animâ*, 55 (his book
De Paradiso has not reached us) ; and Origen, *De Princ*. ii. 11. 6.
On more modern aspects of the derivation of the word, see an
essay by Max Müller.

This ' *tree of life*,' with the privilege to the faithful of eating of its fruits, appears again at the close of this Book (xxii. 2, 14). It is very interesting to note, and no fitter opportunity than this for noting, the fine and subtle bands which knit one part of the Apocalypse to another, the marvellous art, if we may dare to use an earthly word speaking of a heavenly fact, with which this Book is constructed. Especially these seven Epistles, which at first sight might seem, which to some *have* seemed, to be but slightly attached to the other parts of the Book, do yet on nearer examination prove to be bound to them by the closest possible bands. There is not one of the promises made to the faithful in these second and third chapters, which does not look on to, and perhaps first find its full explanation in, some later portion of the Book. Thus the eating of the tree of life, as unfolded farther at xxii. 2, 14, 19; deliverance from the second death (ii. 11) receives its solemn commentary, xx. 14; xxi. 8; the writing of the new name of ii. 17 reappears xiv. 1 ; the dominion over the heathen of ii. 26 at xx. 4 ; the morning star of ii. 28 at xxii. 16; the white garments of iii. 5 at iv. 4; vii. 9, 13; the name found written in the book of life of iii. 5 at xiii. 8; xx. 15 ; the New Jerusalem and the citizenship in it of iii. 12 at xxi. 10; xxii. 14; the sitting upon the throne of iii. 21 at iv. 4.[1]

---

[1] Very beautifully Bengel on this matter, though his words refer not to the seven Epistles only, but to the whole Book: 'Partes hujus libri passim inter se respiciunt. Omnino structura libri hujus prorsus artem divinam spirat; estque ejus quodam modo proprium, ut res futuras multas, et in multitudine varias, proximas, interme- dias, remotissimas, maximas, minimas, terribiles, salutares, ex veteribus prophetis repetitas, novas, longas, breves, easque inter se contextas, oppositas, compositas, seque mutuo involventes, et evol- ventes, ad se invicem ex intervallo parvo aut magno respicientes,

adeoque interdum quasi disparentes, abruptas, suspensas, et postea
de improviso opportunissime sub conspectum redeuntes, absoluto
compendio complectatur; atque his rebus, quæ complectitur liber,
structura libri exacte respondet.   Itaque in omnibus suis partibus
admirabilem habet varietatem, spirasque pulcerrimas, simulque
summam harmoniam, per ipsas anomalias, quæ illam interpellare
videntur, valde illustratam.'

II.

EPISTLE TO THE CHURCH OF SMYRNA.

REV. ii. 8–11.

Ver. 8. '*And unto the Angel of the Church in Smyrna write.*'—The next in order to Ephesus of the seven Churches is Smyrna; the next not only in the spiritual order here, but in the natural as well, lying as it does a little to the north of that city. Smyrna, 'the ornament of Asia' (ἄγαλμα τῆς ᾿Ασίας, as it has been called), was one of the fairest and noblest cities of Ionia (ἡ καλλίστη τῶν ᾿Ιωνικῶν πόλεων, Lucian, *Imagg.* 2), most favourably placed upon the coast to command the trade of the Levant, which alike in ancient and in modern times it has enjoyed. In ecclesiastical history it is chiefly famous as the Church over which Polycarp presided as bishop for so many years. This Church must have been founded at a very early date, though there is no mention of it either in the Acts or in the Epistles of St. Paul.

Tertullian indeed distinctly tells us that Polycarp was consecrated bishop of Smyrna by St. John (*De Præsc. Hæret.* 32); and Irenæus, who affirms that he had himself in his youth often talked with him, declares the same (Eusebius, *H. E.* iv. 14: cf. iii. 36; Jerome, *Catal. Script.* s. v. *Polycarpus*; Jacobson, *Patt. Apostoll.* p. 564; Röthe, *Die Anfänge d. Christl. Kirche*, p. 429). His martyrdom belongs to the principate of Antoninus Pius, and to the year A.D. 154, or 155.[1] (See *On the Epistle of Ignatius to the Smyrnœans*, vol. ii. § 1, p. 285 sq.)

'*These things saith the first and the last, which was dead, and is alive.*'—Being addressed, as this Epistle is, to a Church exposed, and hereafter to be still more exposed, to the fiercest blasts of persecution, it is graciously ordered that all the attributes which Christ here claims for Himself should be such as would encourage and support his servants in their trials and distress. Brightman: 'Titulos sibi sumit [Christus] qui præsenti rerum conditioni conveniunt. Unde varium suæ gloriæ radium in singulis Epistolis spargit, pro variâ fortunâ quâ sunt Ecclesiæ.' For these titles of Christ, '*the first and the last,*' and '*which was dead, and is alive,*' or rather, '*who became dead, and lived again,*' see i. 17, 18. Ἔζησεν here is not '*vixit,*' but '*revixit*' (cf. Ezek. xxxvii. 3; John v. 25; Rev. xiii. 14); death having been for Him only the passage to a more glorious life. How then should his servants fear them who could kill the body, and then had nothing more which they could do? what misgivings should they have in committing their souls to One, who had so triumphantly redeemed and rescued his own?

Ver. 9. '*I know thy works, and tribulation, and poverty; but thou art rich.*'—For the first clause see what has been said already on ver. 2; the words of themselves

---

[1] An important communication recently made by M. Waddington to the French Académie des Inscriptions has put it beyond all doubt that the date of Polycarp's death usually given,—some time, that is, falling within the years A.D. 166-169,—is too late by more than ten years. The best scholars alike in England and abroad have assented to the conclusions at which on this matter he has arrived. Thus Bishop Lightfoot, see the *Contemporary Review*, May, 1875, p. 838; and Renan, *L'Antéchrist*, p. 566.

express neither praise nor blame. The '*tribulation*' refers out of all doubt to the affliction which the Church of
Smyrna endured at the hands of its Jewish and heathen
persecutors and oppressors, θλίβειν and θλῖψις being constant words to express this (1 Thess. iii. 4; Heb. xi. 37;
Acts xx. 23; Rev. i. 9, and often).   So too their '*poverty*'
will probably have come upon them through the spoiling
of their goods (Heb. x. 34), and the various wrongs in
their worldly estate which the profession of the faith of
Christ will have brought with it—'*But thou art rich.*'
How much better this, poor in the esteem of the world,
but rich before Christ, than the condition of the Laodicean
Angel, rich in his own esteem, but most poor in the sight
of Christ (iii. 17).   There can, of course, be no doubt that
'*rich*' here means rich *in grace* (cf. Rom. viii. 32; Col.
ii. 3; 1 Tim. vi. 18), having treasure in heaven (Matt. vi. 20;
xix. 21; Luke xii. 21), as the same word πλούσιος expresses in a similar, but yet a far higher sense, rich *in glory*
elsewhere (2 Cor. viii. 9).   These words, to which Jam.
ii. 5–7 furnishes a remarkable parallel, constitute a very
beautiful parenthesis, declaring as they do the judgment
of heaven concerning this Church of Smyrna, as contra-
distinguished from the judgment of earth.   Men saw nothing there save the poverty, but He who sees not as man
seeth, saw the true riches which this seeming poverty concealed, even as He too often sees the real poverty which
may lie behind the show of riches; for there are both
poor rich-men and rich poor-men in his sight.   Very
beautifully, though of course moving in altogether a
different and lower sphere of thought, the Greek comic
poet writes (Meineke, *Fragm. Com.* p. 765):

> ψυχὴν ἔχειν δεῖ πλουσίαν· τὰ δὲ χρήματα
> ταῦτ' ἐστὶν ὄψις, παραπέτασμα τοῦ βίου.

'*And I know the blasphemy of them which say they are
Jews, and are not, but are the synagogue of Satan.*'—
The most important question which presents itself here is
this—in what sense shall we take the term '*Jews*'? By
'*those which say they are Jews, and are not,*' shall we
understand Jews literally so called, who, being the natural
seed of Abraham, claimed also to be the spiritual; or,
accepting '*Jews*' here as the designation of the true circumcision not made with hands, that is, of Christians,
shall we see in these some who claimed to be Christians,
but whose right to belong to his Church Christ here
denies? The former appears to me the preferable interpretation. The analogy of such passages as Rom. ii. 28,
29; ix. 6; Phil. iii. 2, 3, points this way.[1] Then, again,
these opposers and blasphemers were evidently persecutors to bonds and death of the faithful at Smyrna; but,
extreme shame and disgrace as some of the heretical sects
were bringing on the true Church at this time, there is
no tittle of evidence that they had the power or the desire
to persecute it with the weapons of outward persecution.
It was otherwise, however, with the Jews literally so
named. What their '*blasphemy*' against Jesus of Nazareth, against the Lord of glory, but known to them as
'the hanged one,' was, and still is, we are only too well
aware (see Eisenmenger, *Entdecktes Judenthum*, vol. i.
pp. 61–188). While too the opposition of the heathen
was still languid and fitful, the jealousy of the Roman
state being hardly awakened, the fierceness of *their*
enmity, the eagerness with which *they* sought to stimulate
the enmity of the heathen, almost every page in the Acts

---

[1] There is a long discussion in one of Augustine's letters (*Ep.*
cxcvi. § 6–16), how far Christians, as being the true circumcision,
might rightfully be called 'Jews.'

declares (xiii. 50; xiv. 2, 5, 19 : xvii. 5 ; xxiv. 2 ; 1 Thess.
ii. 14) ; and many a page of early ecclesiastical history no
less. Moreover, this blasphemy and malignant antagonism
of the Jews against the truth displayed itself in bitterest
enmity against this very Church of Smyrna. We learn
from that precious document, the Epistle of the Church of
Smyrna recording the martyrdom of Polycarp, that Jews
joined with heathens in crying out in the amphitheatre
that the Christian bishop should be cast to the lions; and
when there was a difficulty about this, that he should be
burned alive ; which being granted, the Jews, as was their
wont (ὡς ἔθος αὐτοῖς), were foremost and forwardest in
bringing logs for the funeral pile ; they, too, doing all
that lay in their power to hinder the remains of the
martyr from being delivered to his followers for burial
(cap. 12, 13, 17).

In the words which follow, '*but are the synagogue of
Satan,*' I find another proof that Jews, literally so called,
are intended. To them belonged the synagogue, to Christians the Church. Through all the N. T. συναγωγή is
only once used for a Christian place of assembly (Jam. ii.
2), never for the body of the faithful in Christ Jesus.
With this one exception, capable of an easy explanation
(see my *Synonyms of the N. T.*, § 1), the word is abandoned to the Jews. And that congregation of theirs,
which might have been the Church of the living God, is
now '*the synagogue of Satan*'—a hard saying, a terrible
designation on the lips of Him who uses not such words at
random, but a title which they, once the chosen people of
the Lord, had wrought with all their might to deserve.
Nothing else indeed was possible for them, if they would
not be his people indeed ; they could not be as the heathen,
merely *non*-Christian, they must be *anti*-Christian. The

measure of their former nearness to God was the measure
of their present distance from Him. In the height to
which they were lifted up was involved the depth to
which, if they did not continue at that height, they must
inevitably fall; and this, true for them, is true also for
all, for as many as, inheriting their privileges, are therefore exposed to their dangers.—As nothing is accidental
in this Book, so it is worth remarking that as we have
here '*the synagogue of Satan*,' so presently '*the throne
of Satan*' (ii. 13), and then lastly, '*the depths of Satan*'
(ii. 24); '*the synagogue of Satan*' representing the
Jewish antagonism to the Church, '*the throne of Satan*'
the heathen, and '*the depths of Satan*' the heretical.

Ver. 10. '*Fear none of those things which thou shalt
suffer*.'—The great Captain of our salvation never keeps
back or conceals what those who faithfully witness for Him
may have to bear for his name's sake; never entices recruits into his service, or seeks to retain them under his
banner, by the promise that they shall find all things easy
and pleasant there. So far from this, He says of St. Paul
at the outset of his apostolic career, 'I will show him how
great things he must suffer for my name's sake' (Acts
ix. 16; cf. Matt. x. 16-31; Luke ix. 23; John xvi. 2, 33;
Ezek. ii. 3-7; Jer. i. 19)); and in like manner He announces
to the Angel of Smyrna that bonds, and tribulation, and
death itself, are before him and before others, as many as
at Smyrna shall continue faithful to the end. But for all
this they are *not* to fear. Presently He will declare to
them *why* they should not fear; but first He further un-
rolls in their sight the scroll of their sufferings.

'*Behold, the devil shall cast some of you into prison,
that ye may be tried*.'—Ὁ διάβολος (=κατήγωρ, Rev.
xii. 10; 'criminator' as an old Latin version; 'accusator'

in the Vulgate), a name given to Satan by the Alexandrian
translators with reference to the work of *accuser* ascribed
to him, accusing men to God (Job i. 9; ii. 5; Zech. iii.
1, 2; Wisd. ii. 24), and also, which is less often urged,
accusing God to men (Gen. iii. 1, 5): 'Sed et diaboli
nomen meretur, ὡς τὸν Θεὸν πρὸς τοὺς ἀνθρώπους συκο-
φαντῶν, ut loquitur Suidas' (Rhenferd).   How well at his
instigation the Jews played the secondary *rôle* of διάβολοι,
first against the Lord Himself, and then against his servants, appears in the Gospels (Luke xxiii. 2; John xix.
12), in the Acts (xvii. 5-8; xxiv. 2), and in all the early
Church history.   From a multitude of passages in Justin
Martyr's *Dialogue with Trypho*, as from Origen's answer
to Celsus (iii. 1; vi. 27), it is clear that they were the
main authors of the calumnies against the Christians
with which the malice of the heathen world was stimu-
lated and fed, and by which that world sought to justify
itself in the cruelties practised against them.

The manner in which this persecution of the saints
is here traced to the direct agency of Satan, is very well
worthy of observation.   We sometimes assume that Christians were persecuted, because the truth for which they
bore witness traversed the interests, affronted the pride,
would have checked the passions of men; and this is most
true; but we have not so reached to the ground of the
matter.   There is nothing more remarkable in the records
which have come down to us of the early persecutions,
and in this point they singularly illustrate the Scripture
before us, than the sense which the confessors and martyrs
and those who afterwards narrate their sufferings and
their triumphs, entertain and utter, that these great
fights of affliction through which they were called to pass,
were the immediate work of the devil, and no mere result

of the offended passions, prejudices, or interests of men. The enemies of flesh and blood, as mere tools and instruments, are nearly lost sight of by them in a constant reference to Satan as the invisible but most real author of all. And assuredly they had right. So much we might boldly say, even if we had not the warrant of such Scriptures as this. Thus, who that reads that story of the persecution of the saints at Lyons and Vienne, A.D. 177, happily preserved for us by Eusebius (*H. E.* v. 1) in the very words of the survivors (see Renan, *Marc-Aurèle*, p. 302 sqq.), that wondrous tale of persistent inventive cruelty on the part of the heathen, overmatched by a superhuman patience on the part of the faithful, but must feel that there is infinitely more here than a conflict of bad men with good? There is rather on the one side an outbreak from the bottomless pit, the might and malice of the devil, making war against God in the person of his saints; on the other a victory, not over evil men alone, but over Satan, so transcendant that it could only have been surpassed when Christ Himself beheld him fall as lightning from heaven (Luke x. 18). This reference to the devil as the primary author of all assaults upon the Church, the sense of which speaks out so strikingly in these Acts of the Gallic martyrs, speaks out hardly less strongly in others; thus see the *Ep. de S. Polycarpi Mart.* iii. 17, 19; *Mart. Ignat.* 7.

From the fact that our Translators have rendered ἵνα πειρασθῆτε, '*that ye may be tried,*' we may certainly conclude that they contemplated these πειρασμοί rather as the gracious *trials* of God (cf. Jam. i. 2, 3; 1 Pet. i. 7) than the *temptations* of the devil (Job i. 5; ii. 6; Luke xxii. 31). Yet assuredly this is not so; and Tyndale and Cranmer, who translate, '*to tempt you,*' are to be preferred; so

Marckius : ' Ut tentemini : non simplici probatione con-
stantiæ, quo pacto Deus tentat suos, sed incitatione ad
malum et infidelitatem, quo pacto Deus neminem tentat.'
Temptation from the devil, not *trial* or proof from a
Heavenly Father's hand, is that which, according to this
warning word of the Lord, was in store for them. It is
indeed perfectly true that the same event is oftentimes
both the one and the other—God sifting and winnowing the
man to separate his chaff from his wheat, the devil sifting
and winnowing him in the hope that nothing else but chaff
will be found in him (Luke xxii. 31). It is quite true also
that πειράζειν is used in both senses ; sometimes in a sense
closely bordering upon that of δοκιμάζειν, and then ascribed
to God, who, as the supreme δοκιμαστὴς τῶν καρδιῶν,
tempts and proves his servants to show them what of sin,
of infirmity, of unbelief is yet in their hearts ; and showing
them this, to leave them holier than before this temptation
He found them (Heb. xi. 17 ; cf. Gen. xxii. 1 ; Exod. xv. 25 ;
Deut. xiii. 3).   At the same time πειράζειν is much oftener
used of temptation *by the devil*, solicitation on his part
to evil (Matt. iv. 1 ; 1 Cor. x. 13 ; Gal. vi. 1 ; 1 Thess.
iii. 5 ; Heb. ii. 18 ; Jam. i. 13) ; and the words going immediately before, ' *Behold the devil will cast some of you
into prison,*' are decisive that the Lord is here warning
his servants, as He did in the days of his personal ministry
upon earth, against fierce assaults of their ghostly enemy
which were close at hand, that so by watchfulness and
prayer they might be able to stand in the evil day that
was so near.

The temptations of imprisonment He especially adduces
here. In the records of the Church's early conflicts with
the heathen, we constantly find the prison doing its part ;
those who endured torture bravely being returned to prison,

that so it might be seen whether hunger and thirst, darkness a t.l chains, would not be effectual in breaking down
by little and little the courage and the steadfastness which
had resisted manfully the first and more violent onset of
the foe.   Sometimes it would prove so.   The Church's
early story, furnishing in the main a glorious commentary
on these words, furnishes a mournful commentary as well.
When temptations such as the Lord here speaks of arrived,
it would be ever seen that there were many weak brethren,
and some false; and the Church, rejoicing over the
steadfastness of multitudes among her children, had yet to
mourn over the faltering infirmity of some, and the shame-
less apostasy of others (Eusebius, *H. E.* v. 1. 10; Cyprian,
De Laps. 1, 2).

'*And ye shall have tribulation ten days.*'   For ἕξετε
('*ye shall have*') Lachmann and others have received
into the text ἔχητε ('*ye may have*'), which word equally
with πειρασθῆτε will then depend on ἵνα.   These '*ten
days*,' during which the tribulation of Smyrna shall endure,
have been very variously interpreted, some understanding
by them a very long period (cf. Gen. xxxi. 41; Job xix. 3;
Num. xiv. 22); and some a very short (Gen. xxiv. 55;
Num. xi. 19).   Those who interpret in the former sense
have very commonly seen here allusion to the ten persecutions which the Church is often said to have passed
through, during the three hundred years of its conflict
with heathen Rome.   It has been objected that this enumeration of exactly ten persecutions is altogether arbitrary; that, if we include in our list only those which had
some right to be called general, as extending over the
whole Roman empire, the persecutions would not be so
many; if all those which reached any single city or pro-
vince, they would be many more.   But, setting this

objection aside, I am persuaded we must look for something very different here from an announcement of the
great length of time over which the persecution would
extend; the ' *ten days* ' declaring not the length, but the
shortness of time within which all this tyranny would be
overpast. I conclude this from the fact that only so will
the words fall in with the whole temper and spirit of this
verse, which is encouraging and consolatory throughout.
Here, as so often elsewhere, the briefness of the trial is
urged as a motive for its patient endurance (cf. Isai. xxvi.
20; liv. 8; Ps. xxx. 5; Matt. xxiv. 22; 2 Cor. iv. 17;
1 Pet. i. 6; v. 10).

'*Be thou faithful unto death, and I will give thee a
crown of life.*'—More than one of the early Fathers have
written an *Exhortatio ad Martyrium*, but what are they
all, as compared with this? '*Unto death*' here is an in-
tensive, not an extensive, term. Christ does not mean,
'to thy life's end,' contemplating life under aspects of
time; but ' to the sharpest and worst which the enemy can
inflict upon thee, even to death itself.' Dare and endure,
the words would say, the worst which evil men can threaten and inflict, even death itself (Matt. x. 22; xxiv. 13;
Ecclus. iv. 28). Marckius: 'Quam exigit [fidelitatem]
usque ad mortem, non tam terminum temporis notans,
quanquam et ad metæ nostræ finem sit perseverandum,
quam quidem gradum mali, in quo fidelitas nostra demon-
stranda est, ut mortem ipsam in causâ fidei et pietatis
subire non detractemus.'

With the words of the promise which follow, '*and I
will give thee a crown of life,*' compare 2 Esdr. ii. 42–47,
which, however, it can hardly be doubted is the interpola-
tion of some later Christian hand (see Lücke, *Offenb. d.
Johan.* p. 155, 2d edit.). This '*crown of life,*' always

1 2

remaining in its essence the same, is not the less designated by a rich variety of images. Here, and with St. James (i. 12), it is ' a crown of life ; ' with St. Paul, ' a crown of righteousness' (2 Tim. iv. 8; cf. Plutarch, Philop. et Flam. 3 : δικαιοσύνης καὶ χρηστότητος στέφανος), ' a crown of rejoicing ' (καυχήσεως, 1 Thess. ii. 19) ; with St. Peter, ' a crown of glory ' (1 Pet. v. 4 ; cf. Heb. ii. 9) ; with Isaiah, ' a crown of beauty ' (lii. 3, στέφανος κάλλους, LXX ; cf. διάδημα τοῦ κάλλους, Wisd. v. 17) ; with Solomon, ' a crown of graces ' (χαρίτων, Prov. i. 9) ; with the same ' a crown of rich abundance ' (τρυφῆς) ; with the Son of Sirach, ' a crown of exultation ' (ἀγαλλιάματος, Ecclus. vi. 31) ; with the same ' a crown of wisdom ' (σοφίας, i. 18) ; in the Mart. S. Polycarpi, ' a crown of incorruption ' (ἀφθαρσίας, xvii. 19 ; cf. Eusebius, H. E. v. 1 : μέγας τῆς ἀφθαρσίας στέφανος) ; for Ignatius, ' a crown of conflict ' (ἀθλήσεως, Mart. 5, with probable reference to 2 Tim. ii. 5) ; for Philostratus, Vit. Apoll. 7, 14, ' a crown of virtue ' (ἀρετῆς) ; for Clement of Alexandria ' a crown of amaranth ' (Pædag. 2) ; for Sophocles ' a crown of fair fame ' (εὐκλείας, Ajax, 457). Whether Lucian intended a sneer at these glorious promises of the Scripture, when he introduces the impostor Peregrinus, who had been among the Christians, though he died a Cynic, to declare his intention of setting, by a voluntary death, a golden crown on a golden life (χρυσῷ βίῳ χρυσῆν κορώνην ἐπιθεῖναι, De Mort. Pereg. § 33), may be questionable. That he has many such scoffs at the promises of Scripture, as at its miracles and other facts, no one who has at all studied the subject will be disposed to deny.

But a question offers itself here, Is this ' crown ' the diadem of royalty (βασίλειον, 2 Sam. i. 10; 2 Chron.

xxiii. 11, lxx.), or the *garland* of victory, 'Krone' or
'Kranz'? I believe the former. It is quite true that
στέφανος is seldom used in this sense, much oftener
διάδημα (see my *Synonyms of the New Testament*, § 23);
yet the 'golden crowns' (στέφανοι) of ch. v. can only be
royal crowns (cf. ver. 10); στέφανος too is the word by
which all the Evangelists designate the crown of thorns,
evidently a caricature of royalty, which was planted on
the Saviour's brows. Did we indeed meet these words,
'*a crown of life*,' in the Epistles of St. Paul, we should be
justified in saying that in all likelihood the wreath or
garland of the victor in the games, the 'crown' in this
sense, was intended. St. Paul was familiar with the Greek
games, and freely drew his imagery from them (1 Cor. ix.
24–27; Phil. iii. 12; 1 Tim. vi. 12; 2 Tim. ii. 5; iv. 7);
does not fear to contemplate the faithful under the aspect
of runners (θεόδρομοι, as Ignatius, *ad Philad.* c. ii., calls
them) and wrestlers in the games. His universal culture,
his Hellenic as well as Jewish education, exempted him
from any scruples in the employment of illustrations like
these. In the same manner he speaks on two occasions
of being poured out, and poured out as a libation; in
which passages (Phil. ii. 17; 2 Tim. iv. 6) it is difficult
not to think that he had the heathen sacrifices in his eye;
at the same time this cannot be regarded as certain. Not
so, however, the Christians of Palestine. Greek games
and Greek sacrifices were strange to them, or only not
strange, as they were the objects of their deepest abhorrence. This is sufficiently attested in the tumults and
troubles which accompanied the introduction of the games
by Herod the Great at Jerusalem, recorded at length by
Josephus (*Antt.* xv. 8. 1–4). Nor indeed was this then
for the first time seen. A similar attempt at an earlier day

helped not a little to fill up the cup of wrath which at length ran over in the rising of the Maccabees, and over-throw of the Greco-Syrian rule (1 Macc. i. 14; 2 Macc. iv. 12–20).   Tertullian's point of view, who styles them (*Scorp.* 6) 'contentiosa solemnia et superstitiosa certamina Græcarum et religionum et voluptatum,' would very much have been theirs.   And then, to me at least, decisive on this point is the fact, that nowhere else in the Apocalypse is there found a single image drawn from the range of heathen antiquity.   The Book moves exclusively in the circle of Jewish imagery—either sacred or cabalistic; of imagery derived mainly from the inmost recesses of the temple service.   The palms in the hands of the redeemed who stand before the throne (vii. 9) may seem an excep-tion to the universality of this rule; but really are far from so being.   It is quite true that the palm was for Greek and Roman a token of victory, but this ' palmife-rous company,' to use Henry More's words, these happy palmers, do not stand before the throne as conquerors,—Tertullian's exposition, ' albati et *palmis victoriæ insignes* (*Scorp.* 12), being at fault,—but as those who keep the true Feast of Tabernacles, the feast of rest, of all the weary toil in the wilderness accomplished and ended.   As such, and to mark them for what they are, they bear, according to the injunctions of the Old Testament, the branches of palms in their hands (Lev. xxiii. 40; cf. Neh. viii. 15; 2 Macc. x. 7; John xii. 13; Josephus, *Antt.* xii. 13. 5); see some beautiful remarks on this point by Hengstenberg (*in loc.*), in part anticipated by Vitringa.   I must needs then believe that these are *royal crowns* (cf. Ps. xxi. 3; cxxxii. 18), not *victorious garlands*, which the great Rewarder is promising here. [1]

---

[1] The use on two occasions of ἶρις for the rainbow (Rev. iv. 3;

Ver. 11. '*He that hath an ear, let him hear what the Spirit saith unto the Churches; He that overcometh shall not be hurt of the second death.*'—This '*second death,*' setting forth, as it does, the 'vita non vitalis,' the death in life of the lost, as contrasted with the life in death of the saved, is a phrase peculiar to the Apocalypse (cf. xx. 6, 14; xxi. 8); but is not uncommon in the later Jewish theology; indeed frequent in the Chaldee Paraphrase; Vitringa: 'Phrasis nata haud dubie in scholâ sanctorum virorum qui fidem et spem Ecclesiæ post reditum ex exilio Babylonico explicârunt.' But though the *word* is not on the lips of the Lord during his earthly life, He does not shrink from proclaiming the fearful *thing*. The δεύτερος θάνατος of this Book is the γέεννα of Matt. v. 29; Mark ix. 43–48; Luke xii. 5; the κόλασις αἰώνιος of Matt. xxv. 46; and from this Book itself receives this awful interpretation, namely, that it, the second death, is the lake of fire (20. 14). The phrase is itself a solemn witness and protest against the Sadduceeism and Epicureanism, which would make death natural the end-all of man's existence. As there is a life beyond this present life for the faithful, so a death beyond the death which falls under our eye for the wicked; ὁ ὄντως θάνατος, as it is called in the *Epistle to Diognetus,* 10. 'Vita damnatorum mors est,' is the fearful gloss of Augustine; and again (*Serm.* cccvi. § 5): 'Mors vocatur, et nemo ibi moritur; satius et melius dixerim, nemo ibi vivit.' And Philo, though, so far as I am aware, he does not know this phrase, '*the second death,*' has a terrible commentary upon it (*De Præm. et Pœn.* 12): ἄνθρωποι μὲν γὰρ πέρας τιμωριῶν εἶναι νομίζουσι θάνατον· ἐν δὲ τῷ θείῳ δικαστηρίῳ μόγις ἐστὶν

---

x. 1) instead of the more usual τόξον (Gen. ix. 13; Ezek. i. 28) approaches nearer to an exception from the general rule.

οὗτος ἀρχή.   And going on to ask what is the punishment of the ungodly, he answers, ζῆν ἀποθνήσκοντα ἀεί,
καὶ τρόπον τινὰ θάνατον ἀθάνατον ὑπομένειν καὶ ἀτελεύ-
τητον, with more to the same effect; cf. *Leg. Alleg.* i. 33.

So much has been idly written upon names, not a little
most idly on the names of these seven Churches, and the
mystical meanings which they contain, that one shrinks
from any seeming fellowship in such slight and unprofit-
able fancies; and yet it is difficult not to remember here
that σμύρνα, the name of this suffering Church which
should give out its sweetness in persecution and in death,
is a subform of μύῤῥα (Lobeck, *Pathol.* p. 241); and that
myrrh, an aromatic gum of Arabia, served for embalming
the dead (John xix. 39; cf. Herodotus, ii. 40, 86), went up
as incense before the Lord (Exod. xxx. 23), was one of the
perfumes of the bridegroom (Ps. xlv. 8), and of the bride
(Cant. iii. 6).   All this Vitringa has excellently urged:
'Myrrha itaque nobis hîc symbolice figurat graviores Ecclesiæ afflictiones, *amaras* equidem et ingratas carni, πρὸς
τὸ παρόν, quod ad tempus præsens, sed ex quibus fructus
provenit vere *salutaris*.   Solet enim eas Deus suâ provi-
dentiâ Ecclesiæ immittere, ut electos et electorum fidem
præservet a *corruptione*, et illos hoc etiam medio veluti
condiat ad immortalitatem, et *fragrantiam* iis conciliet
egregiam virtutum Christianarum, quarum exercitium
persecutiones Ecclesiæ solent suscitare.'

III.

EPISTLE TO THE CHURCH OF PERGAMUM.

REV. ii. 12–17.

Ver. 12. ' *And to the Angel of the Church in Pergamos write.*'—A word or two may fitly find place here on the name of this city, as it appears in our Authorized Version. In the first place, why do our Translators, writing ' *Pergamos*,' and not ' *Pergamus*,' retain a Greek termination for it, and for it alone, among other similar proper names? ' Assos ' (Acts xx. 13, 14) is not a parallel case, for the Romans wrote ' Assos ' as frequently as ' Assus ; ' and always wrote ' Chios,' which therefore is quite correct (Acts xx. 15). But if ' *Pergamos*,' then, by the same rule, ' Ephesos,' ' Miletos,' ' Timotheos,' and many more. And even against ' *Pergamus*,' though preferable to *Pergamos*,' there would still be something to object. Instances of the feminine, ἡ Πέργαμος (Ptolemy, i. 2), are excessively rare (see Lobeck, *Phrynichus*, p. 422); while the neuter, τὸ Πέργαμον in Greek, and ' Pergamum ' in Latin, occur innumerable times (Xenophon, *Anab.* vii. 8. 8; Polybius, iv. 48. 2 ; Strabo, xiii. 4 ; Pliny, *H. N.* v. 33). I shall speak throughout of the city under this its more usual designation; being that, therefore, which St. John, had the word been employed by him in the nominative, which, however, it is not, would in all likelihood have used. It was another illustrious city of Asia ; ἐπιφανὴς πόλις in the language of Strabo (xiii. 4) ; 'longe clarissimum Asiæ Pergamum' in that of Pliny (*H. N.* v. 33). Although of high antiquity, its greatness, splendour, and dignity did not date very far back. It only attained these under the Διάδοχοι, of whom one made Pergamum the capital of his newly erected kingdom—the same kingdom which a later of his dynasty, Attalus III., bequeathed to the Romans (B.C. 133). It was famous as the birthplace of Galen, next to Hippocrates the most illustrious physician of the ancient world ; famous too for its splendid library, collected in rivalry with that of Alexandria ; our 'parchment' (pergamenum) deriving its name from thence ; for magnificent temples of Zeus, of Athêne, and of Apollo ; but most of all for the worship of Æsculapius (Tacitus, *Annal.* iii. 63 ; Xenophon, *Anab.* vii. 8. 23), the remains of whose temple outside the walls of the city with not a few other magnificent ruins, may still be seen. On the architectural splendours of the city which still survive there is a most interesting paper in the *Revue des Deux Mondes*, April 1881, another in the *Saturday Review*, Dec. 30, 1882 ; while a letter in the *Times* of date Dec. 28 of the same year, is full of information on several of the ruined cities of Asia Minor, this included ; and on all the costly treasures of art which still wait an ingathering there.—'*These things saith He which hath the sharp sword with two edges*,' or, not to make a variation in the English where in the Greek there is none, for '*the sharp sword with two edges*' read '*the sharp two-edged sword*;' cf. i. 16.

Ver. 13. '*I know thy works, and where thou dwellest, even where Satan's seat is.*'—This may not sound, at the first hearing, a reassuring word ; and yet indeed it is eminently such. None of the peculiar difficulties and dangers

which beset the Church at Pergamum are concealed from
Christ. We indeed ask now, and it is not easy to answer
the question, Why should Pergamum more than any other
corrupt heathen city have been ' *Satan's seat*,' or ' *Satan's
throne*,' as in the R. V. it more accurately is rendered ; for
as θρόνος is constantly in this Book translated ' *throne* '
when applied to the powers of heaven (iv. 2, 4, 5, 6, 9,
10 ; v. 1, and often), it should be so also when applied to
the hellish caricature of the heavenly kingdom; to the
kingdom which the rulers of the darkness of this world
seek to set up over against the kingdom of light. The
question has been variously answered. Ewald, and many
before him, find allusion here to the fane of Æsculapius,
—Θεὸς Σωτήρ he was called,—where lying miracles of
healing were vaunted to be performed, Satan seeking by
the aid of these to counterwork the work of the Gospel.
His worship no doubt was very prevalent here (' Pergameus
Deus ' Martial calls him) ; yet for all this the explanation
is quite insufficient. All which we can securely conclude
from this language is that from one cause or another Pergamum enjoyed the bad pre-eminence of being the head-
quarters in these parts of resistance to Christ and his
Gospel. *Why* it should have thus deserved the name of
' *Satan's throne*,' so emphatically repeated a second time at
the end of this verse, ' *where Satan dwelleth*,' must remain
one of the unsolved riddles of these Epistles. Some circumstances, of which no certain notice has reached us, may have
especially stirred up the fanaticism of the heathen there.

 ' *And thou holdest fast my name, and hast not denied
my faith, even in those days wherein Antipas was my
faithful martyr, who was slain among you, where Satan
dwelleth*.'—There is a confused multitude of small variations of reading here, though none seriously affecting the

sense. There was probably an *anacoluthon* in the sentence originally, which transcribers would not let be; but attempted by various devices to palliate or remove (see H. Ewald, *Johan. Script.* vol. ii. p. 67). It is evident from the testimony borne here to the Pergamene Church, that many there, probably the Angel himself, had shown an honourable steadfastness in the faith; had been confessors of it; though possibly only one, Antipas, had resisted, or had been called to resist, unto blood. Eusebius (*H. E.* iv. 15) records several martyrs who at a somewhat later day were at Pergamum faithful to death, and received a crown of life. Attalus also, it may be mentioned, who played so valiant a part in the persecutions of Lyons and Vienne, and who won a foremost place in that noble company of Gallic martyrs, was a Pergamene (*ib.* v. 1, 14, 38, 47).

Of Antipas, except from the glorious record which the Lord bears to him here, we know absolutely nothing. It is difficult to understand the silence of all ecclesiastical history respecting so famous a martyr, one singled out by Christ to such honour as this; for silent in regard of him ecclesiastical history must be confessed to be; that which Tertullian (*Scorp.* 12) and other early writers tell us about him, being merely devised *in fugam vacui*, and drawn exclusively from the passage before us. They manifestly *know* nothing about him except what they find here. Later Latin martyrologies, of course, know a great deal. According to these he was Bishop of Pergamum, and by command of Domitian was shut up, Perillus-like, in a brazen bull, afterwards made red-hot; and by this painful passage entered into life. Hengstenberg has a curious explanation of this name, though it is not perfectly original; he has derived at least the hint of it from

Aretius. Pressing the fact that almost all other names,
he would say all, are symbolic in this Book, as Jezebel,
Balaam, Egypt, Sodom, Babylon, Jerusalem, he urges that
this must be symbolic too. But Ἀντίπας, what is it but a
word formed on the same model as Ἀντίχριστος? and as
this is made up of ἀντί and Χριστός, so Ἀντίπας of ἀντί
and πᾶς, and Antipas is one who for Christ's sake has
dared to stand out *against all*, an ἀντίκοσμος: cf. Jer. xx.
10; xv. 10, 'Woe is me, my mother, that thou hast borne
me a man of strife and a man of contention *to the whole
earth*;' which must be the character and condition of an
eminently godly man set in the midst of a world which
lieth in the wicked one (Jam. iv. 4; Acts iv. 19; v. 29).
A later commentator contemptuously dismisses this with
the observation that Ἀντίπας is only an abbreviation of
Ἀντίπατρος, as Νικόμας of Νικομήδης, Μηνᾶς of Μηνό-
δωρος, and the like. I am certainly not disposed to rate
this explanation higher than an ingenious fancy, a *lusus*
of the critic's art, but see little or no force in this argument against it. Antipas, once formed, enters into all the
rights which its new form confers upon it, irrespective of
the process by which it may have attained this form.
But it is not worth while to vindicate from an insufficient
objection what will not commend itself a whit the more,
even after this objection is set aside.

Ver. 14. '*But I have a few things against thee, because
thou hast there them that hold the doctrine of Balaam, who
taught Balac to cast a stumbling block before the children
of Israel, to eat things sacrificed unto idols, and to commit
fornication.*'—Those 'that hold the doctrine of Balaam'
must be identical with the Nicolaitans of ver. 6, 15; the
latter verse seems to leave no doubt on the matter. The
mention of Balaam as the tempter and seducer would of

itself sufficiently explain the nature of the sins to which he tempted and seduced (Num. xxv. 1–9; xxxi. 15, 16); but the sins are here expressly named. First, however, something may be said on the words ὃς ἐδίδασκε τῷ Βαλάκ, which our version, and I believe rightly, has rendered, '*who taught Balac.*' Hengstenberg indeed, and Bengel before him, on the strength of this dative, a *dativus commodi* as they regard it, joined with the fact that διδάσκειν habitually governs an accusative of the person who is the object of the teaching (thus ver. 20 in this very chapter), argue that we ought to translate '*who taught for Balac,*' that is, in the interests of Balac, to please him. They allege in support of this, that there is no hint in Scripture of Balaam having suggested *to Balac* to put these temptations in the way of the children of Israel; the parting of the two is recorded Num. xxiv. 25, neither is there any reason, they urge, to suppose that they ever met again; it was to the Moabitish women themselves, to Balac's people, but not to Balac himself, that Balaam suggested the placing these stumbling blocks in their way. Assuredly this is a mistake. The construction proposed is much too artificial for the Apocalypse; the dative after ἐδίδασκεν is the penetrating of a Hebrew idiom through the forms of the Greek language; and there is nothing at Num. xxxi. 16 to compel us to understand that Balaam's communication with the daughters of Moab was *immediate,* and not through the intervention of the king; cf. Josephus, *Antt.* iv. 6. 6, who takes this intervention for granted; and Vitringa, *Obss. Sac.* iv. 9. 29.

Two words claim attention here, σκάνδαλον and εἰδωλόθυτον. Σκάνδαλον, a later form of σκανδάληθρον (Aristophanes, *Acharnen.* 686), and σκανδαλίζειν (there is no σκανδαληθρίζειν, see Rost and Palm, *Lex.*), occur only

in the Septuagint and the N. T. and in writings immediately
dependant upon these (see Suicer, *Thes.* s. v.); being
almost always in them employed in a tropical sense;
Lev. xxix. 14 and Judith v. 1 are exceptions. Σκάνδαλον
is properly a trap (joined often with παγίς, Josh. xxiii. 13;
Ps. cxl. 9; Rom. xi. 9), or more precisely that part of the
trap on which the bait is laid, and the touching of which
causes the trap to close upon its prey ('mobile decipulæ
tigillum,' Fritzsche on Rom. xiv. 13); then generally any
loop or noose set in the path, which should entangle the
foot of the unwary walker, and cause him to stumble and
fall; thus σκάνδαλον=πρόσκομμα (Rom. xiv. 13) and
σκανδαλίζειν=προσκόπτειν (Matt. iv. 6; Rom. ix. 32);
and next any stone, or hindrance of any kind (Hesychius
explains it by ἐμποδισμός), which should have the same
effect (1 Pet. ii. 7).   Satan, then, as *the* Tempter, is the
great putter of 'scandals,' 'stumbling blocks,' or offences,'
in the path of men; his sworn servants, a Balaam or a
Jeroboam (1 Kin. xiv. 16), are the same consciously;
while all of us, by careless walking, by seeking what shall
please ourselves rather than what shall edify others (Rom.
xiv. 15–23; 1 Cor. viii. 10), or by counselling our
brethren in the same sense (Matt. xvi. 23), are in danger
of unconsciously, but not unguiltily, being the same.
There is none that is not deeply concerned in the warning
of Matt. xviii. 7.   All have need to ask that they may
prove what St. Paul prayed that the Philippians (i. 10)
might prove, ἀπρόσκοποι themselves (the ἄπταιστοι of
Jude 24 rests on the same image), and that they may put
no πρόσκομμα, no σκάνδαλον, in the path of others.

Εἰδωλόθυτον is a N. T. word to express what the
heathen sacrifices were, as they presented themselves to
the eye of a Christian or a Jew, namely things offered,

not to God, but to idols.[1] The Gentiles themselves expressed the same by ἱερόθυτον (which at 1 Cor. x. 28 is
the better reading, St. Paul there assuming a Gentile to
be speaking, and employing, if not an honourable, yet at
any rate a *neutral*, word), or by θεόθυτον, which the Greek
purists preferred (Lobeck, *Phrynichus*, p. 139). It will
be worth while here to consider under what plea any who
so much as named the name of Christ could consent to
eat of these idol-meats, and yet claim at the same time to
retain allegiance to that royal name. The temptation to
this was one which addressed itself exclusively to the converts from the heathen religion. Of those who attached
themselves to the Church of Christ from the stock of
Abraham, we may be quite sure that there was not one
who was so much tempted to this sin ; their whole previous
education, training them into an abhorrence of such defilement, was for them a sufficient safeguard against it (Num.
xxv. 2 ; Ps. cvi. 28 ; Dan. i. 8 ; Tob. i. 10, 11). It was otherwise with the proselytes from the heathen world ; with the
Gentile Christians gathered in, it might be, to the Church of
Christ out of some corrupt and luxurious Greek city, as
Corinth for example. Refusal to partake in the idol-meats
was for one of these refusal to partake not merely in the
idolatry which he had renounced, but in very much else
which he was not at all so entirely prepared to forego. It
involved abstinence from almost every public and every
private festivity, a withdrawal in great part from the whole

---

[1] It is a notable example of the extreme inconsistency of our
Authorized Version in rendering the same word in different places,
that εἰδωλόθυτα, a word offering no difficulties, is rendered in four
different ways: it is '*meats* offered to idols' (Acts xv. 29); it is
'*things* offered to idols' (Acts xxi. 25); it is 'things *that are* offered
in sacrifice unto idols' (1 Cor. viii. 4); it is 'things *sacrificed* unto
idols' (Rev. ii. 14).

social life of his time; for sacrifice had in one way or other
bound itself up in almost every act of this social life. We
have a singular evidence of this in the fact that 'to kill'
and 'to sacrifice' had in Greek almost become identical;
θύειν, which had originally meant the latter, meaning the
former now. The poor man, offering a slain beast, after
the priest and the altar had received their shares, would
sell the remainder in the market; the rich would give this
which remained over away. From one cause or another
there was a certainty at many entertainments of meeting
these sacrificial meats, there was a possibility of meeting
them at all. The question therefore was one which, like
that of caste at the present day in India, would continually
obtrude itself, which could not be set aside and its presence ignored.[1]

Already we find at the Council of Jerusalem the Apostles resolving that among the few 'necessary things' (Acts
xv. 28) which must be imperatively required of the Gentile converts, abstinence from 'the pollutions of idols'
(ver. 20), or, as in the more formal decree it is expressed,
'meats offered to idols' (ver. 29), was one. Some two
years later various cases of conscience have occurred exactly in that Church where beforehand we might have
looked for them, namely at Corinth, and St. Paul has
been called upon to give his judgment about them. Some
it would seem there, who boasted of their γνῶσις, affirmed
that they saw through the whole heathen idolatry, saw
that it was a fraud and a lie; to them an idol was nothing;
what fear then that they should become partakers with the
idol through partaking of the idol-meats? and these, in

---

[1] See an excellent Essay on this subject in Dean Stanley's *Commentary on the First Epistle to the Corinthians*, with this title,
The Sacrificial Feasts of the Heathen, vol. i. pp. 149-152.

an exaggerated assertion of their liberty, sat openly at
meat in the very idol-temple itself (1 Cor. viii. 10). So
too at a somewhat later date, in Justin Martyr's *Dialogue
with Trypho*, the Jew Trypho makes it a charge against
the Christians that many of them partook of idol-sacrifices,
affirming that they were in no way injured by them (c.
35); to whom the Christian Father replies that these
Marcionites, Valentinians, and the rest, might usurp the
name of Christian, but that the Catholic Church repu-
diated them utterly, in no way acknowledged them as her
children. From Irenæus (i. 6. 3) we learn that they not
merely thus ate of the idol-meats, boasting that they were
in nothing defiled by them, but took a foremost share in
the celebration of the heathen festivals. Others, in an
opposite extreme and excess of scrupulosity, were greatly
troubled lest the meat they innocently bought in the
market, or partook of at the house of a heathen friend,
might have been offered in sacrifice, and they by what
they did unwittingly defiled (1 Cor. x. 25, 27). All will
no doubt remember the wonderful wisdom and love wherewith St. Paul treats these various cases, strengthening and
guiding the weak, rebuking and restraining the strong or
those that thought themselves such. Some, however, of
these latter continued to allow themselves in these dan-
gerous liberties, degenerating only too easily into scanda-
lous excesses; although, after such decisions, first of the
Council at Jerusalem, and afterwards of St. Paul, not any
longer *within* the bosom of the Church, but without it; and
one may see in the Nicolaitans the legitimate spiritual descendants of those Gnostics (Gnostics at least in the bud),
who were not brought back to humbler, more loving, more
self-denying courses by the earnest remonstrances of the
Apostle.—In the same way as we have at Acts xv. 20, the

prohibition of fornication, joined with that of eating
things offered to idols, so here the two sins are linked
together. The impure character of the heathen festivals
caused that the two constantly went hand in hand (Eusebius, *H. E.* iv. 7. 10).

Ver. 15. '*So hast thou also them that hold the doctrine
of the Nicolaitans.*' The concluding words of this verse,
'*which thing I hate,*' have no right to a place in the text,
having been transferred from ver. 6 of this same chapter.
As Balac had Balaam, a false prophet and seducer, so
had the Angel of Pergamum some that held the doctrine
of the Nicolaitans; and whom he notwithstanding endured. In this matter the Angel of Ephesus had more
of the mind of Christ than he had (ver. 6); wanting as
he did that earnest hatred of evil, which should have made
such a presence and such a teaching intolerable to him ;
while of that other Ephesian Angel it could be said, that
what Christ hated, he hated too.

Ver. 16. '*Repent*;' or '*Repent therefore,*'—'*or else I will
come unto thee quickly, and will fight against them with
the sword of my mouth.*'—Out of this feebleness of moral
indignation against evil it had come to pass that this Angel
had not testified with sufficient energy against the Nicolaitans and their doctrine ; he could not say with Paul, 'I
am pure from the blood of all men' (Acts xx. 26). But
now repenting and faithfully witnessing against their
errors, he would either recover them for the truth, or else
drive them wholly from the communion of the Church,—
in either case a gain. But this if he fail to do, the Lord
will come quickly, and fight against them with the sword
of his mouth. We have, I am persuaded, another allusion
here to the history of Balaam, namely to Num. xxxi. 8 (cf.
Josh. xiii. 22): 'Balaam also, the son of Beor, they slew

with the sword;' this sword of the children of Israel
being indeed the sword of God; cf. Num. xxii. 31. Vitringa: 'Verba hæc manifeste respiciunt historiam Bi-
leami: in quâ habemus, primo quidem, Angelum Domini
stricto ense se Bileamo, populo Dei maledicere medi-
tanti, in viâ opposuisse, et, si instituto perseveraret,
exitium illi minatum esse: deinde Bileamum, et Israel-
itas qui consilium illius secuti fuerant, jussu Dei gladio
periisse.'

In that, '*I will fight against them*,' it might seem at
first sight as if there was only a threat for these ungodly
workers; and not for the Angel who had been faithful in
the main, nor for the better portion of the Church. But
this is not so. When God has a controversy with a Church
or with a people, the *tribulation* reaches all, however the
judgment may be only for his foes. The gold and the
dross are cast alike into the furnace, the dross to be
consumed in it, the gold to come out from it purer than
before. The holy prophet is entangled outwardly in the
same doom with the ungodly king (Jer. xxxix. 4; xliii. 6;
cf. Matt. xxiv. 20, 21). There may be, there assuredly
will be, on the part of the faithful, a separation from the
sin—there is seldom an exemption from the suffering—of
such a time. This suffering finds out all. It is well
that so it should be; that there should be nothing in the
usual course of God's judgments to flatter in any the self-
ish hope of avoiding a share in the woe. Enough for any
to escape the woe within the woe, namely, the sense of
this suffering as the utterance of the just wrath of God.

Ver. 17. '*He that hath an ear, let him hear what the
Spirit saith unto the Churches; To him that overcometh
will I give to eat of the hidden manna.*'—Omit the words
'*to eat.*'—Doubtless allusion is here to the manna which

at God's express command Moses caused to be laid up
before the Lord in the Sanctuary (Exod. xvi. 32–34;
cf. Heb. ix. 4). This manna, as being thus laid up in the
Holy Place, obtained the name of ' *hidden*,'—' occultatum '
or ' reconditum,' as Cocceius presses that it should be
rendered, not ' occultum ; ' for it is not κρυπτόν in the
original, but κεκρυμμένον ; not therefore ' *latens* manna '
as in Tertullian (*Scorp.* 12), but ' *absconditum* ' as in the
Vulgate. It is true that many commentators, as Hengstenberg, omit any reference to this, and some expressly
deny that any such reference exists; but Vitringa rightly :
' Ducit autem phrasis nos manifeste ad cogitandum de
mannâ illo, quod ex jussu Dei in urnâ reponendum erat in
sacratissimo Tabernaculi conclavi, per divinam providen-
tiam ab omni corruptione præservandum ; quod manna
vere symbolum fuit Christi virtute obedientiæ suæ in cæ-
lum translati, et ibi delitescentis, usque quo Ecclesia
ipsius luctam suam in his terris absolverit.' The question,
what we shall exactly understand by this ' *hidden manna*,'
and the eating of it, has not always been answered with
precision. Origen characteristically understands by it the
inner mystical sense of Scripture as distinguished from
the outward form and letter (*Hom.* 9 *in Exod.*): ' Urna
mannæ reposita, intellectus Verbi Dei subtilis et dulcis.'
For the Mystics it is in general that grace and goodness of
God which can only be known by those who have themselves
actually tasted it ; thus one of these : ' Hujus spiritualis
et occulti mannæ sapor latet in occulto, nisi gustando sen-
tiatur.' I take it, however, that this ' *hidden manna*
represents a more central benefit even than these ; moreover, like all the other promises of these Epistles, it represents a benefit pertaining to the future kingdom of glory,
and not to the present kingdom of grace. I would not

indeed affirm that this promise has not prelibations which
will be tasted in the present time; for the life eternal
commences on this side of the grave, and not first on the
other; and here in the wilderness Christ is the bread
from heaven, the bread of God, the true manna, of which
those that eat shall never die (John vi. 31-33, 48-51).
Nay, more than this; since his Ascension He is in some
sort a '*hidden manna*' for them now. Like that manna
laid up in the Sanctuary before the Testimony, He too,
withdrawn from sight, but in a human body, and bearing
our flesh, is yet exempted from the law of corruption
under which all other children of men have lain (Exod.
xvi. 20, 33, 34; Acts ii. 27, 31). But this promise of the
gift of '*the hidden manna*' is misunderstood, or at any
rate is scanted of its full meaning, unless we look on to
something more and higher than this. The words imply
that, however hidden now, it shall not remain hidden evermore; and the best commentary on them is to be found
at 1 Cor. ii. 9; 1 John iii. 2. The seeing of Christ as He
is, of the latter passage, and through this beatific vision the
being made like to Him, is identical with this eating of
the hidden manna; which shall, as it were, be then brought
forth from the sanctuary, the Holy of Holies of God's immediate presence, where it was withdrawn from sight so
long, that all may partake of it; the glory of Christ, now
shrouded and concealed, being then revealed at once *to*
his people and *in* them (Col. iii. 4). Alcuin: 'Apte ergo
illa satietas cælestis gloriæ manna [absconditum?] vocatur, quia juxta Pauli vocem nec oculus vidit, nec in cor
hominis ascendit, quæ præparavit Deus diligentibus se.'
Richard of St. Victor quotes in illustration Ps. xxx. 20:
'Quam magna multitudo dulcedinis tuæ, Domine, quam
abscondisti timentibus te.'

There has been, and there will be again, occasion to observe, that in almost all these promises there is a peculiar adaptation of the promise to the self-denial by which it will have been won. Witsius notes this here, and draws out very beautifully the inner sweetness of this promise (*Miscell. Sac.* vol. i. p. 692): ' Eas [profanas epulas] si quis generosâ fidei constantiâ, una cum omnibus blandientis seculi deliciis atque illiciis fortiter spreverit, sciat se satiatum iri suavissimis divinæ tam gratiæ quam gloriæ epulis, quarum suavitatem nemo rite æstimare novit, nisi qui gustavit. Propterea autem *mannæ absconditæ* comparantur, id est, illi quæ in urnâ aureâ in abdito loco asservanda, coram facie Jehovæ seposita fuit, I. Quia quod præcipuum est in illâ dulcedinis Christi participatione reservatur cum Christo in cælis (Col. iii. 3 ; 2 Tim. i. 12). II. Quia mundanorum hominum nemo dulcedinem hujus novit (Joh. xiv. 17) ; immo ne ipsi fideles quidem antequam experiantur (1 Joh. iii. 2). III. Quia communio ista non in diem est, uti manna quotidiana, sed perpetua, uti illa quæ seposita coram Domino a putrefactione et vermibus immunis erat (Joh. vi. 27), et propterea profanis Pergamensium epulis immensum anteferenda.'

' *And will give him a white stone, and in the stone a new name written, which no man knoweth saving he that receiveth it.*'—' *White*' is everywhere the colour and livery of heaven ; and nowhere with a greater or so great an emphasis, or with so frequent iteration, as in this Book. Thus of the Son of God we are told, ' His head and his hairs were *white* like wool, as *white* as snow ' (i. 14). Then besides this ' *white* stone ' we have ' *white* raiment ' (iii. 5), ' *white* robes ' (vii. 9), ' a *white* cloud ' (xiv. 14), ' fine linen clean and *white* ' (xix. 8, 14), ' *white* horses ' (xix. 11, 14), 'a great *white* throne' (xx. 11). With these passages compare Dan. vii. 9 ; Matt. xvii. 2 ; xxviii. 3 ; Mark. ix. 3 ; xvi. 5 ; John xx. 12 ; Acts i. 10. The sense of the fitness of white to serve as a symbol of absolute purity speaks out in many ways ; it would do so singularly in the Latin ' castus,' if Döderlein's suggestion (*Lat. Syn.* vol. iii. p. 196) that 'castus' is a participle of 'candeo' could be admitted. It may be well to observe that '*white*' as this colour of heaven, is not the mere absence of other colour, not the dull ' albus,' but the bright ' candidus ; ' glistering white—as is evident from many passages ; for instance, from a comparison of Matt. xxviii. 3 and Luke xxiv. 4 with John xx. 12 ; of Rev. xx. 11 ($\lambda \epsilon \nu \kappa \delta s \ \theta \rho \acute{o} \nu o s$) with its original, Dan. vii. 9 ($\theta \rho \acute{o} \nu o s \ a \dot{\nu} \tau o \hat{\nu} \ \phi \lambda \delta \xi \ \pi \nu \rho \acute{o} s$) ; and from those passages just now referred to, which relate to the Transfiguration. It is the character of intense white to be shining ; thus ' niteo ' (= 'niviteo ') is connected with ' nix ;' $\lambda \epsilon \nu \kappa \acute{o} s$ with ' lux ' (see Donaldson, *New Cratylus*, § 269 ; Pott, *Etym. Forsch.* vol. iii. p. 247) ; $\lambda \epsilon \nu \kappa \acute{o} s$ and $\lambda a \mu \pi \rho \acute{o} s$ are used as convertible terms, Rev. xix. 8, 14 ; while at Acts x. 30, $\lambda \epsilon \nu \kappa \hat{\eta}$ and $\lambda a \mu \pi \rho \hat{a}$ are different readings ; and at Cant. v. 11, the Septuagint has $\lambda \epsilon \nu \kappa \acute{o} s$ and Symmachus $\lambda a \mu \pi \rho \acute{o} s$.

And as '*white*,' so also '*new*' belongs eminently to this Book ; being one of the key-words of it ; He who is the giver of this revelation everywhere setting forth Himself as the only renewer of all which sin had made old ; the author of a new creation even in the midst of a decaying and dying world ; and thus we have besides the '*new* name' here (cf. iii. 12), the '*new* Jerusalem' (iii. 12), the '*new* song' (v. 9), the '*new* heaven and the *new* earth' (xxi. 1), and finally ' all things *new*' (xxi. 5) ; with all which we may profitably compare Ps. xxxiii. 3 ; cxliv. 9 ;

Isai. xlii. 10; lxii. 2; lxv. 17; Jer. xxxi. 31; Ezek. xi.
19; xxxvi. 26.

But though it is not difficult to fix the symbolic significance of '*white*' and '*new*' in this Book, it must be
freely admitted that we still wait an entirely satisfactory
explanation of this '*white stone*' with the '*new name*'
written in it. The greater number of expositors, especially
the older ones, start from an assumption to which no objection can be made, namely, that there was in ancient
times something festal, fortunate, of good omen, in white
pebbles or beans.   Thus the Greek phrase λευκὴ ἡμέρα,
or λευκὸν ἦμαρ (Æschylus, *Pers.* 305), is commonly derived from a custom ascribed to the Scythians or Thracians, of indicating each happy day which they spent with
a white stone placed in an urn, each unhappy with a black.
After death, as those or these exceeded in number, their
lives were counted happy or miserable (Pliny, *H. N.* vii.
41; the Younger Pliny, *Ep.* vi. 11; Martial, ix. 53: 'Dies
nobis Signandi melioribus lapillis,' xii. 34).   Or there is
another explanation of the ' white day,' connecting it still
with the white stone or bean, I mean that given by Plutarch in his *Life of Pericles*, c. 64.   At the siege of Samos,
fearing that his soldiers would be weary with its length (I
quote North's translation), 'he divided his army into eight
companies, whom he made to draw lots, and that company
which lighted upon the white bean, they should be quiet
and make good cheer, while the other seven fought.   And
they say that from thence it came that when any have
made good cheer, and taken pleasure abroad, they do yet
call it *a white day*, because of the white bean.'

But how, it may be asked, is all this brought to bear
on the promise of the '*white stone*' to the faithful here?
The earliest attempt to find help in this quarter is that

of the Greek commentator Andreas. He sees allusion in
these words to the white pebble, by placing which in the
ballot-box the Greek judges pronounced the sentence of
acquittal ($\psi\hat{\eta}\phi o\iota$ $\sigma\acute{\omega}\zeta o\upsilon\sigma a\iota$ they were therefore called), as
by the black of condemnation ; a custom expressed in the
well-known lines of Ovid (*Metam.* xv. 41, 42) :—

> ' Mos erat antiquus, niveis atrisque lapillis,
>   His damnare reos, illis absolvere culpæ.'

But, not to speak of a grave fault, of which I shall
presently speak, common to this and almost every other
explanation of these words which is offered, this one is
manifestly inadequate ; the absolving pebble was not *given
to* the acquitted, as this is to the victor, nor do we hear of
any name written upon it.

Others see allusion to the *tessera* (it too was called
$\psi\hat{\eta}\phi o s$), which the conquerors at the Olympic or other
solemn games (the $\grave{o}\lambda\upsilon\mu\pi\iota o\nu\hat{\iota}\kappa a\iota$, $\iota\varepsilon\rho o\nu\hat{\iota}\kappa a\iota$) received from
the master of the games ; which $\psi\hat{\eta}\phi o s$ gave ever after to
him who received it certain honorary distinctions and privileges, as for example, the right of free access to the public
entertainments.   So Arethas, Gerhard (*Loci Theoll.* vol. ii.
p. 327), and others ; while Vitringa is obliged to confess
that he can only explain the symbol by combining together these two customs of the absolving pebble, and
the *tessera* given to the victor in the games ; which two
in the higher interpretation must be blended into one :
' Ut tamen verum fatear, probabile videri possit Dominum
orationem suam hoc loco ita temperâsse, ut non ad simplicem
aliquem ritum, apud Græcos receptum, hic loci alluserit, sed
phrasin suam mutuatus sit a duobus illis ritibus supra com-
memoratis, inter se compositis, qui licet diversi fuerint gen-
eris, in tertio tamen, quod dicitur, inter se conveniebant.'

But all these explanations, and others which it would

be tedious to enumerate, even if they were more satisfactory, and they appear to me most unsatisfactory, are af-
fected with the same fatal weakness, namely, that they are
borrowed from *heathen* antiquity, while this Book moves
exclusively within the circle of sacred, that is, of Jewish,
imagery and symbols ; nor is the explanation of its symbols in any case to be sought beyond this circle.   All which
on this matter was said in respect of the ' *crown of life* '
(ii. 10) finds its application here.   It is true that Hengstenberg, whose interpretation I have not yet mentioned,
avoids this mistake, but only by, in fact, denying that the
' *white stone* ' means anything at all.   It has for him no
significance or independent value of its own, being introduced merely for the sake of the ' *new name* ' which is
written upon it, and that it may serve as a vehicle for this
name, being as such entirely subordinate to it.   Few, I am
persuaded, reading the words of the promise, with the emphasis which the Lord lays on the twice-repeated mention
of the stone, and noting the independent place which it
occupies as itself a gift, whatever other gifts might be
associated with it, will be content to acquiesce in this, or
to regard as a solution what is in fact merely an evasion,
of the difficulty which the words present.

But to return.   The first necessary condition of any interpretation which should be accepted as satisfactory being
this, that it should be sacred and not heathen, at the same
time this is not the only one.   There appear to me two
other necessary conditions, the non-fulfilment of which is
fatal to any exposition ; the fulfilment of them, on the
contrary, not being itself proof that the right interpretation has been seized ; but only a *conditio sine quâ non*,
and up to a certain point implying a probability that this
has been attained.   Besides thus being Hebrew or sacred,

and not heathen or profane, which I believe is the universal law of all Apocalyptic symbolism, the solution must in this particular instance refer to the wilderness period of Jewish history, in the same way as the '*hidden manna*' does. I must ask the reader to suspend his demand for a proof of this assertion till we have reached the very last of the promises, when the course, order, and succession of them all will be considered. And, in the second place, it must be capable of being brought into some unity with that other promise, '*To him that overcometh will I give to eat of the hidden manna*;' there must be some bond of connexion between the two. I conclude this not merely from the natural fitness of things, but from the analogy of all the other promises made to the other Churches. In every other case the promise is either absolutely single, as at ii. 7, 11; iii. 21; or single in its central idea, as at ii. 26–28; iii. 5, 12, which I shall have the opportunity of showing. This being so, it is very improbable that the present should be an exception to the rule, and that here two entirely disparate promises should be arbitrarily linked together.

The only solution I know which fulfils all these conditions, is one proposed by Züllig (*Offenb. Johannis*, vol. i. pp. 408-454). It has found no favour or acceptance whatever, having been indeed by him encumbered with so many absurdities that this could scarcely have been otherwise. Fully acknowledging my obligations to him for the original suggestion of it, and for some of the arguments by which it is supported, I must yet claim to set it forth independently of him, nor is he in any way responsible for my statement of it.

Starting then from a reconsideration of the word ψῆφος, this, it may be observed, is sometimes used in the later Greek for a *precious* stone; thus ψῆφος δακτυλική, the gem in a seal-ring worn on the finger. Neither is there in the epithet λευκός (not ' albus,' but ' candidus ') anything which renders this unlikely here, but rather the contrary; a diamond, for instance, being of the purest glistering white. The ψῆφος λευκή then may be, not what we commonly begin with taking for granted it must be, a white pebble, but a precious stone, shining white, a diamond. But may not the mysterious Urim and Thummim have been exactly this? First, let me observe, by way of preoccupying a difficulty on the threshold, that whatever this may have been, it was not two things, but two names for one and the same thing (see Bähr, *Symbolik d. Mos. Cult.* vol. ii. pp. 109, 110); often therefore called only the Urim (Num. xxvii. 21; 1 Sam. xxviii. 6). Sparing my readers the learning which might easily be transcribed to any amount from the many elaborate treatises devoted to the inquiry as to what this Urim and Thummim might be, I will state the conclusions to which those who have studied the matter most profoundly have arrived. They are agreed that it was some precious thing which the High Priest bore within the *Choschen*, or square breastplate of judgment; this being doubled back upon itself, to the end that like a purse it might contain the treasure committed to it (Exod. xxviii. 15–30; Lev. viii. 8), and with all its costly jewellery and elaborate workmanship existing for this object, quite as much as the ark existed for the sake of the tables of the law. But what precious thing this Urim may have been is shrouded in mystery; only as that in the purse, and for which the purse was made, is likely to have been *more* precious than the purse itself, if *that* was set with its twelve precious stones, each with the name of a tribe engraven on

it, in *this* we are led to look for a stone rarer and more
costly than them all; and it is certainly very noticeable
that among the twelve stones of the breastplate the diamond does not appear; for the mention of it in our Version (Exod. xxviii. 18) is confessedly a mistake ;—as though
this stone had been reserved for a higher honour and dignity still.

Then further, no one knows, probably no one ever
knew, what was graven on the Urim; except indeed the
High Priest; who, consulting it that he might in some
way obtain through it lively oracles from God, in matters
which greatly concerned the weal or woe of the people
(Num. xxvii. 21 ; 1 Sam. xxiii. 9–12 ; xxx. 7, 8), could not
have remained ignorant of this.   It is generally conjectured,
however, to have been the holy Tetragrammaton, the in-
effable name of God.   It is difficult to conceive it to have
been anything else.   I need hardly ask the reader who
has followed me thus far to note how well this agrees with
the words before us, '*and in the stone a new name written,
which no man knoweth saving he that receiveth it.*'   Many
are led away from the right interpretation of these last
words, by referring this '*receiveth it*' to the '*name,*' and
not to the '*stone*;' they read as though it was written,
'*saving he that receiveth this name,*'—when, as I feel sure,
we ought to read it, '*saving he that receiveth this stone.*'
They assume the overcomer's *own name* to be that written
on this stone; and draw from these words an intimation
that, just as the mystery of regeneration is known only to
the new-born, so the yet higher glory of heaven only to
him that is partaker of it (1 Cor. xiii. 9); which all is most
true, and a new name is often used to express a new
blessedness (Isai. lxii. 2 ; lxv. 15); but yet it is not the
truth of the promise here.   The '*new name*' here is

something even better than this. It is the new name
of God or of Christ, ' *my new name* ' (cf. iii. 12) ; some
revelation of the glory of God, only in that higher state
capable of being communicated by Him to his people,
and which they only can understand who have actually
received ; for it is a *knowing* which is identical with a
being ; and that word in old time ascribed to the Lord,
' My mystery is for Me, and for the sons of my house ' (cf.
Isai. xxiv. 10), stands fast, whether actually spoken by
Him, or only ascribed to Him (Clement of Alexandria,
Strom. v. 10. 64).

How excellently well the promise, so understood,
matches with the other promise of ' *the hidden manna*,'
which goes hand in hand with it. It was said at the outset of this inquiry, that there ought to be an inner bond
between the two parts of the promise ; and such, according
to this interpretation, there will be. ' *The hidden manna* '
and the ' *white stone* ' are not merely united in time, belonging both to the wilderness period of the history of
God's people ; but they are united as both representing
high-priestly prerogatives, which the Lord should at length
impart to all his people, kings and priests to God, as He
will then have made them all. If any should be privileged
to eat of ' *the hidden manna*,' who but the High Priest,
who alone had entrance into the Holy Place where it was
laid up ? If any should have knowledge of what was
graven on the Urim, who but the same High Priest, in
whose keeping it was, and who was bound by his very
office to consult it ? The mystery of what was written
there, shut to every other, would be open to him. In lack
of any more satisfying explanation of the promise of the
' *white stone* ' with the ' *new name* ' written upon it, I
venture to suggest that the key to it may possibly be here.

IV.

EPISTLE TO THE CHURCH OF THYATIRA.

REV. ii. 18-29.

Ver. 18. '*And unto the Angel of the Church in Thya-tira write.*'—The Roman road from Pergamum to Sardis left Thyatira, as we are told by Strabo (xiii. 4), a little to the left; St. John is led 'in the Spirit' by the same route which he may often in time past have travelled in the course of his apostolic visitations. Thyatira, a city of no first-rate dignity, 'inhonora civitas' the Elder Pliny goes so far as to call it (v. 33), was a Macedonian colony (Strabo, xiii. 4); and it may be regarded as a slight and unintentional confirmation, in a minute particular, of the historic accuracy of the Acts, that Lydia, a purple-seller of Thyatira, is met in the Macedonian city of Philippi (Acts xvi. 14), this being precisely what was likely to happen from the close and frequent intercourse maintained be-tween a mother city and its daughter colonies. From this Lydia, whose heart the Lord had opened to attend to the things spoken of Paul (Acts xvi. 14), the Church at Thyatira may have drawn its beginnings. She who had gone forth for a while, to buy and sell and get gain, may when she returned home have brought back with her far richer merchandise than any she had looked to obtain.

'*These things saith the Son of God, who hath his eyes*

like unto a flame of fire, and his feet are like fine brass.
The attributes which the Lord claims are again drawn
from the description of the first chapter, ver. 14, 15, which
see. The title '*Son of God*' (cf. xix. 13) is not indeed
expressly and in so many words there ; but it is involved
in, and is the sum total of the impression left by, the whole
description. The actual form of this title is here drawn
from the second Psalm, ver. 9 ; as is plain from more than
one reference to that Psalm before this Epistle is ended ;
thus compare ver. 26 with Ps. ii. 8 ; and ver. 27 with ii. 9.
He who will presently give dominion to his servants, first
claims this dominion for Himself. The heathen have been
given to Him for an inheritance, else He could not give
them to his servants. If these servants of his are to rule
them with a rod of iron, and break them in pieces like a
potter's vessel, it is only as partakers in a power which He
has Himself first received.

Ver. 19. '*I know thy works, and charity, and service,
and faith, and thy patience, and thy works; and the last
to be more than the first.*'—Omit '*and thy works*' on its
second occurrence, which has no right to a place in the
text, and which mars the symmetry of all. We shall then
have two pairs. First, '*thy charity and thy service,*' for
the article prefixed to all these words shows that the concluding σοῦ belongs to them all,—the '*charity,*' or love,
being the more inward thing, the '*service*' (διακονία) the
outward ministrations, the helps of all kinds shown first to
the household of faith, and then to all others, in which
this '*charity*' found its utterance (Acts xi. 29 ; 1 Cor.
xvi. 15 ; Heb. vi. 10). As the first pair have a very close
inner connexion, so have also the next pair, '*and thy faith
and thy patience.*' It needs but to refer in proof to
Heb. xi. 27 : '*He endured, as seeing Him that is invisible;*'

L

and indeed Scripture everywhere declares that faith is the root and source of all patient continuance in well-doing.— '*And the last to be more than the first.*' The faithful in Thyatira were growing and increasing in this service of love, this patience of faith; herein satisfying the desire of Him, who evermore desires for his people that they should abound more and more in all good things. How much better this τὰ ἔσχατα πλείονα τῶν πρώτων than that of which St. Peter elsewhere speaks as the state of some, τὰ ἔσχατα χείρονα τῶν πρώτων (2 Pet. ii. 20: cf. Matt. xii. 45), which, as regarded the most excellent grace of all, the Lord has just declared to be the condition of the Ephesian Church (ver. 4).

Ver. 20. '*Notwithstanding I have a few things against thee, because thou sufferest that woman Jezebel, which calleth herself a prophetess, to teach and seduce my servants to commit fornication, and to eat things sacrificed unto idols.*'—Omit '*a few things*' (ὀλίγα), which has no business in the text, having been brought here from ver. 14; and change, as a consequence of this, '*because*' into '*that*' —but do not change '*that woman*' into '*thy wife*,' the authority for the insertion of σοῦ after τὴν γυναῖκα being insufficient to justify this; however there may be 'many authorities, and some ancient, in its favour' (R.V.) see Lee, *On the Revelation*, pp. 527, 535. How many of the early heretical leaders led about with them one who was neither a wife nor a sister is sufficiently known to all, as a Simon Magus his Helena, that we speak not of others. The whole condition of things at Thyatira was exactly the reverse of the condition at Ephesus. There much zeal for the maintenance of sound doctrine, a stiff orthodoxy, but little love, and as a consequence, no doubt, few ministrations of love. Here the activity of faith and love, but insufficient zeal for the maintenance of godly discipline and doctrine, a patience of error even where there was not a participation in it. Each of these Churches was weak in that wherein the other was strong.

But whom shall we understand by ' *that woman Jezebel, which calleth herself a prophetess,*' whom the Lord proceeds presently to threaten with so terrible a doom? It may be well here to consider first the position which the literal and historic Jezebel occupies in the history of the Church of the Old Testament. As Balaam, in the earlier history of the children of Israel, was the author of the great attempt to introduce heathenism with all its train of attendant impurities into the heart of the Church of God (Rev. ii. 14; Num. xxv.), so Jezebel in the later period of that same history. She was a daughter of Ethbaal, king of Sidon (1 Kin. xvi. 13). The identity of this Ethbaal and Εἰθώβαλος, mentioned in a fragment of the *Tyrian Annals* of Menander, preserved by Josephus (*Con. Apion.* i. 18), is sufficiently made out, and is not, I believe, called in question by any. Of this Ethbaal we there learn that he was a priest of Astarte, and, by the murder of his predecessor Pheles, made his own way to the throne and kingdom. Jezebel, so swift to shed blood (1 Kin. xvii. 4; xix. 2; xxi. 10), is a worthy offshoot of this evil stock. Nor less does she attest herself the daughter of the priest of Astarte. Hitherto the worship of the Calves had been the whole extent of the departure of the Ten Tribes from the Levitical institutions,—the true God worshipped still, although under symbols which He had expressly forbidden; the law of Moses in the main allowed and kept, however there might be a certain amount of sinful will-worship mingling with and infecting all. But from the time of Ahab's marriage with the daughter of Ethbaal the apostasy of Israel assumes altogether a different character; the guilt of it is of quite another and an infinitely deadlier kind (1 Kin. xvi. 31; xxi. 25, 26). A fanatical promoter of the Baal worship (1 Kin. xviii. 19), overbearing with her stronger will the weak will of her despicable husband, having made her own the substance of a power whereof only the shadow remained to him (1 Kin. xxi. 7, 8), animated with the fiercest hatred against the prophets of Jehovah, the last witnesses for Him in Israel, now that the Levitical priesthood had been abolished there (1 Kin. xxi. 31), she seeks utterly to exterminate these (1 Kin. xviii. 13). She was probably herself, like her moral name-sake here, a false prophetess; a priestess of that foul enthusiasm. Many arguments make this probable at the least. As much seems implied in the answer to Joram's question, 'Is it peace?' which Jehu makes, 'What peace, so long as the whoredoms of thy mother Jezebel, and *her witchcrafts* are so many' (2 Kin. ix. 22)? So too, when we keep in mind the essentially impure character of the Phœnician idolatries which she introduced,—Ashtaroth or Astarte was the Phœnician Aphrodite,—we have an explanation of the 'whoredoms' which Jehu further lays to her charge, and which may thus have set a hideous contradiction between her and her name, if indeed that derivation which would make it etymologically to signify The Chaste (our *Agnes*) is the true one (see Gesenius, *Hebrew and Chaldee Lexicon*, p. 37). Nor is this the only passage where these impurities are ascribed to her. There is at Jeremiah iv. 30 an allusion, often overlooked, but, so soon as attention is called to it, not to be gainsaid, to 2 Kin. ix. 30; and there the lovers or paramours of Jezebel appear.

Such was the elder Jezebel; the female Antichrist of

the Old Testament. And the later, assuredly not a sect of evil-workers personified, but some single wicked woman in the Church of Thyatira (Jablonski, *De Jezabele, Thyatirenorum pseudoprophetissâ, Opusc.* vol. iii. p. 225), inheriting from her this name of infamy in the Church of God, would seem to have followed hard in the steps of her Jewish prototype (for a like transfer of an evil name see Isai. i. 10; Ezek. xvi. 3). Witsius: 'Facile ex hoc loco concluditur fuisse Thyatiræ principem aliquam atque illustrem fœminam, simulacricolam, veneficam, meretricem, geminam germanam antiquæ illius Jezebelis, hoc tamen instructiorem ad perniciem, quod hæc palam sese hostem ac persecutricem Ecclesiæ ostendebat, illa autem videri voluit prophetissa, raptus fatidicos mentiens, in Nicolaïtarum ludo ad omnem nequitiam edocta.' Not only did she give herself out for a prophetess, but in one sense, as I take it, was such,—no mere *teacher* of perverse things, employing her intellectual faculties in the service of Satan and not of God; but claiming inspiration, and probably possessing it, wielding spiritual powers, only they were such as reached her from beneath, not such as descended on her from above; for as at this time miraculous gifts of grace and power were at work in the Church, so were also the devilish counterfeits of these. And thus, by aid of these, she seduced the servants of Christ '*to commit fornication, and to eat things sacrificed to idols;*' see ver. 14. To restrain '*servants*' here to those who hold office in the Church is certainly a mistake. Δοῦλος may very well have this narrower meaning at i. 1; but that δοῦλοι includes the whole body of the faithful at vii. 3; xxii. 3, is evident. A comparison of this verse with ver. 14–16 leaves no doubt that the Jezebelites, and Balaamites, and Nicolaitans, with secondary differences no doubt, were yet substantially the same;—all libertine sects, disclaiming the obligations of the moral law; all starting with a denial that Jesus Christ was come in the flesh, and that in the flesh therefore men were to be holy; all alike false spiritualists, whose highflying pretensions did not hinder them from ending in the foulest fleshly sins; being themselves rather the means of entangling men therein.

Ver. 21. '*And I gave her space to repent of her fornication; and she repented not.*'—The fact that punishment does not at once overtake sinners is constantly misunderstood by them as an evidence that it never will overtake them (Eccl. viii. 11; Isai. xxvi. 10; Ps. xxvi. 11); that God does not see, or, seeing, does not care to avenge. Christ opens out here another aspect under which this delay in the divine revenges may be regarded. The very time during which ungodly men are heaping up for themselves greater wrath against the day of wrath, was a time lent them for repentance (Rom. ii. 4; 2 Pet. iii. 9), if only they would have understood the object and the meaning of it.

Ver. 22. '*Behold, I will cast her into a bed,*[1] *and them that commit adultery with her into great tribulation, except they repent of their deeds.*'—These last words imply that even now the day of grace was not expired for these transgressors, however near at hand the close of it might be.

---

[1] A curious testimony to the entire disappearance of Greek, and of the power of appealing to Greek copies of Scripture, probably to the well-nigh total absence of such in Western Europe to appeal to, and the consequent exclusive dependence on the Vulgate, occurs here in the *Commentary* of Richard of St. Victor, one of the most learned men of perhaps the most learned monastic foundation in France. He observes that some copies of the Latin here read 'lectum,' some 'luctum;' discusses at length the several advantages and probabilities of the two readings, without one word implying the possibility of settling the question at once by a reference to the original. It is, as it were, extinct to him.

'*I will cast her into a bed*;' there where she has sinned (cf. Isai. lvii. 7, 8) shall she also be punished (cf. 1 Kin. xxi. 19); the bed of sin shall be the bed of languishing, of sickness, and of death ; cf. 1 Macc. i. 5 (ἔπεσεν ἐπὶ τὴν κοίτην = 'he fell sick'); 1 Cor. xi. 30. The allusion which Vitringa traces here to the bed on which Ahab cast himself down 'heavy and displeased' (1 Kin. xxi. 4) is ingenious, but exceedingly far-fetched.

Ver. 23. '*And I will kill her children with death.*'— If her lovers, those '*that commit adultery with her*' (ver. 22), can only mean the chief furtherers and abettors of those evil things (she may have seduced them to fleshly as well as spiritual wickedness), '*her children*' must be rather the less prominent, less forward members of the same wicked confederacy, more the deceived while the others were the deceivers (Isai. lvii. 3), who yet should be involved with them in a common doom (Isai. ix. 16; xlvii. 9; Ezek. xxiii. 47). The words '*with death*' must plainly be accepted as emphatic; some understand with pestilence and plague (see Jer. xxi. 7), relying mainly on Rev. vi. 8; where, however, θάνατος cannot be proved to mean this; a reference to 2 Sam. xxiv. 13, 15; Ezek. xiv. 19, 21 ; xxxiii. 27, LXX, would have been more to the point. Hengstenberg detects an allusion here to the death of the adulteress (Lev. xx. 10; Ezek. xvi. 38-41; cf. John viii. 5); but this can scarcely be ; for it is the '*children*' of the adulteress, not the adulteress herself, who are here threatened with death. Others find an allusion to the two sweeping catastrophes which overtook the priests and votaries of Baal at exactly that period of Jewish history to which the mention of Jezebel here points (1 Kin. xviii. 40; 2 Kin. x. 25);—but more probably the words contain nothing more than a general threat that their doom

should be a signal one, that they should 'die of grievous
deaths' (Jer. xvi. 4), and not the common death of all
men, nor be visited after the visitation of all men
(Num. xvi. 29).

'*And all the Churches shall know that I am He which
searcheth the reins and hearts.*'—The judgment on this
brood of transgressors shall be so open and manifest, their
sin shall so plainly find them out, that, not the wicked, for
God's judgments are far above out of their sight, but '*all
the Churches*,' all who ponder these things and lay them
to heart, shall confess that He who moves up and down in
the midst of his Church, beholding the evil and the good,
is a God of knowledge (see ii. 2), who is not mocked;
'*which searcheth the reins and hearts*' (ταῖς ἐννοίαις ἐμ-
βατεύων, as Olympiodorus explains it). '*The reins*'
are probably regarded here as the seat of the passions
(Delitzsch, *Psychologie*, p. 220), '*the heart*' of the affec-
tions; cf. Jer. xvii. 10; xx. 12; and Basil the Great,
Hom. in Ps. vii. § 6. But this searching of the hearts
and reins being, as it is, a prerogative of Deity (Mark
ii. 8), God only knowing the thoughts of men (ὁ καρδιο-
γνώστης Θεός, Acts xv. 8; i. 24; 1 Kin. viii. 39; 1 Chron.
xxix. 17; Ezek. xi. 5), it is plain that Christ, challenging
this power for Himself, is implicitly claiming to be God;
even as others do the like for Him, when they make this
claim on his behalf (Heb. iv. 12, 13).—'Ερευνᾶν is used
in this same sense of searching, Rom. viii. 27, and
always expresses a *careful* investigation, a following up of
tracks or indications as far as they will lead, as the dog
the footprints of the chase, the miner the veins of the
metal (Gen. xxxi. 35; 1 Kin. xx. 6; Prov. xx. 27; 1 Cor.
ii. 10; 1 Pet. i. 11). Expressing, as the word does, this
laborious and even painful investigation, leading step by

step to its result, as every other *discursive* act, can only ἀνθρωποπαθῶς be ascribed to God; to whom by absolute and immediate intuition all hearts at all times lie open and manifest; who needs not to search out, and in this way to find, that which He always knows. For ἐρευνῶν the Septuagint Translators prefer ἐτάζων (Ps. vii. 10; 1 Chron. xxix. 17; Ps. cxxxviii. 22; Jer. xvii. 10), which rests on a different image,[1] and does not occur in the New Testament; though ἐξετάζειν more than once (Matt. ii. 8; John xxi. 12).

'*And I will give unto every one of you according to your works.*'—This promise, or this threat, for it may be either, is one which nowadays we too commonly keep in the background; but it is one which we should press on ourselves and on others with the same emphasis and iteration wherewith Christ and his Word presses it upon us all (Ps. lxii. 13; Matt. xvi. 27; Rom. ii. 6; 1 Pet. i. 17; 2 Cor. v. 10; Job xxxiv. 11; Eccles. xii. 14; Prov. xxiv. 12; Jer. xxxii. 19). It is one of the gravest mischiefs which Rome has bequeathed to us, that in a reaction and protest, itself absolutely necessary, against the false emphasis which she puts on works, unduly thrusting them in to share with Christ's merits in our justification, we often shrink from placing upon them the true; being as they are, to speak with St. Bernard, the 'via regni,' however little they may be the 'causa regnandi;' though here too it must never be forgotten that it is only the good tree which brings forth good fruit; and that no tree is good until Christ has made it good.

---

[1] Basil the Great: Ἐτασμὸς κυρίως ἐστὶν ἡ μετὰ πασῶν βασάνων προσαγομένη ἔρευνα παρὰ τῶν κριτῶν τοῖς ἐξεταζομένοις, ἵνα οἱ κρύπτοντες παρ' ἑαυτοῖς τὰ ἐπιζητούμενα, τῇ ἀνάγκῃ τῶν πόνων εἰς τὸ ἐμφανὲς καταστήσωσι τὸ λανθάνον.

Ver. 24. '*But unto you I say, and unto the rest in Thyatira, as many as have not this doctrine, and which have not known the depths of Satan, as they speak; I will put upon you none other burden.*'—Leave out the καὶ with which the second clause in the sentence begins, and read, '*But unto you I say, the rest in Thyatira, &c.*' The Gnostics, starting probably from 1 Cor. ii. 10, were ever boasting their acquaintance with mysteries, the deep things of God; could speak much about the βυθός, 'vere cæcutientes, qui profunda Bythi adinvenisse se dicunt' (Irenæus; cf. Tertullian, *Adv. Valentin.* § 1). A question is often here raised, whether these evil-workers spoke of '*depths of Satan;*' or only of '*depths,*' while '*of Satan*' is a further characteristic of these '*depths,*' added by the Lord Himself; who thus intimates with a severe irony what was the real character of those '*depths*' into which they professed themselves to have entered, and into which they sought to guide others. In this last way the words are generally understood, the Lord declaring what, in his all-seeing eye, was the true nature of the μεγαλορρημοσύναι (such Ignatius, *Ep. ad Ephes.* 10, calls them), the 'great swelling words of vanity' which these Gnostics vented; promising liberty to others, while they were themselves servants of corruption. I should be disposed, however, to think with Hengstenberg, that it was they themselves who talked of '*depths of Satan,*'—the position of ὡς λέγουσι seems to imply as much,—that in that fearful sophistry wherein they were such adepts, and whereby they sought to make a religion of every corrupt inclination of the natural mind, they talked much of '*depths of Satan,*' which it was expedient for them to fathom. They taught, as we know, that it was a small thing for a man to despise pleasure and to show himself superior to it, while at the same

time he fled from it. The true, the glorious victory was,
to remain superior to it even while tasting it to the full;
to give the body to all the lusts of the flesh, and yet with
all this to maintain the spirit in a region of its own, un-
injured by them; and thus, as it were, to fight against
pleasure with the arms of pleasure itself; to mock and
defy Satan even in his own kingdom and domain. We
have an anticipation of this sophistry of sin, with its
flatteries at once of the pride and corruption of the human
heart, in the well-known *mot* of Aristippus, the Cyrenaic
philosopher, who being upbraided on the score of his
relations with a Corinthian courtesan, defended himself
with the reply, difficult adequately to render in English,
Ἔχω Λαΐδα, οὐκ ἔχομαι ὑπ' αὐτῆς (Clement of Alexandria,
Strom. ii. 20; Diogenes Laertius, ii. 8. 75). Here, however, were but the germs of that which in some of the
Gnostics appears fully blown.

'For you,' says the Lord, 'who have not gone to this
satanic school, who have been content with the simple
knowledge of the good, and not thought it needful to
know the evil as well, not good and evil, but only good,
I will put upon you none other burden.' If it be asked,
'*none other burden*' than what?—the answer no doubt
is, none other than a continued abstinence from, and
protest against, these abominations. It was the master-
stroke of the antinomian Gnostics to exaggerate, to distort,
to misapply, all which St. Paul had spoken about the
freedom of the Christian man from the law. They were
the ultra-Paulines, who caricatured his doctrine, till of
God's truth they had made a devil's lie. St. Paul had
said of the law that it was not the ground of the Christian
man's justification (Romans, Galatians), nor yet the source
of his holiness (Colossians): they made him to say that

it was not the rule of his life; as though the Apostle had rejected it altogether as a burden no longer to be borne by the redeemed. The Lord takes up this word '*burden*;'—'I do lay on you a burden, but it is a burden which it is your blessedness to bear, and over and above which I will impose no other.' Compare Matt. xi. 30, where, however, φορτίον, not βάρος, stands in the original, and Acts xv. 28, 29, where βάρος occurs in this very sense of abstinence from idol-meats and fornication; and where exactly in the same sense, and almost in the same words, the Apostles declare that they will lay on the faithful of the Gentiles 'no greater burden than these necessary things.' I cannot but think that Christ's words here have direct reference to that solemn decree of the Church.

Ver. 25. *But that which ye have already hold fast till I come.*'—It is on this condition that He will impose on them no additional burden. What they have of sound doctrine, of holy living, this they must hold fast, must so grasp it that none shall wrest it from them, till the day when the Lord shall come, and bring this long and painful struggle for the maintenance of his truth to an end. Ever and ever in Scripture, not the day of death, but the day of the Lord Jesus, is put as the term of all conflict.

Ver. 26. '*And he that overcometh, and keepeth my works unto the end, to him will I give power over the nations.*'—On the nominative absolute here (ὁ νικῶν . . . δώσω αὐτῷ) and at iii. 12, 21, see Winer, *Gramm.* § 28. 3 ; and for other examples of the same, Ps. x. 4; Hos. xii. 7; Matt. x. 32; Acts vii. 40. By '*my works*' we must understand 'works which I have commanded, in which I find pleasure, which are the fruits of my Spirit;' cf. John vi. 28, where 'the works of God' are to be understood in the same sense as 'godly works.' Here again that which

is praised, that which will be crowned, is the keeping of
these his works '*unto the end*;' for Christ, the great
ἐπιστάτης in the games, of which the Father is the
ἀγωνοθέτης, and, still to keep the language of Tertullian
(*ad Mart.* 3), the Holy Ghost the ξυστάρχης, eternal life
the βραβεῖον, promises here this reward, not to him who
enters the lists and endures for a time, but to him who,
having begun well, continues striving lawfully to the last.
'*To him will I give power over the nations.*' The royalties of Christ shall by reflection and communication be
the royalties also of his Church. They shall reign ; but
only because Christ reigns, and because he is pleased to
share his dignity with them (iii. 21 ; Rom. v. 17 ; 2 Tim.
ii. 12). When we ask ourselves in what sense, at what
time, and in what form this '*power over the nations*'
shall be the prerogative of the Church, we must find our
answer in such passages as Rev. xx. 4 ; xxii. 5 ; 1 Cor. vi. 2 ;
Dan. vii. 22, 27 ; Ps. cxlix. 6-9 ; and above all Matt. xix.
28 ; cf. also Wisd. iii. 8 ; Ecclus. iv. 15. For '*power*'
the R. V. has substituted '*authority*,' which is an improve-
ment. There is very commonly a *moral* element implied in ἐξουσία (Matt. xxi. 23 ; Mark i. 22 ; John xvii.
2), which in δύναμις would be looked for in vain.

Ver. 27. '*And he shall rule them with a rod of iron ;
as the vessels of a potter shall they be broken to shivers.*'—
As this is a dignity which is originally Christ's (Ps. ii. 9 ;
cx. 2 ; Rev. xii. 5 ; xix. 15), and only by Him made over
to his servants, it is needful first to inquire what it means
in respect of Him ; and we may then understand what it
means in respect of them. The passage in the second
Psalm is no doubt that on which the three in this Book
ultimately rest. It is there, ' Thou shalt *break* them with
a rod of iron ; ' but this Book of Revelation is in agree-

ment with the Septuagint, 'Thou shalt *rule* [ποιμανεῖς]
them with a rod of iron.' The Hebrew word for 'Thou
shalt *break*,' and that for 'Thou shalt *rule*,' only differ in
their vowels; their consonants are identical; at the same
time the parallelism of the latter half of the verse, 'Thou
shalt dash them in pieces like a potter's vessel,' leaves
no doubt that 'Thou shalt break' was the intention of the
Psalmist. Shall we therefore conclude not merely that
the Septuagint Translators mistook, which happens too
frequently to be a matter to us of any serious wonder, but
that the Lord set his seal to their error? By no means.
He indeed accepts the pregnant and significant variation
which they, intentionally or unintentionally, drew out of
the language before them; and which was justified by the
root common to both words; and instead of the mere
unmingled judgment which lay in the passage as it originally stood in that Psalm, He expresses by it now judgment
mingled with mercy, judgment behind which purposes of
grace are concealed, and only waiting their due time to
appear. Such a παιδευτικὴ ἐνέργεια, as Theodoret terms
it, must be recognized in the ποιμαίνειν; which our '*Thou
shalt rule*,' and the Latin 'reges,' only imperfectly give
back; as, in regard of the Latin, Hilary (*in Ps.* ii.) urged
long ago: 'Reges eos in virgâ ferreâ; quanquam ipsum
reges non tyrannicum neque injustum sit, sed ex æquitatis
ac moderationis arbitrio regimen rationale demonstret,
tamen molliorem adhuc regentis affectum proprietas
Græca significat. Quod enim nobiscum est, *reges eos*,
cum illis est ποιμανεῖς αὐτούς, id est, *pastoraliter* reges,
regendi scilicet eos curam affectu pastoris habiturus.'
For a still tenderer use of ποιμαίνειν see John xxi. 16;
Acts xx. 28. No doubt the words do contain a threat for
the nations; but it is a threat of love (cf. 1 Cor. iv. 21).

Christ shall rule them with a sceptre of iron, so to make
them capable of being ruled with a sceptre of gold;
severity first, that grace may come after; they are broken
in pieces, that they may know themselves to be but men;
that, their fierceness and pride being brought down, they
may accept the yoke of Christ (Ps. lxxxiii. 16). And
indeed how often the great tribulations of a people have
been the προπαιδεία, the preparatory discipline, stern but
indispensable, whereby the Son of God has broken their
pride, and made them capable of receiving his gospel,
which, but for these, they would in their presumption and
self-confidence have rejected to the end. Thus what a
ruling with a rod of iron was the enforced conversion of
the Saxons by Charlemagne; what a bruising and breaking
of their pride and self-confidence, while yet it was the
beginning for them of a higher life, which except for this
they might have never known.

Our Translators have only rendered ῥάβδος by 'sceptre'
on a single occasion in the New Testament (Heb. i. 8).
It were to be wished they had done so here, and at xii. 5;
xix. 15. The word in the second Psalm שֵׁבֶט has this
meaning; cf. Ps. xliv. 8, where in like manner it occurs;
and everything else speaking of royalty here, this should
do the same. It may be urged, indeed, that royal sceptres
are not usually of iron, but of wood overgilded, or of silver,
or of gold. This may be quite true, but only makes more
striking the exception in the present instance. '*He
shall rule them with a sceptre of iron,*' which, harder and
stronger than any other, shall dash them who oppose
themselves to it in pieces like a potter's vessel; this image
implying the ease with which all resistance shall be overcome, the utter destruction which shall overtake all them
who attempt it (Jer. xix. 11; Isai. xxx. 14). Ewald:

'Imago regis hostes suos facillimâ operâ conterentis et dispergentis.'

' *Even as I received of my Father*.'—There was one who offered to inaugurate Him at once in the possession of all the kingdoms of the world and the glory of them; and the Lord had repelled him and his offer with indignation (Luke iv. 5–8), not because these were not his just expectation and his due inheritance; but because He would receive them at no other hands than his Father's. And now we find that He *has* received them at these hands, and they are his; his to impart to his servants; and that which was a lying boast on the lips of the usurper, namely, that he could give them to whom he would, is a truth on the lips of the rightful Lord. Even while upon earth He could say to his own, in prophetic anticipation of his completed work (and the words constitute a very remarkable parallel to these), 'I appoint unto you a kingdom, as my Father hath appointed unto Me' (Luke xxii. 29). Richard of St. Victor: 'Magna promissio, magnum donum: hoc promittit, hoc tribuit, quod Ipse accepit.'

Ver. 28. ' *And I will give him the morning star*.'— Cf. xxii. 16, where the Lord Himself is ' the bright and morning star ' (ὁ ἀστὴρ ὁ λαμπρὸς ὁ πρωϊνός); and the glorious hymn in the *Ranæ* of Aristophanes (343) where Dionysus is described as νυκτέρου τελετῆς φωσφόρος ἀστήρ. Whether He is meant by ' the day-star' (φωσφόρος) of 2 Pet. i. 19, may be a question. This star, as light-bringer, herald and harbinger of day, goes by many names; it is ἀστὴρ ἑωθινός (Ecclus. l. 6), ὁ ἑωσφόρος ὁ πρωὶ ἀνατέλλων (Isai. xiv. 12, ' Lucifer, son of the morning,' A. V.); the beauty and transcendant brightness of it being continually celebrated by poets, as by Homer (*Il.* xxii. 317: ἕσπερος, ὃς κάλλιστος ἐν οὐρανῷ ἵσταται ἀστήρ); by Virgil (*Æn.* viii. 389); by Ovid (*Trist.* i. 3. 71: ' cælo nitidissimus alto '); and by Milton (*Par. Lost,* iv. 605:

> ' Hesperus, that led
> The starry host, *rode brightest* ').

Thus does He who is ' fairer than the children of men ' claim all that is fairest and loveliest in creation as the faint shadow and image of his perfections. A comparison with that other passage in this Book referred to already (xxii. 16) conclusively proves that when Christ promises that He will give to his faithful ones the morning star, He promises that He will give to them Himself, that He will impart to them his own glory and a share in his own royal dominion (cf. iii. 21); for the star, as there has been already occasion to observe, is evermore the symbol of royalty (Matt. ii. 2), being therefore linked with the sceptre (Num. xxiv. 17). All the glory of the world shall end in being the glory of the Church, if only this abide faithful to its Lord. Witsius very beautifully, though placing his emphasis not precisely as I have done : ' Stellæ matutinæ datio significat, I. communionem arctiorem cum Christo penes quem fons lucis est (Ps. xxxvi. 10), et qui se ipsum stellam illam matutinam et splendidam nuncupat (Rev. xxii. 16). II. Quod exinde consequitur lucis et cognitionis spiritualis incrementum, immo consummationem sapientiæ cælestis (cf. 2 Pet. i. 19). III. Gaudium gloriosum et ineffabile, quod frequenter luci comparatur (Esth. viii. 16; Job xxx. 26; Ps. xcvii. 11), et imprimis luci matutinæ, quæ quum caliginosæ noctis horrori proxime succedat, omnium est gratissima (Job ii. 17; 2 Sam. xxiii. 4; Jes. viii. 20).'

Ver. 29. ' *He that hath an ear, let him hear what the Spirit saith unto the Churches.*'—Compare ii. 7.

M

V.

EPISTLE TO THE CHURCH OF SARDIS.

Rev. iii. 1–6.

Ver. 1. '*And unto the Angel of the Church in Sardis write.*'—Sardis, now Sart, was situated on the side of Mount Tmolus, upon the river Pactolus. The ancient capital of Lydia ('Crœsi regia Sardis,' Horace, *Ep.* i. 11. 2), it maintained a certain portion of its old dignity and splendour in the time of the Persians, being the residence of the Satrap, and had not wholly lost it in the Roman period. For the things in which the Sardians gloried the most, see Tacitus, *Annal.* iv. 55. Melito, whose name we hear seldom now, but the titles of whose works, one of these being a *Commentary on the Apocalypse*, are alone sufficient to inspire us with a lively regret for their almost entire loss, was bishop of Sardis in the latter half of the second century, being the only illustrious name connected with this Church (Routh, *Reliquiæ Sacræ*, vol. i. p. 109 sqq.; Neander, *Kirch. Gesch.* i. 3, p. 1140; *Theol. Stud. und Krit.* 1838, p. 54; Renan, *Marc-Aurèle*, pp. 178–191). Renan only needed a little more material to work on to have made a most interesting sketch of Melito's life and work; but his materials are *too* scanty, and even *his* ingenuity fails him here. See further Donaldson's *Critical History of Christian Literature and Doctrine*, vol. iii. p. 221 sqq.

'*These things saith He that hath the seven Spirits of God, and the seven stars.*'—There has been already occasion (i. 4) to speak of '*the seven Spirits of God*,' and to claim for these that they in this complex can set forth no other than the one Holy Spirit, the third Person of the ever-blessed Trinity, in his sevenfold operation. Augustine (*In Joan. Tract.* 122) speaks confidently on this matter : 'Quid in Apocalypsi, nonne septem spiritus Dei dicuntur, cum sit unus atque idem Spiritus, dividens propria unicuique prout vult ? Sed operatio septenaria unius Spiritûs sic appellata est ab eodem Spiritu, qui scribenti adfuit, ut septem spiritus dicerentur.' It only remains to consider the relation in which Christ, declaring that it is He '*that hath the seven Spirits of God*,' claims to stand to these seven. How entirely He '*hath*' them, by how intimate a right they are his, may best be understood by the comparison of other words, presently occurring in this same Book : 'I beheld a Lamb as it had been slain, having seven horns and seven eyes, which are the seven Spirits of God sent forth into all the earth ' (v. 6 ; cf. Zech. iii. 9 ; iv. 10). It needs hardly to be observed how important a witness this verse, when the right interpretation of '*the seven Spirits*' has been seized, bears to the faith of the Western Church on that great point upon which it is at issue with the Eastern, in respect, namely, of the procession of the Holy Ghost. He is indeed the Spirit of the Father *and the Son*. The Son '*hath the seven Spirits*,' or the Spirit ; not because He has received ; for though it is quite true that in the days of his flesh He did receive (Matt. iii. 16 ; John iii. 34 ; Heb. i. 9), yet now it is the Son of God, a giver therefore, and not a receiver, who is speaking ; who '*hath*' the Spirit ; '*hath*' to the end that He may impart it. If, too, the Spirit be admitted to be

God, then the Son, who '*hath*' the Spirit, must be God likewise; as is well argued, though not with reference to this particular verse, by Augustine (*De Trin.* xv. 26): '*Quomodo Deus non est, qui dat Spiritum Sanctum? Immo quantus Deus est, qui dat Deum?*' There is a special fitness in the assumption of this style by the Lord in his address to the Angel of the Church of Sardis. To him and to his people, sunken in spiritual deadness and torpor, the lamp of faith waning and almost extinguished in their hearts, the Lord presents Himself as having the fulness of all spiritual gifts; able therefore to revive, able to recover, able to bring back from the very gates of spiritual death those who would employ the little last remaining strength which they still retained, in calling, even when thus *in extremis*, upon Him.

In the words which follow, '*and the seven stars*,' is the only approach to a repetition in the titles of the Lord throughout all the Epistles. He has already proclaimed Himself as '*He that holdeth the seven stars in his right hand*' (ii. I), and now He is '*He that hath the seven stars*.' But the repetition is only apparent. '*The seven stars*' are brought into entirely different combinations there and here. There '*He that holdeth the seven stars*' is set forth as the same '*who walketh in the midst of the seven golden candlesticks*;' here '*He that hath the seven Spirits of God*' hath also '*the seven stars*.' But since '*the stars are the Angels of the seven Churches*' (i. 20) we must see in this combination a hint of the relation between Christ, as the giver of the Holy Spirit, and as the author of a ministry of living men in his Church; this ministry of theirs resting wholly on these gifts, even as the connexion between the two is often brought out in the New Testament. The *locus classicus* on this matter is

Ephes. iv. 7-12 ; but see further John xx. 22, 23 ; Acts i.
8 ; xx. 28. His are the golden urns from which these
' *stars*,' if they would at all shine, must continually draw
their light. They need not fear to be left destitute of his
manifold gifts, for He hath the Holy Spirit in all his
sevenfold operations, wherewith evermore to furnish them
to the full. With a deep insight into this truth the
Church orders that hymn, ' Come, Holy Ghost, our souls
inspire,' to be sung at the ordination of her ministers.
Cocceius : ' Per hanc descriptionem Christus vult se nosci
caput Ecclesiæ, suppeditatorem Spiritûs Sancti, et datorem
Ministrorum.'

' *I know thy works, that thou hast a name that thou
livest, and art dead.*'—A passage which at once suggests
itself as parallel to this, is 1 Tim. v. 6, where St. Paul, of
a woman living in pleasure, says, ζῶσα τέθνηκε : and compare, in the same sense, Matt. viii. 22 ; Luke xv. 24 ;
Rom. vi. 13 ; Ephes. ii. 1, 5 ; Heb. vi. 1 ; ix. 14. Bengel
suggests, and earlier commentators had anticipated the
suggestion, that the name of this Angel may have contained some assertion of *life* ; which stood in lamentable
contradiction with the realities of *death* which the Lord
beheld in him ; a name therefore which in his case was
not the utterance of a truth, but a lie ; no *nomen et omen*,
but the reverse ; the name affirming and implying that he
was alive, while in truth he was dead ; Ζώσιμος would be
such a name in Greek, Vitalis in Latin. Hengstenberg
considers the suggestion not improbable ; Marckius brands
it as ' inanissima conjectura ; ' even as it appears to me
exceedingly improbable and far-fetched. The use of
' *name* ' as equivalent to fame, reputation, character, is as
common in Greek as in English. The fact that Sardis
should have had this name and fame of life is very start-

ling, and may well summon each and all to an earnest heart-searching. There would be nothing nearly so startling, if Sardis had been counted by the Churches round about as a Church fallen into lethargy and hastening to decay and death. But there is no appearance of the kind. Laodicea, we know, deceived herself (iii. 17), but nothing implies that she deceived others; counted herself rich, when she *was* most poor; but there is no hint to make us think that others counted her rich as well; but Sardis had a name that she lived, was well spoken of, regarded, we may well believe, as a model Church, can therefore have been by no means wanting in the outer manifestations of spiritual life ; while yet all these shows of life did but conceal the realities of death ; so He, before whose eyes of fire no falsehood can stand, too surely saw.

Ver. 2. ' *Be watchful, and strengthen the things which remain, that are ready to die.*'—Translate rather, ' *Become watchful*,' or, if this be not too familiar, ' *wake up* ' (γίνου γρηγορῶν). The passages are many in which activity or vigilance of spirit is set forth under this same image, often by this very word (Matt. xxiv. 42, 43; xxv. 13; xxvi. 41 ; Mark xiii. 37 ; Acts xx. 31 ; 1 Cor. xv. 34; xvi. 13 ; 1 Thess. v. 6; 1 Pet. v. 8; Rev. xvi. 15). Not a few of our commentators are agreed that τὰ λοιπά here should be rendered not ' *the things which remain* ' (' quæ huc usque tibi mansere virtutes,' Ewald); but rather, ' *those which remain*,' or ' *the rest* ' (=τοὺς λοιπούς, or τοὺς καταλοίπους, Jer. xxiii. 3), as many as are not yet dead, however they may be now at the point of death. We gather from these words that, with few exceptions, the entire Sardian Church shared in this deadness of its chief pastor ; while he, in seeking to revive their life, to chafe their dead limbs, would best revive and recover the warmth of his

own (Ps. li. 13). Their present abject and fallen condition
is excellently expressed by the use of the neuter (cf. 1 Cor.
i. 27 ; Ezek. xxxiv. 4; Zech. xi. 9) ; nor indeed need the
use of it surprise us, even without the sufficient explanation
which this supplies. It is not here only that στηρίζειν is
employed in this sense of establishing, confirming in the
grace of God (see Luke xxii. 32 ; Rom. i. 11 ; 2 Thess. iii.
3 ; 1 Pet. v. 10) ; βεβαιοῦν too often occurs in the same
sense (1 Cor. i. 8; 2 Cor. i. 21 ; Col. ii. 7) ; θεμελιοῦν
(Eph. iii. 17; Col. i. 23; 1 Pet. v. 10), and ῥιζοῦν
(Ephes. iii. 18; Col. ii. 7) as well. This command to
the Sardian Angel implies that the νεκρὸς εἶ of ver. 1
must not be taken in all its force. The dead can bury
their dead, but this is all which such can do; they must
be themselves alive, who are bidden to impart a savour of
life to others. The fire of grace may burn very low in
their hearts ; but it cannot be quite extinguished; for
how in that case could they kindle any flame in the
hearts of others ?

'*For I have not found thy works perfect before God.*'—
The word here employed is not that which we commonly
render '*perfect* ;' not τέλεια, but πεπληρωμένα ; so that
the Lord contemplates the works prepared and appointed
in the providence of God for the faithful man to do as a
definite sphere (Ephes. ii. 10), which it was his duty and
his calling to have *fulfilled* or *filled to the full*,—the same
image habitually underlying the uses of πληροῦν and πλη-
ροῦσθαι (Matt. iii. 15 ; Rom. xiii. 8). This sphere of appointed duties the Sardian Angel had not fulfilled ; not, at
least, '*before God* ;' for on these last words the emphasis
must be laid. Before himself and fellow men his works
may very likely have been '*perfect* ;' indeed, we are expressly told that he had '*a name to live*' (ver. 1); for we

all very easily satisfy ourselves concerning our own works,
neither is it very difficult to satisfy the world concerning
them. But to have our works '*perfect before God,*' to
fill up the measure of those that He has ordained, so to
have them πεπληρωμένα, that is quite a different and a
far harder thing. Very striking and very searching words
on this matter are those of one whose own devotion to his
work gave him a right to speak—Juan d'Avila, the apostle
of Andalusia : 'Tot tantæque sunt pastorum obligationes,
ut qui vel tertiam earum partem reipsâ impleret, sanctus
ab hominibus haberetur ; cum tamen eo solo contentus,
gehennam non esset evasurus ;' and few, who have read,
will forget some words of Cecil very nearly to the same
effect—for holy men have in their holiness a marvellous
bond of union, when everything else seems to separate
them,—that a minister of Christ is very often in highest
honour with men for the performance of one half of his
work, while God is regarding him with displeasure for the
neglect of the other half.

It is a very instructive fact, that everywhere else, in
the Epistles to all the Churches save only to this and to
Laodicea, there is mention of some burden to be borne, of
a conflict either with foes within the Church or without,
or with both. Only in these two nothing of the kind
occurs. The exceptions are very significant. There is no
need to assume that the Church at Sardis had openly
coalesced and joined hands with the heathen world ; this
would in those days have been impossible ; nor yet that it
had renounced the *appearance* of opposition to the world.
But the two tacitly understood one another. This Church
had nothing of the spirit of the Two Witnesses, of whom we
read that they ' *tormented* them that dwelt on the earth '
(Rev. xi. 10), tormented them, that is, by their witness

for a God of truth and holiness and love, whom the
dwellers on the earth were determined not to know. There
was nothing in it to provoke from the heathen, in the
midst of whom it sojourned, any such words as those which
the author of the *Wisdom of Solomon* puts into the mouth
of the ungodly men (ii. 12–16). The world could endure
it, because it too was a world. On the not less significant
absence of all heretical perversions of the truth in these
Churches, there will be something to say when we have
reached the Epistle to Laodicea.

Ver. 3. ' *Remember therefore how thou hast received
and heard, and hold fast, and repent.*'—This ' *how* ' is by
some interpreters referred to the *manner* of their former
receiving, and by some to the *matter* which they formerly
received and heard. Now if the character of the charge
which the Lord is making against Sardis were that of
holding, or even tolerating, any erroneous doctrine, contrary to ' the faith once delivered to the saints,' I should
certainly side with them who referred this ' *how* ' to the
matter, to the form of sound words which they had accepted at the first, and to which Christ would recall them
now ; I should see in these words a parallel to such passages as Col. ii. 6; 1 Tim. vi. 20 ; 2 Tim. i. 14. But the
charge against Sardis is not a perverse holding of untruth,
but a heartless holding of the truth ; and therefore I cannot but think that the Lord is graciously reminding her of
the heartiness, the zeal, the love with which she received
this truth at the first. Then, no doubt, there was great
joy in that city (Acts viii. 8) ; but now all was changed ;
compare St. Paul's words, 1 Thess. i. 5–10, where, however,
there is no such painful comparison to draw between the
present and the past of his Thessalonian converts; also
the same Apostle to the Galatians (iv. 13–15), a completer

parallel to the words before us, seems to imply that St. Paul is contrasting there their present disaffection and coldness of heart toward him and the Gospel of the grace of God which he brought, with the zeal and warmth and love wherewith they first received these glad tidings at his lips, the ' *how* ' of their present holding with the ' *how* ' of their past receiving. But this ' *how thou hast re-ceived*' refers to something more, besides *their* joyful loving acceptance of the truth in times past. They are bidden, no doubt, in these words to remember as well ' *how* ' that truth itself came, that they *might* receive it ; with what demonstration of the Spirit and of power from the lips of those ambassadors of Christ, whoever they may have been, who first brought it to Sardis ; how holily, how unblamably these went in and out among them. And remembering all this, let them not guiltily suffer that to go, which came so commended to them, which was so joyfully embraced by them, but rather hold it with a firm grasp. ' Prize now '—this is what the warning word of a gracious Lord would say—' that which thou didst once prize at so high a rate, which came to thee so evidently as a gift from God, accompanied with the Holy Ghost from heaven ; and repent thee of all the coldness and heartless-ness wherewith thou hast come to regard it ' (2 Pet. i. 9).

' *If therefore thou shalt not watch, I will come on thee as a thief, and thou shalt not know what hour I will come upon thee.*'—Augustine has pointedly said, ' Latet ultimus dies, ut observetur omnis dies.' But should this Angel refuse thus to observe and watch, the Lord takes up against him and repeats here his own words, twice spoken, with slight variations, in the days of his ministry on earth (Matt. xxiv. 42, 43 ; Luke xii. 39, 40) ; words which must have profoundly impressed themselves on those who heard

them, and on the early Church in general, as is evidenced
from the frequent reference to them in other parts of the
New Testament; as by St. Paul (1 Thess. v. 2, 4) ; by St.
Peter (2 Ep. iii. 10); and by St. John (Rev. xvi. 15). It is
the *stealthiness* of Christ's advent, and thus his coming
upon the secure sinner when least He is looked for, which
is the point of the comparison, not the violent taking away
of the worldling's goods.   In that case, He would be the
λῃστής rather than the κλέπτης, the robber, and not the
thief which here He is (cf. Matt. xxiv. 36–51 ; xxv. 13).
That grand ancient proverb, which ascribed to the aveng-
ing deities feet shod with wool, ' Dii laneos habent pedes,'
awfully expressed the sense which the heathen had of this
noiseless approach of the divine judgments, of Justice
(ὀπισθόπους Δίκη, as one called her of old), oftentimes
so near at the very moment when thought so remote.
So too in that sublime fragment of some Greek tragic
poet, the very turn of the phrase in the conclusion reminds one of these words of Christ :

> δοκεῖς τὰ θεῶν σὺ ξυνετὰ νικῆσαί ποτε,
> καὶ τὴν Δίκην που μάκρ' ἀπῳκίσθαι βροτῶν ;
> ἡ δ' ἐγγύς ἐστιν, οὐχ ὁρωμένη δ' ὁρᾷ,
> ὃν χρὴ κολάζειν τ', οἶδεν· ἀλλ' οὐκ οἶσθα σύ
> ὁπόταν ἄφνω μολοῦσα διολέσῃ κακούς.

Ver. 4. ' *Thou hast a few names even in Sardis which
have not defiled their garments.*'—' But ' (ἀλλά), with
which this verse begins, and about whose right to a place in
the text there is not a question, has been carelessly omitted
here by our Authorized translators. ' *Names*' cannot here
be slightingly used, any more than at Acts i. 15 ; cf. Rev.
xi. 13 ; Num. i. 2, 18, 20; iii. 40, 43 ; xxvi. 53 ; it must
be simply equivalent to persons ;—or there may be a tacit
reference to ver. 1.   The Angel of Sardis had a ' *name* '

that he lived, and was dead; but there were some there,
however few, whose ' *names* ' were more than names; who
had not merely the *form* of godliness (2 Tim. iii. 5;
μόρφωσις there=ὄνομα here), but the *power*. It is very
beautiful to observe the gracious manner in which the
Lord recognizes and sets his seal of allowance to the good
which anywhere He finds. Abraham said, 'to slay the
righteous with the wicked, that be far from Thee' (Gen.
xviii. 25); but it is far from Him no less even to seem to
include the righteous and the wicked in a common blame.
He, the same who delivered Noah, a preacher of righteousness, from the destruction of the old world, who drew just
Lot out of Sodom, who could single out from the whole
wicked family of Jeroboam, and take from the evil to come,
Abijah, ' because in him there was found some good thing
toward the Lord God of Israel ' (1 Kin. xiv. 13), beholds the
few faithful in Sardis that had not defiled their garments,
will not suffer them to suppose that they are overlooked
by Him, or that his condemnation was intended to include
them. The ' *garments* ' which these are thus declared not
to have ' *defiled*,' are not to be identified with the ' *white
raiment* ' of the next verse, nor with the ' *white* ' in the
next clause of this. The ' *white raiment* ' there is the
garment of *glory*,—this the garment of *grace*; that in-
capable of receiving a stain, being part of an inheritance
which in all its parts is ἀμίαντος (1 Pet. i. 4); this one
which σπίλοι (Ephes. v. 27 ; Jam. iii. 6), μιάσματα (2 Pet.
ii. 20), μολυσμοί (2 Cor. vii. 1), can only too easily deform ;
that keeping itself, for nothing that defileth enters where
it is worn (Rev. xxi. 27); this needing to be kept above
all keeping (Rev. xvi. 15), if the glory and brightness are
not quite to depart from it. This, itself a wedding garment (Matt. xxii. 11, 12), but not *necessarily* identical with

'the fine linen, clean and white, the righteousness of saints'
(Rev. xix. 8), is put on at our entrance by baptism into
the kingdom of grace; that at our entrance by the resurrection, if not before, into the kingdom of glory.

There were those at Sardis, a little remnant, who had
thus kept their garments; or, according to his testimony
'who seeth in secret,' had '*not defiled*' them. Absolutely,
and in the highest sense, no one has thus kept his garments, save only He who received more than a garment
of grace at baptism; having been sanctified in his mother's
womb, and thus a 'holy thing' (Luke i. 35), not from his
birth only, but from his conception. Yet, in a secondary
sense, and as compared with too many, there are those
who have not defiled these garments; or, in the equivalent
language of St. James, 'kept themselves unspotted from
the world' (i. 27). These are they who, if they do contract any defilement upon these, yet suffer it not to harden
or become ingrained in their garments; but go at once to
the fountain open for all uncleanness, wash those garments and make them white again in the blood of the
Lamb (Rev. vii. 14).—Μολύνειν differs from μιαίνειν, as
'inquinare' from 'maculare' (see my *Synonyms of the
New Testament*, § 31), being not so much to stain with
colour as to besmear or besmirch with filth (Cant. v. 3;
Gen. xxxvii. 30). Hengstenberg is convinced we are to
find in this μιαίνειν (= 'sordidare'), a covert allusion to
the name of this city, Sardis or Sardes, which is so near
to *sordes*; Christ saying that, with the few exceptions
which He has made, Sardes is become *sordes* ('*Sardes* ist
sordes geworden'). But a *Latin* pun, and such a wretched
one, in the Apocalypse! A Hebrew, or even a Greek, play
on words, is quite conceivable there. Such an one lies
in the name 'Nicolaitans,' given to the libertines of the

apostolic period (see ii. 6). A deep sense of the significance of words and names will often find its utterance in
such; but a Latin jeu d'esprit, and that with no slightest
hint to set any looking for such, is about the unlikeliest
thing in the world to encounter there. Not a few expositors, bringing this passage into connexion with Jude 23,
find reference in both to those ceremonial uncleannesses
spoken of in Lev. xv. and elsewhere, which so very easily
may be moral uncleannesses as well. I do not think this
to lie in the words; but that *every* defilement (μολυσμός) of
the flesh and spirit (2 Cor. vii. 1) is here intended.

'*And they shall walk with Me in white : for they are
worthy.*'—The use of περιπατεῖν to express a *moral* walking
seems restricted to sacred Greek; at least I cannot remember any example of this elsewhere. But to proceed.
Here are many promises in one. The promise of life, for
only the quick or living walk, the dead are still; of liberty,
for the free walk, and not the fast bound; of beauty, for
the grace and dignity of long garments only appears to
the full, when the wearer of them is in motion ; therefore
is it that 'the Scribes *desire to walk* in long robes' (Luke
xx. 46). And all this has its corresponding truth in the
kingdom of heaven. God's saints and servants here in
this world of grace, and no doubt also in that world of
glory, are best seen, and most to be admired, when they
are engaged in active services of love. And such they
shall have. They shall walk (cf. Zech. iii. 7) with their
Lord, shall be glorified together with Him (Rom. viii. 17;
John xvii. 24); his servants shall serve Him (Rev. xxii.
3). And why? '*for they are worthy.*' God does not
refuse to ascribe a *worthiness* to men (Matt. x. 10, 11;
xxii. 8; Luke xx. 35; xxi. 36; 2 Thess. i. 5, 11; Wisd.
iii. 5); although this worthiness must ever be contemplated

as *relative*, and not *absolute*; as resting on God's free acceptance of an obedience which would fain be perfect, even while it actually *is* most imperfect, and on this his acceptance and allowance of it alone. There are those who '*are worthy*' according to the rules which free grace *has* laid down, although there are none worthy according to those conditions which strict justice *might have* laid down; and God is 'faithful' (1 John i. 9), in that having set forth these conditions of grace, He will observe and abide by them. Vitringa well: 'Dignitas hîc notat proportionem et congruentiam, quæ erat inter statum gratiæ quo fuerant in his terris, et gloriæ quam Dominus ipsis decreverat, *æstimandam ex ipsâ lege gratiæ*.' Compare Bishop Bull's Sermon, *The worthiness of the partakers of future glory* (*Works*, vol. i. p. 216). There is another very fearful 'they are worthy' in this Book (xvi. 6), where no such observation would need to be made, where no such mitigation of the word's force would be required; for see the antithesis between death as the *wages* (ὀψώνια) of sin, and eternal life as the *gift* (χάρισμα) of God, Rom. vi. 23.

Ver. 5. '*He that overcometh, the same shall be clothed in white raiment.*'—A repetition of the promise of the verse preceding. They who have kept their garments here, as a few in Sardis to whom the Lord bears testimony (ver. 4) had done, shall have brighter garments given to them there, 'vestes vitæ,' as in the book of Enoch they are called. Of white as the colour of heaven, and of *white* garments as *shining* garments of glory, there has been already occasion to speak; see on ii. 17. Add the words of Grotius: 'λευκὰ ἱμάτια, hoc loco et infra, iii. 18; iv. 4, sunt vestes *coruscantes*, et sic sume στολὰς λευκάς, infra, vi. 11; vii. 9, 13.' It is not in Scripture merely that white is thus presented as the

colour of heaven, and white garments the suitable investiture of the blessed inhabitants of heaven. The same,
out of a deep inborn symbolism, repeats itself in heathen
antiquity as well; thus see Plato, *Legg.* xii. 956; Cicero,
Legg. ii. 18; Virgil, *Æn.* vi. 665; Ovid, *Fast.* iii. 363;
iv. 419, 420; *Metam.* x. 432. As '*raiment*' in the
literal sense of the word is inconceivable in heaven, we
must understand by it here, that clothing with light *as
with a garment*, which shall be theirs who shall then
'*shine out* (ἐκλάμψουσι, Matt. xiii. 43; cf. Dan. xii. 3)
as the sun in the kingdom of their Father;' this vesture
of light being indeed their raiment, and yet for all this
not something external to them, but the expression outwardly of all which now inwardly they are. The glorified
body, defecated of all its dregs and impurities, whatever
remained of these having been *precipitated* in death, and
now a body transformed and transfigured into the likeness
of Christ's body (Phil. iii. 21), this σῶμα ἐπουράνιον, as
contrasted with the σῶμα ἐπίγειον and χοϊκόν which we
now wear (1 Cor. xv. 40, 47), with its robe, atmosphere,
and effluence of light, is itself, I believe, the '*white raiment*,'
which Christ here promises to his redeemed. There are
some beautiful observations on this matter in Delitzsch, *Bibl.
Psychologie*, p. 374.

I have noted already (see ii. 10) the frequency, as it
appears to me, of the scoffing side-glances at Scripture
which occur in the writings of Lucian. It would be curious
to know whether he intended a mock at this glorious hope
of the Christian, when, relating the tales current about
Peregrinus, and the fiery passage of this charlatan in the
fashion of Empedocles to a mock immortality, he makes
one of this impostor's followers assure his hearers that
shortly after the disappearance of Peregrinus in his funeral

pile, he beheld him *walking in a white garment, shining*, and crowned with a garland of olive (ἐν λευκῇ ἐσθῆτι περιπατοῦντα, φαιδρόν, κοτίνῳ τε ἐστεμμένον, *De Mort. Pereg.* 40). The coincidence of one or two such passages we might attribute to accident; but they recur too often for any such explanation. See a very good article by Planck, *Lucian und das Christenthum*, in the *Theol. Stud. und Krit.* 1851, pp. 826–902; where also there are references to some earlier essays on the same subject.

'*And I will not blot out his name out of the book of life.*'—It is much more than a simple negative; οὐ μὴ ἐξαλείψω = '*nequaquam* delebo.' Our Translators have elsewhere given to this οὐ μὴ its full force; thus John vi. 37 ('in no wise'); viii. 51; xiii. 8 ('never'); but this only too rarely; for see Luke xxi. 33; Rev. ii. 11. We read of a '*book of life*,' Exod. xxxii. 32, 33; Ps. lxix. 29; Dan. xii. 1; Phil. iv. 3; Rev. xiii. 8; xx. 15; xxi. 27; of those 'written among the living' (γραφέντες εἰς ζωήν) of Isai. iv. 3; and resting on the same image, our Lord speaks of some whose names 'are written in heaven' (Luke x. 20; cf. Heb. xii. 23). These are the τεταγμένοι εἰς ζωήν of Acts xiii. 48. Famous cities of this world, great Italian above all, Florence and Genoa for example, have had, or still may have, their 'book of gold' (*libro d'oro*), in which to be written has implied participation in all the privileges, rights, honours, and advantages which that city could confer; while to be blotted out from this book would mark a man as infamous, stript of all the honours and dignities which once he called his own. These at their best are but weak earthly copies of the glory or the shame which are the portion of those who bear themselves worthily or unworthily of that heavenly polity to which they have been called. The intimation here given that

there are names, which, having been once written in that
book, might yet be afterwards blotted out of it, has proved
not a little perplexing to followers of Augustine, who will
not be content in this mystery of predestination with
having *some* Scriptures on their side, and leaving the
reconciliation of these and those others which are appa-
rently contradictory to these, for another and a higher
state of knowledge; but who would fain make it appear
that *all* Scripture is with them (see Turretine, *De Libro
Vitæ*, pp. 9–22). If this passage had stood by itself, it
would not have been hard for them to answer, as indeed
they *do* answer, that *all* who 'are written in the book of
life' overcome; therefore that this promise holds good for
them all, and none who are therein written have their
names blotted out from this book. But, unfortunately,
beside and behind this passage, there are others, not capable of this solution, and principally Exod. xxxii. 32; Ps.
lxix. 29; Rev. xxii. 19. How much violence they are
obliged to use, before they can compel such Scriptures as
these within the limits of their system, may be judged
from Augustine's own comment on the second of them
(*Enarr. in Ps.* lxix.): 'Deleantur de libro viventium, et
cum justis non scribantur, non sic accipere debemus quod
quemquam Deus scribat in libro vitæ, et deleat illum; si
homo dixit, Quod scripsi scripsi, Deus quemquam scribit
et delet? . . . . Isti ergo quomodo inde delentur, ubi
nunquam scripti sunt? Hoc dictum est *secundum spem
ipsorum, quia ibi se scriptos putabunt.* Quid sit, deleantur de libro vitæ? Et ipsis constet non illos ibi esse.
The warning is surely an instructive one, when so holy
and truth-loving a man as Augustine can, in favour of a
foregone conclusion, *thus* violently deal with a word of
God's.

'*But I will confess his name before my Father, and before his Angels.*'—Christ had spoken when on earth of confessing those who confessed Him, before his Father in heaven (Matt. x. 32, 33), and before the Angels (Luke xii. 8, 9). That 'in heaven' is of course omitted now, for there is no longer any contrast between the Father *in heaven* and the Son *on earth*; but the two confessions, which were separated before, appear united now; and in general we may observe of this Epistle that in great part it is woven together of sayings which the Lord had already uttered once or oftener in the days during which He pitched his tabernacle among men; He now setting his seal from heaven upon his words uttered on earth. On these costly mosaic-works of Scripture, which in our careless reading of it we so often overlook, there are some beautiful remarks in Delitzsch, *Commentar über den Psalter*, on Ps. cxxxv.; which Psalm is itself, as are also Psalms xcvii. xcviii. notable examples of the skill of a divine Artificer herein.

Nor will it be inopportune to observe further what signal internal evidence this same fact, analysed a little closer, will supply on another point; upon this, namely, that these Epistles are what they profess themselves to be, namely Epistles directly, and in their form no less than their substance, from Christ the Lord. With no unworthy thought about their inspiration, we might very easily come to regard them as having passed though the mind of St. John, and having been recast, in their form at least, in the passage. What they would have been, if they had undergone any such modifying process as this, St. John's own Epistles tell us. But nothing of the kind has found place. It is the Lord Himself who speaks throughout; who not merely suggests the thoughts, but dictates the words. That

St. John is here merely his organ, that the Master is speaking and not the servant, is, I say, remarkably attested in the fact of the numerous points of contact and coincidence between these seven Epistles and the words of Christ as recorded in the Gospels, in the three synoptic Gospels above all. Had these coincidences been all or nearly all with St. John's own Gospel, this might have suggested quite a different explanation. But it is mainly the three earlier Gospels which furnish them. Thus in this Sardian Epistle alone, where, it is true, the points of resemblance are more numerous than anywhere else, spiritual activity is set forth as a watching, ver. 3; with which compare Matt. xxiv. 42; xxv. 13; xxvi. 41; Mark xiii. 37. Christ likens his unlooked-for coming to that of a thief (ibid.); He does the same, Matt. xxiv. 43; Luke xii. 39. He speaks here of blotting out a name from the book of life (ver. 5), there of names written in the book of life (Luke x. 20); here of confessing his servants before his Father (ibid.), the parallels of which from the Gospels have just been given. The remarkable reappearance in this and in all these Epistles of the words so often on our Lord's lips, according to the three first Gospels, but never noticed in the fourth, '*He that hath an ear, let him hear*' (Matt. xi. 15; xiii. 9, 43; Mark iv. 9, 23; vii. 16, 33; Luke viii. 8; xiv. 35), has been dwelt on already, p. 95.

Ver. 6. '*He that hath an ear, let him hear what the Spirit saith unto the Churches.*'—Compare ii. 7.

VI.

EPISTLE TO THE CHURCH OF PHILADELPHIA.

REV. iii. 7-13.

Ver. 7. '*And to the Angel of the Church in Philadelphia write.*'—Philadelphia, at the foot of Mount Tmolus,
on the banks of the little river Cogamus, which not far
from the city falls into the Hermus (Pliny, *H. N.* v. 29,
30), was built by Attalus Philadelphus, king of Pergamum
(he died B.C. 138), from whom it derives its name. Φιλ-
αδελφία τῆς 'Ασίας St. Ignatius calls it in the salutation
of *his* Epistle, § 1 ; to distinguish it from other cities
like-named. No city of Asia Minor suffered more, or so
much, from violent and often-recurring earthquakes—
πόλις σεισμῶν πλήρης Strabo calls it (xiii. 4), and describes it as almost depopulated in consequence of these.
In the great earthquake in the reign of Tiberius, which
wasted so wide a range of some fairest regions of Asia,
Philadelphia was nearly destroyed (Tacitus, *Ann.* ii.
47). Despite of all drawbacks, it still retains a Christian
population, sustains several churches and an active commerce.

'*These things saith He that is Holy.*'—Christ claims
here to be ὁ ῞Αγιος, The Holy One; at Dan. ix. 24 He
is ἅγιος ἁγίων: cf. Acts ii. 27 ; xiii. 35 ; Heb. vii. 26. In
these latter passages, however, ὅσιος, not ἅγιος, stands in

the original; nor are these words perfectly identical,
though we have but the one word 'holy' by which to
render them both. The ὅσιος, if a man, is one who
diligently observes all the sanctities of religion; anterior,
many of them, to all law, the 'jus *et fas*,' with a stress
on the latter word; thus in the *Euthyphro* of Plato
ὁσιότης is continually used as equivalent to εὐσέβεια.
If applied to God, as at Deut. xxxii. 4; Rev. xv. 4;
xvi. 5, and here, He is One in whom these eternal sanctities reside; who is Himself the root and ground of them
all. The ἅγιος is the separate from evil, with the perfect
hatred of that evil from which he is separate. But holiness in this absolute sense belongs only to God; not to
Angels, for 'He charged his Angels with folly' (Job iv.
18), and certainly not to men (Jam. iii. 2; Gen. vi. 5;
viii. 21). He then that claims to be '*The Holy One*,'—
a name which Jehovah in the Old Testament continually
claims for his own (Isai. vi. 3; xl. 25; xliii. 15),—implicitly claims to be God; takes to Himself a title which is
God's alone, which it would be blasphemy for any other to
appropriate; and, unless we are prepared for the alternative that He is guilty of this, can only be accepted as
Himself God (see my *Synonyms of the New Testament*,
§ 88).

'*He that is true*.'—We must not confound ἀληθινός
(='verus') with ἀληθής (='verax'). God is ἀληθής
(= ἀψευδής, Tit. i. 2), as He cannot lie, the truth-speak-
ing and truth-loving God; with whom every word is Yea
and Amen; but He is ἀληθινός, as fulfilling all that is
involved in the name God, in contrast with those who are
called gods, but who, having the name of gods, have
nothing of the truth, wicked spirits, or dead idols. That
is ἀληθινός which fulfils its own idea to the highest

possible degree; as Origen (*In Joan.* tom. ii. § 4) well puts it: ἀληθινός, πρὸς ἀντιδιαστολὴν σκιᾶς καὶ τύπου καὶ εἰκόνος. Nor is ἀληθινός only, as when thus predicated of God, the true as contrasted with the absolutely false; but as contrasted with the subordinately true, with all imperfect and partial realizations of the idea; thus Christ is φῶς ἀληθινόν (John i. 9; 1 John ii. 8), ἄρτος ἀληθινός (John vi. 32), ἄμπελος ἀληθινή (John xv. 1); there is a σκηνὴ ἀληθινή in heaven (Heb. viii. 2). In each of these cases the antithesis is not between the true and the false, but between the perfect and the imperfect, the idea fully, and the idea only partially, realized; for John the Baptist also was a light (John v. 35), and Moses gave bread from heaven (Ps. cv. 40), and Israel was a vine of God's planting (Ps. lxxx. 8), and the tabernacle pitched in the wilderness, if only a figure of the true, was yet pitched at God's express command (Exod. xxv.). Christ then, in declaring Himself ὁ ἀληθινός, declares that whatever names, titles, offices He assumes, these in Him are realized to the full, reach their culminating glory; that the idea and the fact in Him are, what they never are nor can be in any other, absolutely commensurate.

' *He that hath the key of David, He that openeth and no man shutteth; and shutteth, and no man openeth.*'— Let us note here, but only that we may avoid, a not uncommon error of interpretation, namely, the identifying, or confounding, of this '*key of David*' with the '*key of knowledge,*' which in the days of his earthly ministry Christ accused the Scribes that they had taken away (Luke xi. 52). They who thus identify the two regard Him as here claiming to be the One who unlooses the seals of Scripture, opens the closed door into its inner chambers; who by his advent first made intelligible the dark and obscure prophecies of the Old Testament, and by his Spirit opens and enlightens the eyes of men to see and understand the deep things which are written in his Word. Into this erroneous interpretation Origen not unfrequently falls, bringing Rev. v. 7–9 into relation with these two passages as a third, having the same import; thus *In Joan.* tom. v. § 4; *Sel. in Psalm.* Ps. i.; Hilary no less (*Prol. in Libr. Psalm.* §§ 5, 6); and Jerome (*Ep.* 50, *de Stud. Script.*). But '*the key*' is ἐξουσίας σύμβολον (Andreas), the symbol of power (cf. xx. 1); and '*the key of David*' is 'the key of the house of David,' of that royal household whereof David was chief, and all his servants members. Cocceius: 'Clavem Davidis vocat, quia ea regia clavis, et is tempore ministerii sui clausit et aperuit, typum Christi gerens; vide Ps. ci. 4–8.' But David being a type of Christ, so eminent a one, that Christ more than once actually bears his name (Ezek. xxxiv. 23, 24), 'the house of David' alluded to thus can mean nothing less than the heavenly house, the kingdom of heaven; and the Lord is, in fact, declaring, 'I have the keys of the kingdom of heaven.' Those keys which He committed to Peter and his fellow Apostles (Matt. xvi. 19), He announces here to be in the highest sense his own. It depends on Him, the supreme κληδοῦχος in the house of God, who shall see the King's face, and who shall be excluded from it. Men are admitted into, or shut out from, that presence according to the good pleasure of his will; for it is He, and no other, '*that openeth, and no man shutteth; that shutteth, and no man openeth.*' Christ, as we learn here, has not so committed the keys of the kingdom of heaven, with the power of binding and loosing, to any other, his servants, but that He still retains the highest administration of them in his own hands. If at any time there is error in their

binding and loosing, if they make sad the heart which He
has not made sad, if they speak peace to the heart to
which He has not spoken peace (Ezek. xiii. 19), then his
sentence stands, and not theirs. For the promise that
He would ratify and confirm in heaven the judgments of
his Church on earth, could only be absolute and uncon-
ditional so long as the Church retained such a discern-
ment of spirits as was never at fault. When once this
had departed from it, when therefore it was exposed to
possible mistake and error, from that moment the promise
could be only conditional. From the highest tribunal
upon earth there lies an appeal to a tribunal of yet
higher instance in heaven; to his '*that openeth, and
no man shutteth; that shutteth, and no man openeth*;'
and when through ignorance, or worse than ignorance,
wrong has been done to any of his servants here, He
will redress it there, disallowing and reversing in heaven
the mistaken or unrighteous sentences of earth. It was
in faith of this that Hus, when the greatest Council which
Christendom had seen for a thousand years delivered his
soul to Satan, did himself confidently commend it to the
Lord Jesus Christ. In the same confidence, many a
faithful confessor at Rome or Madrid has walked to the
stake, his yellow *san-benito* all painted over with devils
in token and prophecy of those with whom his portion
should be; but has never doubted the while that his lot
should be indeed with Him who retains in his own hands
'*the key of David*;' who therefore could open for him, and
who would, though all who visibly represented here the
Church had shut him out with extreme malediction at
once from the Church militant on earth and the Church
triumphant in heaven.

That the substrate of this language, and, so to say, the

suggestion of this thought, is to be sought at Isai. xxii.,
there can be no reasonable doubt. The prophet there
describes the shameful dismissal of Shebna, the major-
domûs or chief οἰκονόμος of the king, who had occupied
for a while the place of highest dignity and honour (1
Kin. iv. 6; xviii. 3; 2 Chron. xxvi. 21), but whom the
Lord beheld as unworthy of this, and from which He puts
him down with shame and dishonour, with the substitu-
tion of Eliakim in his room, and the installation of the
one into the honours and dignities which the other had
lost. It needs only to quote the words as they occur in
the Septuagint: δώσω αὐτῷ τὴν κλεῖδα οἴκου Δαυὶδ ἐπὶ
τῷ ὤμῳ αὐτοῦ, καὶ ἀνοίξει καὶ οὐκ ἔσται ὁ ἀποκλείων,
καὶ κλείσει καὶ οὐκ ἔσται ὁ ἀνοίγων (ver. 22). The
prophet describes all this with an emphasis and fulness,
which, however highly we may conceive of Eliakim, is
surprising and inexplicable, until we look beyond that
present, and read in that Scripture not merely the history
of a revolution in the royal palace or house of David,—a
putting down of one and setting up of another; but, over
and above this, the type and real prophecy of an event
immeasurably greater, the indignant rejection of all those
unworthy stewards who in God's spiritual house had
long abused their position, with the exaltation of the true
Steward of the mysteries of God, who should be faithful
in all his house, in their room. Vitringa (*Comm. in Esai.*
xxii.): 'Quæ Eliakimo promittitur prærogativa dignitatis,
fore ut claves gerens Domûs Davidis clauderet et aperiret
solus, et omnis ab eo suspenderetur sarcina et decus
Domûs Davidis (in quam hîc cadit emphasis): tam magni-
fice et ample dictum est, ut plus dixisse videretur Propheta
quam debebat, si id in aliquo subjecto nobiliore, cujus
Eliakimus typum gerere poterat, olim illustrius non con-

sequeretur exemplum. Certe sunt verbi prophetici recessus profundi.'

Ver. 8. '*I know thy works: behold, I have set before thee an open door, and no man can shut it.*'—This '*open door*' is best explained by a reference to 1 Cor. xvi. 9; 2 Cor. ii. 12; Acts xiv. 27; Col. iv. 3. Vitringa: 'Notat commodam Evangelii prædicandi occasionem.' To this Philadelphian Church, weak probably in numbers, enjoying few worldly advantages, God had opened 'a great door and effectual' for the declaring of his truth; and, though there were many adversaries, none could shut it. For was not He who opened, the same who had '*the key of David*'? and when He opened, none could shut; when he made room for his truth in the heart of one or of many (Acts xvi. 14; Job xxxiii. 16), none could hinder it from having free course and being glorified; even as, if He shut and withheld a blessing, all other might and power would be wholly unavailing to make for it an entrance there.

'*For thou hast a little strength, and hast kept my word, and hast not denied my name.*'—They were probably but a little flock, poor in worldly goods, of small account in the eyes of men (cf. 1 Cor. i. 26–28), having '*little strength*'—not '*a little strength*,' which would rather be an acknowledgment of power than of weakness—the fitter therefore that God should be glorified in them and by them; even as He *had* been; for, put to the proof, they had kept his word, and had not denied his name (Zech. xii. 8; Isai. lvi. 4, 5). The aorists, ἐτήρησας, οὐκ ἠρνήσω, refer to some distinct occasions in the past, when, being thus put to the test, they had approved themselves faithful to Him.

Ver. 9. '*Behold, I will make them of the synagogue of*

*Satan, which say they are Jews, and are not, but do lie;
behold, I will make them to come and worship before thy
feet, and to know that I have loved thee.'*—Here is the
reward of their faithfulness, of the entrance which they
had made by that '*open door*' which the Lord set before
them. The promise to Philadelphia, in respect of Jewish
adversaries, is larger and richer than that to Smyrna. All
which Christ there promised was, that these enemies should
not prevail against *them* (ii. 9, 10); but here are better
promises, namely, that *they* shall prevail against their
enemies; and that with a victory the most blessed of all,
in which victors and vanquished should be blessed alike,
and should rejoice together. In reward of their faithfulness, they should see some of these fierce gainsayers and
opposers, some of this '*synagogue of Satan*' (see ii. 9;
cf. Jer. ix. 2 : σύνοδος ἀθετούντων), falling on their faces,
and owning that God was with them of a truth. The
'*worship*' before their feet, of course, does not mean more
than this; cf. Isai. xlix. 23; lx. 14; Matt. viii. 2; 2 Kin.
ii. 15; Dan. ii. 46. This act of homage, the προσκυνεῖν,
may imply much more (John iv. 21; Rev. xiv. 19; Acts
viii. 27); but manifestly does not so here. It is only *some*
of their adversaries who shall worship thus; for there is
no promise during the present dispensation that *all* Israel,
but only that a remnant, shall be saved (Rom. ix. 27).
In our Version we have failed to express, that they are
only *some* '*of the synagogue of Satan*' who should thus
acknowledge the presence of God in the Church of his
dear Son, should look at Him whom they had pierced
(Zech. xii. 10), and own that this Jesus of Nazareth was
indeed He of whom Moses and the prophets wrote, the
promised Messiah, the King of Israel, that should turn
iniquity from Jacob. In connexion with this promise,

there is an interesting passage in the Epistle of Ignatius to this same Philadelphian Church (c. 6), implying the actual presence in the midst of it, of converts from Judaism, who now preached the faith which once they persecuted. We may say too that this same promise has been gloriously fulfilled to other Churches in our own days, or almost in our own days, as we call to mind the many of Germany's noblest theologians and philosophers, her Neanders and her Stahls; who, being of the stock of Abraham, have yet had the veil taken from their hearts, and owned of the Church of Christ that God was with it of a truth. It is a singular evidence of the complete change in the relations between the Jew and Gentile, and of both to the kingdom of God, that exactly this same promise should find place under the Old Covenant, while yet the parts are exchanged which the one and the other should fulfil (Isai. xlv. 14; xlix. 23; lx. 14).

Ver. 10. '*Because thou hast kept the word of my patience, I also will keep thee from the hour of temptation, which shall come upon all the world, to try them that dwell upon the earth.*'—What does the Lord exactly mean here by '*the word of my patience*'? There are some who find reference to certain special words and sayings of Christ's, in which He has exhorted his servants to patience, or declared the need they would have of it; such words as occur at Luke viii. 15; Matt. x. 22; xxiv. 13; cf. Rev. i. 9. Much better, however, to take the whole Gospel as '*the word of Christ's patience,*' everywhere teaching, as it does, the need of a patient waiting for Christ, till He, the waited-for so long, shall at length appear. Observe the *benigna talio* of the kingdom of God: '*because thou hast kept*' (ἐτήρησας), therefore '*I also will keep*' (τηρήσω); '*because thou hast *kept* my word,

therefore in return I will *keep* thee.' The promise does
not imply that the Philadelphian Church should be exempted from persecutions which should come on all other
portions of the Church; that by any special privilege they
should be excused from fiery trials through which others
should be called to pass.   It is a better promise than this;
and one which, of course, they share with all who are
faithful as they are—to be kept *in* temptation, not to be
exempted *from* temptation ($\tau\eta\rho\epsilon\hat{\iota}\nu\ \dot{\epsilon}\kappa$ not being here $=\tau\eta\rho\epsilon\hat{\iota}\nu$
$\dot{\alpha}\pi\acute{o}$, Jam. i. 27; Prov. vii. 5; cf. 2 Thess. iii. 3); a bush
burning, and yet not consumed (cf. Isai. xliii. 2).   They
may take courage; the blasts of persecution will indeed
blow; but He who permits, uses, and restrains them, will
not suffer his barn-floor to be winnowed with so fierce a
wind that chaff and grain shall alike be swept away.
This '*hour of temptation*' is characterized as coming '*upon
all the world, to try them that dwell upon the earth.*'   These
that dwell on the earth, according to the constant use of the
Apocalypse, include all mankind, with the exception of the
$\dot{\alpha}\pi\alpha\rho\chi\acute{\eta}$ of the Church (vi. 10; xi. 10; xiii. 8, 14); who
all of them are contemplated as already seated in heavenly
places with Christ Jesus (Ephes. ii. 6).   The great catastrophes which come upon the earth are ' *temptations*' to the
world no less than to the Church.   God is then putting
' *them that dwell upon the earth*' to proof, whether now at
length they will not repent, and, when his judgments are in
the world, learn righteousness, however they may in times
past have hardened themselves against Him.   So too such
times of great tribulation are trials or ' *temptations*,' because
they bring out the unbelief, hardness of heart, blasphemy
against God, which were before latent in the children of
this world; hidden from others, hidden from themselves,
till that ' *hour of temptation*' came and revealed them

(Rev. ix. 20, 21; xvi. 9, 11, 21).   Thus Moses speaks of
the plagues as the 'temptations of Egypt' (Deut. iv. 34;
vii. 19; xxix. 3); and they were such, inasmuch as they
brought out the pride and obduracy that were in Pharaoh's
heart and in his servants,' as these would never in any other
way have been revealed either to themselves or to others.
Voltaire tells us that half the population of Southern
Europe lost its faith in God as a result of the terrible
earthquake that overthrew Lisbon.

Ver. 11. ' *Behold, I come quickly: hold that fast which
thou hast, that no man take thy crown.*'—This announcement of the speedy coming of the Lord, the ever-recurring
key-note of this book (cf. xxii. 7, 12, 20), is sometimes
used as a word of fear for those who are abusing the
Master's absence, wasting his goods and ill-treating their
fellow-servants; careless and secure as men for whom no
day of reckoning is in store (Matt. xxiv. 48–51; 2 Thess.
i. 7–9; 1 Pet. iv. 5; cf. Jam. v. 9; Rev. ii. 5, 16); but
sometimes as a word of infinite comfort for those who
with difficulty and painfulness hold their ground.   He
that should bring the long contest at once to an end; who
should at once turn the scale, and for ever, in favour of
righteousness and truth, is even at the door (Jam. v. 8;
Phil. iv. 5; 2 Thess. i. 20; Heb. x. 37; 2 Pet. iii. 14).
Such a word of comfort is this announcement here: ' Yet
a little while, and thy patience shall have its full reward;
only in the interval, and till I come, *hold that fast which
thou hast.*'   That which Philadelphia ' *had* ' we have just
seen—zeal, patience, with little means accomplishing not a
little work.

' *That no man take thy crown.*'—These last words some
have explained, 'that no man step into that place of glory
which was designed for thee;' after the manner, for

example, that Jacob stepped into Esau's place (Gen. xxv. 34; xxvii. 36); Judah into Reuben's (Gen. xlix. 4, 8); David into Saul's (1 Sam. xvi. 1, 13); Eliakim into Shebna's (Isai. xxii. 15-25); Benaiah into Joab's (1 Kin. ii. 35); Zadok into Abiathar's (ibid.); Matthias into Judas's (Acts i. 25, 26); Gentiles into the place of Jews (Matt. 21, 43; Rom. xi. 11); men into that of angels; the number of the elect, as Augustine concludes from these words, remaining still the same, and having been determined from the beginning, only some filling the places which others have left empty, and thus taking their crown: *De Corrept. et Grat.* c. 13, 'Si enim alius non est accepturus, nisi iste perdiderit, certus est numerus'; cf. Gregory the Great, *Moral.* xxxiv. 20. But these thus adduced *received* indeed a privilege or prerogative—a '*crown*' we may call it, which others lost; they did not *take* it from those others (the 'accipiat' of the Vulgate is wrong here; it should be rather 'auferat'); and it is quite inconceivable that any who should ever himself wear the crown, should be set forth as *taking* it from another. This taking, or seeking to take, the crowns from others' brows is the part, not of the good who would wear them on their own, but of the wicked who would see others discrowned and disinherited like themselves. Instead of ascribing to the words any such meaning, we must regard them as exactly equivalent to those of St. Paul: 'Let no man *beguile you of your reward*' (καταβραβευέτω ὑμᾶς, Col. ii. 18); but not as giving the slightest hint that what this Angel lost, another would gain; the crown which he forfeited, another would wear; and that other one who had despoiled him of it. Neither, again, may we understand '*thy crown*' as the crown 'which thou hast,' but the crown 'which thou mayest have' (cf. 2 Tim. iv. 8: ἀπόκειταί μοι ὁ τῆς

δικαιοσύνης στέφανος). ' Let no man,' Christ would say,
' deprive thee of the glorious reward laid up for thee in
heaven, of which many, my adversaries and thine, would
fain rob thee; but which only one, even thyself, can ever
cause thee to forfeit indeed.'

Ver. 12. '*Him that overcometh will I make a pillar in
the temple of my God, and he shall go no more out.*'—It
need hardly here be said, except that some have denied it,
that this is a promise, as are all the others in these Epistles,
of *future* blessedness, belonging not to the members of the
Church militant here on earth, but of the Church triumphant in Heaven. Marckius brings out here excellently
well the force of the words, '*I will make*': 'Nec illud hîc
prætermittendum est quod Christus *se facturum* suos tales
dicit, cum præter gratiam Christi ad hoc prorsus necessa-
riam sic innuatur naturalis omnium a templo hoc abalien-
atio, debilitas summa, et fœditas non minor.' Compare
Matt. iv. 19 : ' I will make you fishers of men.' '*Pillar*'
(στῦλος) is not to be interpreted here exactly as it is at
Gal. ii. 9. The ' pillars ' there are certain eminent Apostles,
the main supports, under Christ, of the Church in its militant condition here upon earth ; and, as such, towering
above the rest of the faithful. But there is no such com-
parative preëminence indicated here ; as is evident from
the fact that the promise *to every one* of the faithful, to
each that has overcome, is, that he shall be made ' *a pillar
in the temple of God*; ' Christ so speaks, as Jerome (*in
Gal.* ii. 9) says well, ' docens *omnes* credentes qui adver-
sarium vicerint, posse columnas Ecclesiæ fieri.' To find
any allusion here, as Vitringa and others have done, to the
two monumental pillars, Jachin and Boaz, which Solomon
set up, not in the temple, but in the open court before the
temple (1 Kin. vii. 21 ; 2 Chron. iii. 15, 17 ; Jer. lii. 17),

is altogether beside the mark ; the words which follow, ' *and
he shall go no more out*, making this well nigh impossible.
These famous pillars were *always without* the temple;
they would therefore have served very ill to set forth the
blessedness of the redeemed, who shall be *always within*
it. Other pillars might set forth this, but scarcely these,
contradicting in their position the central intention of
Christ's words here, which is to declare that he who over-
comes shall dwell *in the house of God* for ever. ' *He shall
go no more out*;' for, as the elect angels are *fixed* in
obedience, and have over-lived the possibility of falling,
have attained what the Schoolmen call the *beata necessitas
boni*, so shall it be one day with the redeemed.   Gerhard
(*Locc. Theoll.* xxxii. 2): ' Erit perpetuus heres æternorum
bonorum, nec ullius ἐκπτώσεως ipsi imminebit periculum,
qui columna est, symbolum immobilitatis in statu gloriæ
cælestis.' Once admitted into the heavenly kingdom, they
have their place there for ever ; the door is shut (Matt.
xxv. 10; cf. Gen. vii. 16) ; not merely to exclude others,
but safely to include them, who shall thus be ' ever with
the Lord' (1 Thess. iv. 17).   In that heavenly household
the son, every son who has once entered, abideth for ever
(John viii. 35 ; cf. Isai. xxii. 23) ; no wonder, therefore,
that Augustine should exclaim, ' Quis non desideret illam
Civitatem, unde amicus non exit, quo inimicus non intrat ? '

' *And I will write upon him the name of my God, and
the name of the City of my God, which is New Jerusalem,
which cometh down out of heaven from my God.*'—Christ
will write these names, of his God, and of the City of his
God, upon *him* that overcometh—not upon *it*, the pillar.
It is true indeed that there were sometimes inscriptions
on pillars,—which yet would be στῆλαι rather than στῦλοι.
—but the image of the pillar is now dismissed, and only

the conqueror remains. In confirmation of this, that it is the person and not the pillar, whom the Lord contemplates now, we find further on the redeemed having the name of God, or the seal of God, on their foreheads (vii. 3; ix. 4; xiv. 1; xxii. 4), with probable allusion to the golden plate inscribed with the name of Jehovah, which the High Priest wore upon his (Exod. xxviii. 36–38). In the 'kingdom of priests' this dignity shall not be any more the singular prerogative of one, but the common dignity of all. Exactly in the same way, in the hellish caricature of the heavenly kingdom, the votaries of the Beast are stigmatics, having *his* name upon their foreheads (xiii. 16, 17; xvii. 5; and cf. xx. 4).—What the name of this '*City of my God*' is, we are told Ezek. xlviii. 35: 'The Lord is there' (cf. Isai. lx. 14; Jer. xxxiii. 16). Any other name would but faintly express its glory; 'having the glory *of God*' (Rev. xxi. 11, 23). He that hath the name of this City written upon him is thereby declared free of it. Even while on earth he had his true πολίτευμα ἐν οὐρανοῖς (Phil. iii. 20; see Ellicott thereon); the state, city, or country to which he belonged was a heavenly one; but still his citizenship was latent; he was one of God's hidden ones; but now he is openly avouched, and has a right to enter in by the gates into the City (xxii. 14). This heavenly City, the City which hath the foundations, and for which Abraham looked (Heb. xi. 10), the 'continuing City' (xiii. 14), is but referred to here; the full and magnificent description of it is reserved as the fitting close of the Book (xxi. 10—xxii. 5); and not of this Book only, but of the whole Bible. It goes by many and glorious names in Scripture. 'That great City, the holy Jerusalem,' St. John calls it (xxi. 10); claiming for it this title of 'holy,' which the earthly Jerusalem once possessed (Matt. iv. 5), but which it had forfeited for ever. 'Jerusalem which is above,' St. Paul calls it (Gal. iv. 26); while elsewhere for him, or for another writing in his spirit, it is 'the City of the living God, the heavenly Jerusalem' (Heb. xii. 22). It is the true Καλλίπολις, ἡ ἄνω Καλλίπολις, as Cyril of Alexandria has strikingly named it; being indeed that *Beautiful City*, of which Plato did but dream, when he devised this name (*Rep.* vii. 527 c); the Οὐρανόπολις, as Clement of Alexandria (*Pæd.* ii. 12) has so grandly called it, recovering and reclaiming for the City of God this magnificent title; which Greek sycophants in profane flattery had devised for quite another city (Athenæus, i. 36), for one 'rerum pulcherrima' as Virgil has not scrupled to call it, but if we may trust the pictures of it drawn by those who saw it closest and knew it best, far better deserving a name drawn from beneath than from above.

The epithet '*new*,' given here to the heavenly Jerusalem, sets it in contrast with the old, worn-out, sinful city bearing the same name; for καινός expresses this antithesis of the new to the old *as the out-worn;* its true antithesis being not ἀρχαῖος, but παλαιός; thus καινὸς ἄνθρωπος (Ephes. ii. 15), καινὴ κτίσις (2 Cor. v. 17; Gal. vi. 15), καινὸν ἱμάτιον (Matt. ix. 16), while νέος would but express that which had recently come into existence, as contrasted with that which had subsisted long; thus Νεάπολις, the city *recently* founded (see my *Synonyms of the New Testament,* § 60). There would therefore have been no fitness in this last epithet here, for this New Jerusalem, 'whose builder and maker is God,' is at once new, in that sin has never wasted it, and at the same time the oldest of all, dating as far back as the promise of Gen. iii. Bengel has pertinently observed, that St. John writes always in his Gospel Ἱεροσόλυμα, in the

Apocalypse always Ἱερουσαλήμ; and gives, no doubt, the true explanation of this : ' Non temere Johannes in Evangelio omnibus locis scribit Ἱεροσόλυμα de urbe veteri : in Apocalypsi semper Ἱερουσαλήμ de Urbe Cælesti. Ἱερουσαλήμ est appellatio Hebraica, originaria et sanctior ; Ἱεροσόλυμα deinceps obvia, Græca, magis politica.'

Strange conclusions have been drawn from the words that follow : ' *which cometh down out of heaven from my God.*' The fancy of an actual material city to be let down bodily from heaven to earth, an ' aurea atque gemmata in terris Hierusalem,' as Jerome somewhat contemptuously styles it (*In Esai. Præf. ad Lib.* 18; cf. Origen, *De Princ.* ii. 11. 2), has been cherished in almost all ages of the Church by some, who have been unable to translate the figurative language of Scripture into those far more glorious realities of the heavenly πολιτεία, whereof those figures were the outward garment and array. Thus the Montanists believed that the New Jerusalem would descend at Pepuza in Phrygia, the head-quarters of their sect; and already, according to Tertullian (*Adv. Marc.* iii. 24), there were vouchsafed from time to time signs and prophetic outlines in heaven of the fabric of the City which should thus be let down to earth. For forty days, he assures us, morning and evening, the splendid vision and sky-pageant of this City had been seen suspended in the air. But if only it be a City ' in which righteousness dwelleth,' it will little matter whether we go to it, or it come to us; and in this shape assuredly it will *not* come.[1]

---

[1] Glorious things have been spoken of this City of God, and not in the sacred Scriptures only, but also in the writings of uninspired men, in whose hearts, while they have mused on that Heavenly Jerusalem, the fire has kindled, and they have spoken with their tongues. Thus our own ' Jerusalem, my happy home,'

'*And I will write upon him my new name.*'—This
'*new name*' is not 'The Word of God' (xix. 13), nor yet
'King of kings, and Lord of lords' (xix. 16), as some will
have it. It is true that both of these appear in this
Book as names of Christ; but for all that neither of them
could be called his '*new name*;' the faithful having been
familiar with them from the beginning. The '*new name*'
is that mysterious, and in the necessity of things uncom-
municated, and for the present time incommunicable,
name, which in that same sublimest of all visions is
referred to : 'He had a name written, that no man knew,
but He Himself' (xix. 12); for none except God can

---

in all its different shapes, is worthy of no mean place among
spiritual songs. But the German and the Latin hymnologies are
far richer, both indeed are extraordinarily rich, in these hymns
celebrating the glories of the New Jerusalem. Thus in German
how lovely is Meyfart's (1590-1642) 'Jerusalem, du hochgebaute
Stadt' (Bunsen, *Gesangbuch*, no. 495); but grander still, and not
in Bunsen's collection, Kosegarten's (1758-1818) 'Stadt Gottes,
deren diamantnen Ring'—and in the Latin, Hildebert (not to speak
of Prudentius, *Psychom.* 823-887, Bernard of Clugny, *Laus Patriæ
Cælestis*, and many others), has set forth the beauty and the
blessedness of that City of the living God, and his own longing to
be numbered among the citizens of it, in verses beautiful as these
(see my *Sacred Latin Poetry*, 3rd edit. p. 337) :

Me receptet Sion illa,	Super petram collocata,
Sion, David urbs tranquilla,	Urbs in portu satis tuto,
Cujus faber auctor lucis,	De longinquo te saluto,
Cujus portæ lignum crucis,	Te saluto, te suspiro,
Cujus muri lapis vivus,	Te affecto, te requiro :
Cujus custos Rex festivus.	Quantum tui gratulantur,
In hâc urbe lux solennis,	Quam festive convivantur,
Ver æternum, pax perennis ;	Quis affectus eos stringat,
In hâc odor implens cælos,	Aut quæ gemma muros pingat,
In hâc semper festum melos ;	Quis chalcedon, quis jacinthus,
Non est ibi corruptela,	Nôrunt illi qui sunt intus.
Non defectus, non querela ;	In plateis hujus urbis,
Non minuti, non deformes,	Sociatus piis turbis,
Omnes Christo sunt conformes.	Cum Moÿse et Eliâ,
Urbs cælestis, urbs beata,	Pium cantem Alleluia.'

search out the deep things of God (1 Cor. ii. 12; cf.
Matt. xi. 27; Judg. xiii. 18). But the mystery of this
'*new name*,' which no man by searching could find out,
which in this present condition no man is so much as
capable of receiving, shall be imparted to the saints and
citizens of the new Jerusalem. They shall know, even
a. they are known (1 Cor. xiii. 12).

Ver. 13. '*He that hath an ear, let him hear what the
Spirit saith unto the Churches.*'—Cf. ii. 7. I cannot leave
this Epistle, so full of precious promises to a Church,
which, having little strength, had yet held fast the word
of Christ's patience, without citing a remarkable passage
from Gibbon (*Decline and Fall*, c. lxiv.), in which he
writes like one who almost believed that the threatenings
and promises of God did sometimes fulfil themselves in
history: ' In the loss of Ephesus the Christians deplored the
fall of the first Angel, the extinction of the first candlestick,
of the Revelations; the desolation is complete; and the
temple of Diana or the Church of Mary will equally elude
the search of the curious traveller. The circus and three
stately theatres of Laodicea are now peopled with wolves
and foxes; Sardes is reduced to a miserable village; the
God of Mahomet, without a rival or a son, is invoked in
the mosques of Thyatira and Pergamus, and the populous-
ness of Smyrna is supported by the foreign trade of the
Franks and Armenians. Philadelphia alone has been
saved by prophecy, or courage. At a distance from the sea,
forgotten by the emperors, encompassed on all sides by
the Turks, her valiant citizens defended their religion and
freedom above fourscore years, and at length capitulated
with the proudest of the Ottomans. Among the Greek
colonies and Churches of Asia, Philadelphia is still erect—
a column in a scene of ruins,—a pleasing example that the
paths of honour and safety may sometimes be the same.'

VII.

EPISTLE TO THE CHURCH OF LAODICEA.

Rev. iii. 14–22.

Ver. 14. '*And unto the Angel of the Church of the Laodiceans write.*'—Laodicea, called often 'Laodicea on the Lycus,' to distinguish it from other cities (they were no less than six in all) bearing the same name, was a city in Southern Phrygia (Phrygia Pacatiana), midway between Philadelphia and Colosse. Its nearness to the latter city is more than once assumed in St. Paul's Epistle to the Colossians (iv. 13, 15, 16). Its earliest name was Diospolis, then Rhoas (Pliny, *II. N.* v. 29); being rebuilt and adorned by Antiochus II., king of Syria, he called it Laodicea, after his wife Laodice, by whom he was afterwards poisoned. In Roman times it was a foremost city among the many of second rank in Asia Minor; 'celeberrima urbs,' Pliny calls it. Its commerce was considerable, being chiefly in the wools grown in the region round about, which were celebrated for their richness of colour and fineness of texture. The city suffered grievously in the Mithridatic War, but presently recovered again; it was overthrown by an earthquake in the reign of Nero (A.D. 61; but restored by the efforts of its own citizens, without any help sought from the Roman senate (Tacitus, *Annal.* xiv. 27).

Some have supposed that the negligent Angel of the
Laodicean Church was that Archippus, for whom St. Paul,
writing to the Colossians, adds the message, ' And say to
Archippus, Take heed to the ministry which thou hast
received in the Lord, that thou fulfil it ' (Col. iv. 17).
Bishop Lightfoot does not think it improbable. The
urgency of this monition certainly seems to imply that St.
Paul was not altogether satisfied with the manner in which
Archippus was then fulfilling the ' ministry,' whatever
that might be, which he had undertaken ; and affording
support to this conjecture is the fact that in the *Apo-
stolical Constitutions* (viii. 46), which with much of later
times also contain much of the very earliest, Archippus is
distinctly named as first bishop of Laodicea. Let him
have been the son of Philemon (Philem. 2), a principal
convert in the Colossian Church, whose son therefore
might very probably have been chosen to this dignity
and honour, more perhaps for his father's merits than his
own ; and it would be nothing strange to find him some
thirty years later holding his office still ; while it would
be only too consonant with the downward progress of
things, that he who began slackly, who so soon required
that ' Take heed ' of St. Paul, should in the lapse of years
have grown more and more negligent, till now he needed
and received this sharpest reproof from his Lord. Whether
the rebukes and threatenings contained in this Epistle
did their work or not, it is only for Him who reads all and
remembers all to know. But it is certain that the Church of
Laodicea was in somewhat later times, so far as man's eye
could see, in a flourishing condition. In numbers it increased so much that its bishop obtained metropolitan
dignity ; and A.D. 361 an important Church Council, that
in which the Canon of Scripture was finally settled, was

held at Laodicea, and thence derives its name. But this at best was only a transient revival. All has perished now. He who removed the candlestick of Ephesus, has rejected Laodicea out of his mouth. The fragments of aqueducts and theatres spread over a vast extent of country tell of the former magnificence of this city; but of this once famous Church nothing survives. Recent travellers with difficulty discovered one or two Christians in the poor village which stands on the site occupied by Laodicea of old.

'*These things saith the Amen, the faithful and true Witness.*'—'*The Amen*' (the word only here is used as a proper name, or as a substantive, but compare Isai. lxv. 16) is He who can add a ' Verily, verily,' an ' Amen, amen,' to every word which He utters; as so frequently He does —the double 'Amen' indeed only in the Gospel of St. John (i. 51; iii. 3, 5, 11, and often; cf. Num. v. 22; Neh. viii. 6). He is '*the faithful and true Witness*' in that He speaks what He knows, and testifies what He has seen. The thought is a favourite and ever-recurring one in the Gospel of St John (iii. 11, 32, 33); but does not appear in any other. It may be interesting here to call to mind how the confessors of Lyons and Vienne, referring to these very words, put back from themselves the name of ' witnesses' (μάρτυρες), when others would have given it to them, saying that Christ was '*the faithful and true Witness*,' that this title was not theirs, but His alone (Eusebius, *H. E.* v. 2).

Of the two epithets, the first, πιστός, expresses his entire trustworthiness. The word is employed in two very different senses in the New Testament as elsewhere, in an active and a passive,—now as trusting or believing (John xx. 27; Acts xiv. 1), now as trustworthy or to be believed

(2 Tim. ii. 13 ; 1 Thess. v. 24 ; 1 John i. 9). Men may be
πιστοί in both senses, the active and the passive, as exercising faith, and as being worthy to have faith exercised
in them ; God can be πιστός only in the latter. The
Arians found this epithet applied to Christ (Heb. iii. 2),
and, as though the word was and could be only used in
the former sense, in that of exercising faith upon some
higher object, itself of course a creaturely act, they drew
from the application of this epithet to the Son an argument against his divinity. I quote the clear and excellent
answer of Athanasius (*Library of the Fathers, Treatises
against Arianism*, p. 289) : ' Further, if the expression,
" Who was faithful," is a difficulty to them from the
thought that " faithful " is used of Him as of others, as
if He exercises faith and so receives the reward of faith,
they must proceed to find fault with Moses, for saying,
" God faithful and true," and with St. Paul for writing,
" God is faithful, who will not suffer you to be tempted
above that ye are able." But when the sacred writers spoke
thus, they were not thinking of God in a human way, but
they acknowledged two senses of the word " faithful " in
Scripture, first believing, then trustworthy, of which the
former belongs to man, the latter to God. Thus Abraham was faithful because he believed God's word ; and
God faithful, for, as David says in the Psalm, " The Lord
is faithful in all his words," or is trustworthy, and cannot
lie. Again, " If any faithful woman have widows," she is
so called for her right faith ; but, " It is a faithful saying,"
because what He hath spoken hath a claim on our faith,
for it is true, and is not otherwise. Accordingly the words,
" Who is faithful to Him that made Him," imply no parallel with others, nor mean that by having faith He became well-pleasing, but that, being Son of God the True,

He too is faithful, and ought to be believed in all He says and does.'

It will be seen that the *truthfulness* or veracity of Christ as a Witness is asserted in the πιστός, not, as might at first sight be assumed, in the ἀληθινός that follows, or at least in it only as one quality among many. Christ is a μάρτυς ἀληθινός (not ἀληθής), in that He realized and fulfilled in the highest sense all that belonged to a witness. Three things are necessary thereunto. He must have been αὐτόπτης; must have seen with his own eyes that which he professes to attest (Acts i. 21, 22). He must be competent to relate and to reproduce this information for others. He must be willing faithfully and truthfully to do this. The meeting of these three conditions in Christ, and not the presence of the last only, constitutes Him a '*true Witness*,' or one in whom all the highest qualities of a witness met.

'*The beginning of the creation of God.*'—There are two ways in which *grammatically* it would be possible to understand ἀρχή here (see Pott, *Etym. Forsch.* vol. iii. p. 744; Delitzsch *On Proverbs*, p. 141). The word *might* imply that Christ was passively this '*beginning of the creation of God*,' as the first and most excellent creature of God's hands, his *chef-d'œuvre*; thus Jacob addresses Reuben as ἀρχή τέκνων μου (Gen. xlix. 3; cf. Deut. xxi. 17). Or the words might declare of Christ that He was the active source, author, and, in this sense, '*beginning*' and beginner of all creation; thus, in the Book of Proverbs, Wisdom claims to be ἀρχὴ ὁδῶν τοῦ Θεοῦ, viii. 22; as in the words of the Creed, ' by whom all things were made.' But while both meanings are possible so long as the words are merely considered by themselves, and without reference to any other statements concerning Christ, the analogy of faith imperatively demands the adoption of the latter. The Catholic Church has ever rejected the other as an Arian misuse of the words; impossible to accept, because it would set this passage in contradiction with every passage in Scripture which claims divine attributes, and not creaturely merely, for the Son. To go no further than these seven Epistles, all the titles which Christ claims for Himself in them are either necessarily divine, or, at any rate, not inconsistent with his divinity; and this must be so no less. He is not, therefore, the 'principium *principiatum*,' but rather the 'principium *principians*,'—not He whom God created the first, but He who was the fountain-source of all the creation of God, by whom God created all things (John i. 1–3; Col. i. 15, 18); even as throughout this Book Christ appears as the Author of creation (v. 13). The Arians, as is well known, explained these words in the same way as they explained Col. i. 15, which is, indeed, the great parallel passage, as though ἀρχή was 'the begun,' and not '*the beginning*;' and they brought Job xl. 19 into comparison. But for the use of ἀρχή in the sense and with the force which we here demand for it, as ' principium,' not ' initium ' (though these Latin words do not adequately reproduce the distinction), compare the *Gospel of Nicodemus*, c. 25, in which Hades addresses Satan as ἡ τοῦ θανάτου ἀρχὴ καὶ ῥίζα τῆς ἁμαρτίας; and further, Dionysius the Areopagite (c. 15): ὁ Θεὸς ἐστὶν πάντων αἰτία καὶ ἀρχή; and again, Clement of Alexandria (*Strom.* iv. 25): ὁ Θεὸς δὲ ἄναρχος, ἀρχὴ τῶν ὅλων παντελής. Add from Tertullian (*Adv. Hermog.* 19): ' Principii vocabulum, quod est ἀρχή, non tantum ordinativum, sed et potestativum capit principatum.' He is not merely the first in order, but dynamically the beginning, the author. These and innumerable other passages abundantly vindi-

cate for ἀρχή that active sense which, as I have said, the
analogy of faith compels us to claim for it here. On the
words of St. Paul which exactly say over again of Christ
what He here says of Himself, πρωτότοκος πάσης κτίσεως
(Col. i. 15), the reader is referred to the grand discussion
in Bishop Lightfoot's *Colossians*, in loco.

Ver. 15. '*I know thy works, that thou art neither cold
nor hot: I would thou wert cold or hot.*'—Ζεστός, from
ζέω, ferveo, cf. Acts xviii. 25; Rom. xii. 11 (ζέοντες τῷ
πνεύματι), love to God being a divine heat, a divine fire
(Cant. viii. 6; Luke xxiv. 32). Ὄφελον, properly the
second aorist of ὀφείλω, but now grown into an adverbial
use (='utinam'), has so far forgotten what at the first it
was, as to be employed promiscuously in all numbers and
all persons; cf. 1 Cor. iv. 8; 2 Cor. xi. 1. It governs an
indicative, not an optative, here (ἦς, not εἴης, is the right
reading, and '*wast*' should replace '*wert*' in our Version),
inasmuch as the Lord is not desiring that something even
now *might be*, but only that something *might have been*.
In form a *wish*, it is in reality a *regret*.

Shall we take this '*I would thou wert cold or hot*,'
merely as the expression of a holy impatience at the half-
and-half position of this Laodicean Angel; without push-
ing the matter further, or attempting to explain to ourselves *how* the Lord should have put coldness as one of
two alternatives to be desired; as though He had said, 'I
would thou wouldst take one side or other, be avowedly
with me, or avowedly against me, ranged under my banner,
or under that of my enemies, that so I might understand
how to deal with thee'? Hardly so. This impatience,
looked at more closely, would not deserve to be called
holy. It is the impatience of sinful man, not of the Son
of God; to whom indecision between good and evil must

be preferable to decision for evil. The state of lukewarmness must be in itself worse than even that of coldness,
before the Lord could thus deliberately desire the latter
as a preferable alternative. But how? for this certainly
demands an explanation. Lukewarmness is greatly inferior
to heat, but *seems* preferable to absolute coldness in the
things of God. To have only half a heart for these
things is bad; but wherein is it better to have no heart
at all? How shall we then understand this exclamation,
'*I would thou wert cold or hot*'? Best, I think, in
this way, namely, by regarding the '*cold*' here as one
hitherto untouched by the powers of grace. There is
always hope of such an one, that, when he does come
under those powers, he may become a zealous and earnest
Christian. He is not one on whom the grand experiment
of the Gospel has been tried and has failed. But the
'*lukewarm*,' is one who has tasted of the good gift and of
the powers of the world to come, who has been a subject
of Divine grace, but in whom that grace has failed to
kindle more than the feeblest spark. The publicans and
harlots were '*cold*,' the Apostles '*hot*.' The Scribes and
Pharisees, such among them as that Simon in whose house
the Lord sat and spake the parable of the fifty and the
five hundred pence (Luke vii. 36-47), they were '*lukewarm*.' It was from among the '*cold*,' and not the
'*lukewarm*,' that He drew recruits; from among them
came forward the candidates for discipleship and apostle-
ship and the crown of life, Matthew, and Zacchæus, and
the Magdalene, and the other woman that had been a
sinner (if indeed another), and all those, the publicans
and harlots, that entered into the kingdom of heaven,
while the Scribes and Pharisees continued without; and
above all Paul the Apostle, who, having been a persecutor

and injurious, was changed into a preacher of that faith
which he persecuted before. That woman 'which was a
sinner,' for example, having been '*cold*,' passed from that
coldness to the fervency of a divine heat, at which there is
little likelihood that the '*lukewarm*' Simon ever arrived
(Luke vii. 47 ; Matt. xxi. 28–31).

It is thus that Gregory the Great explains these words
(*Reg. Past.* iii. 34) : 'Qui enim adhuc in peccatis est,
conversionis fiduciam non amittit. Qui vero post conversionem tepuit, et spem, quæ esse potuit de peccatore, sub-
traxit. Aut calidus ergo quisque esse, aut frigidus quæ-
ritur, ne tepidus evomatur, ut videlicet aut necdum conversus, adhuc de se spem conversionis præbeat, aut jam
conversus in virtutibus inardescat.' Compare Origen (*De
Princip.* iii. 4) : 'Forte utilius videatur obtineri animam
a carne, quam residere in suis propriis voluntatibus.
Namque quoniam nec calida dicitur esse, nec frigida, sed
in medio quodam tepore perdurans, tardam et satis diffi-
cilem conversionem poterit invenire. Si vero carni ad-
hæreat, ex his ipsis interdum malis quæ ex carnis vitiis
patitur, satiata aliquando et repleta, velut gravissimis
oneribus luxuriæ ac libidinis fatigata, facilius et velocius
converti a materialibus sordibus ad cælestium desiderium
et spiritualem gratiam potest.' Jeremy Taylor, too, in
the second of his sermons, *Of Lukewarmness and Zeal*,
discusses this point, namely, *why* the Lord preferred
either '*hot*' or '*cold*' to '*lukewarm*,' at considerable
length ; and urges well that it is the '*lukewarm*,' not as a
transitional, but as a *final* state, which is thus the object
of the Lord's abhorrence : 'In feasts or sacrifices the ancients did use *apponere frigidam* or *calidam* ; sometimes
they drank hot drink, sometimes they poured cold upon
their gravies or in their wines, but no services of tables or

altars were ever with lukewarm. God hates it worse than
stark cold; which expression is the more considerable,
because in natural and superinduced progressions from
extreme to extreme, we must necessarily pass through the
midst; and therefore it is certain a lukewarm religion is
better than none at all, as being the doing some parts of
the work designed, and nearer to perfection than the
utmost distance could be; and yet that God hates it more,
must mean, that there is some appendant evil in this state
which is not in the other, and that accidentally it is much
worse : and so it is, if we rightly understand it; that is, if
we consider it not as a being in, or passing through, the
middle way, but as a state and a period of religion. If it
be in motion, a lukewarm religion is pleasing to God; for
God hates it not for its imperfection, and its natural
measures of proceeding; but if it stands still and rests
there, it is a state against the designs and against the
perfection of God : and it hath in it these evils.'

I must not leave these words without observing that
there is another way of explaining this, '*I would thou
wert cold or hot*,' which has found favour with some in
modern times. Urging that food, when *either* cold or hot,
is pleasant to the taste, and only when tepid unwelcome,
they make *both* the ' *cold* ' and the '*hot*' to express spiritual conditions absolutely acceptable in themselves, the
only *tertium comparationis* being the nausea created by
the tepid, and they affirm that nothing further has a right
here to be pressed. But assuredly there is much more in
these words than this.

Ver. 16. '*So then because thou art lukewarm, and
neither cold nor hot, I will spue thee out of my mouth.*'—
The land of Canaan is said to have *spued out* its former
inhabitants for their abominable doings; the children of

P

Israel being warned that they commit not the same, lest in like manner it *spue* out them (Lev. xviii. 28 ; xx. 22). But the threatening here is more terrible still. It is nothing less than to be spued *out of the mouth of Christ*, to be rejected as with moral loathing and disgust, by Him ; to exchange the greatest possible nearness to Him for the remotest distance. At the same time, in the original the language is not quite so severe as in our Version ; the threat does not present itself as one about to be put into *immediate* execution. The long-suffering of Christ has not been all exhausted : μέλλω σε ἐμέσαι, 'I am about,' or 'I have it in my mind, to spue thee out of my mouth,' as the Vulgate seeks to express it, '*incipiam te evomere* ;' that is, ' unless thou so takest to heart this threat that I shall never need to execute this threat' (Jon. iii. 10 ; 1 Kin. xxi. 29). But if executed, it implies nothing less than absolute rejection, being equivalent to that '*I will remove thy candlestick out of his place*' (ii. 5), uttered against the Ephesian Angel. Not very different is the tropical use of πτύειν, καταπτύειν, and in Latin of 'respuere,' 'conspuere,' as = ' repudiare,' ' abhorrere ab aliquâ re.' Χλιαρός, aptly rendered in our Version '*lukewarm*,' is a word with which we are familiar enough in Homer ; but it there appears in an old Ionic subform as λιαρός (*Il.* ix. 477 ; *Od.* v. 268).

Ver. 17. '*Because thou sayest, I am rich, and increased with goods* (or as it is in the R. V., '*and have gotten riches*'), *and have need of nothing ; and knowest not that thou art wretched, and miserable, and poor, and blind, and naked.*'—There is a question whether this verse coheres the most closely with what goes before, or what follows after,—that is, whether Christ threatens to reject him from his mouth, because he says, '*I am rich,*

and increased with goods, and have need of nothing;'
or whether, because he says he is all this, therefore Christ
counsels him to buy of Him what will make him rich
indeed (ver. 18). Our Translators regard the latter connexion as the right one; and, by the punctuation which
they have adopted, join this verse with that which follows
after it, not with that which went before it. I doubt
whether in this they have correctly done. I should prefer
to place a colon at the end of ver. 16, and a full-stop at
that of ver. 17, instead of the reverse, which has been
their course.—These riches and other goods in which the
Laodicean Church and Angel gloried we must understand
as *spiritual* riches, in which they fondly imagined they
abounded. Some interpreters take it in another sense,
that they boasted of their worldly prosperity, their flourishing outward condition, and found in this a sign and
token of God's favour towards them. But assuredly this
is a mistake. It is in the sphere of spiritual things that
the Lord is moving; and this language in this application is justified by numerous passages in Scripture: as by
Luke xii. 21; 1 Cor. i. 5; 2 Cor. viii. 9; above all, by
two passages of holy irony, 1 Cor. iv. 8 and Hos. xii. 8;
both standing in very closest connexion with this; I can
indeed hardly doubt that there is intended a reference to
the latter of these in the words of our Lord. The Laodicean Angel, and the Church which he was drawing into
the same ruin with himself, were walking in a vain show
and imagination of their own righteousness, their own
advances in spiritual insight and knowledge. That this
may go hand in hand with the most miserable lack of all
real grace, all true and solid advances in goodness, we
have a notable example in the Pharisee of our Lord's parable (Luke xviii. 11, 12; cf. xvi. 15; 1 Cor. xiii. 1); and

so it was here. Rightly Richard of St. Victor: ' Dicis quod sum dives et locupletatus, sive videlicet per scientiæ cognitionem, sive per Scripturæ prædicationem, sive per secularis eloquentiæ nitorem, sive per sacramentorum administrationem, sive per pontificalis apicis dignitatem, sive per vulgi laudem inanem.'

Such was their estimate of themselves: but now follows the terrible reality, namely, Christ's estimate of them: ' *And knowest not that thou art wretched, and miserable, and poor, and blind, and naked.*' Here, as so often, our Version, to its loss, has taken no note of the article which, going before the two first adjectives, raises them to the dignity of substantives, while the three which follow are added as qualifying adjectives. An exact parallel, and, singularly enough, much more than a mere verbal parellel, occurs Isai. xlvii. 8 (LXX): νῦν δὲ ἄκουε ταῦτα, τρυφερά, ἡ καθημένη, ἡ πεποιθυῖα, ἡ λέγουσα ἐν καρδίᾳ αὐτῆς, Ἐγώ εἰμι, καὶ οὐκ ἔστιν ἐτέρα, κ.τ.λ. Best therefore to translate, ' *And knowest not that thou art the wretched and the miserable one, and poor, and blind, and naked.*' Ταλαίπωρος, ' *wretched,*' in the New Testament occurs only here and Rom. vii. 24: it is commonly derived by the grammarians from τλαω, and πῶρος in the sense of grief, but thought now to be a poetical recasting of ταλαπείριος, in which case we should find πειρά, a sharp piercing point, in the latter syllables. Ἐλεεινός, a later form of the word whose Attic form is ἐλεινός (Lobeck, *Phrynichus*, p. 87), occurs only here and 1 Cor. xv. 19; it sets him forth as an object of extremest pity (ἐλέους ἄξιος, Suidas), as in certain peril of eternal death, if he should remain what he was. The charge of blindness would seem to imply that the Laodicean Church boasted of spiritual insight. Like some before them, being blind they yet said, ' We see' (John ix. 41). This blindness, of course, was not absolute and complete; else the 'eye-salve' which the Lord presently bids them to obtain of Him would have profited little. They were μυωπάζοντες, blinking, as St. Peter describes some, he too joining τυφλός and μυωπάζων (2 Pet. i. 9).

Ver. 18. '*I counsel thee to buy of Me gold tried in the fire, that thou mayest be rich; and white raiment, that thou mayest be clothed, and that the shame of thy naked-ness do not appear, and anoint thine eyes with eyesalve, that thou mayest see.*'—Marckius: 'Triplici malo pauper-tatis, nudidatis, et cæcitatis, triplex opponitur merx, aurum igne coctum, vestimenta alba, et collyrium.' There is a slight touch of irony, but the irony of divine love, in the words. He who might have commanded, prefers rather to counsel; He who might have spoken as from heaven, conforms Himself, so far as the outward form of his words reaches, to the language of earth. To the merchants and factors of this wealthy mercantile city He addresses Him-self in their own dialect. Laodicea, on the great high road of Oriental commerce, was a city of extensive money transactions; so that Cicero, journeying to or from his pro-vince, proposes to take up money there (*Epp. ad Div.* ii. 17; iii. 5). Christ here invites to dealings with Himself. He has gold of so fine a standard that none will reject it. The wools of Laodicea, of a raven blackness, were famous throughout the world. He has raiment of dazzling white for as many as will receive it at his hands. There were ointments for which many of the Asiatic cities, perhaps Laodicea among the number, were famous; but He, as He will presently announce, has eyesalve more precious than them all. Would it not be wise to transact their chief business with Him? Thus Perkins (*Exposition upon*

Rev. i. ii. iii., *Works*, vol. iii. p. 363): 'Christ saith, "*I counsel thee to buy of Me*;" where He alluded to the outward state of this city, for it was rich, and also given to much traffic, as histories record, and therefore He speaks to them in their own kind, as if He should say, Ye are a people exercised in much traffic, and delighted with nothing more than buying and selling. Well, I have wares that will serve your turn, as gold, garments, and oil; therefore come and *buy of Me*.'

We must not fail to put an emphasis on that '*of Me*.' ' In Me,' Christ would say, ' are hidden all the treasures of wisdom and knowledge.' His Apostle once already had reminded the Colossians, neighbours of the Laodiceans, that this was so; and that there was no growth for the Church, or for any member of the Church, except through holding the Head (Col. ii. 3, 19); that all self-chosen ways of will-worship might have a show of wisdom, but puffed up, and did not build up (ii. 10–15); and out of the deep anxiety which he evidently felt for both these sister Churches alike (ii. 1), he had desired that the Epistle to the Colossians should be read also in the Church of the Laodiceans (iv. 16). But they of Laodicea had not learned their lesson. St. Paul's 'great conflict' for them had been well nigh in vain; and now the Lord, repeating his servant's lesson, gathers up into a single point, concentrates in that single phrase, 'buy *of Me*,' the whole lesson of the Epistle to the Colossians.

The invitation to '*buy*' of Him, who is so much more frequently set forth as making a free gift of all which He imparts to men (Rom. vi. 23; Rev. xxii. 17), is drawn from Isai. lv. 1, with which we may compare Prov. iii. 14; xxiii. 23; Matt. xiii. 44, 46. The price which they should pay was this, the renunciation of all vain reliance on their own righteousness and wisdom; the price which in another Epistle St. Paul declared he had so gladly paid, that so he might himself win Christ (Phil. iii. 7, 8); the ἀπο-τάσσεσθαι πᾶσι, which the Lord long before had declared to be the necessary condition of his discipleship (Luke xiv. 33). This is the price, contemplated rather in its negative aspect; on its positive side it is the earnest striving after, and longing for, the gift, the reaching out after it, the opening of the mouth wide that He may fill it. Vitringa: 'Quæ beneficia Dominus vult ut emant, h. e. secundum conditiones fœderis gratiæ pro iis expendant pretium abnegationis sui ipsius et mundanarum cupiditatum; quod hic non habet rationem meriti, sed tamen pretii, quia in regeneratione homo aliis quibusdam rebus sibi hactenus caris renunciat, ut pretioso dono justitiæ Christi potiatur.'

What does the Lord counsel this Angel that he shall ' *buy*; ' what precious things name, the which when he has made his own, he shall be no longer '*poor, and blind, and naked*'? They are three. And first, as he is '*poor*'—'*gold tried in the fire, that thou mayest be rich.*' A comparison with 1 Pet. i. 7 (cf. Zech. xiii. 9; Mal. iii. 3; Prov. xvii. 3; Jam. i. 3) teaches us that by this ' *gold* ' we must understand faith; for faith being a gift of God, must therefore be bought of Christ (Luke xvii. 5; cf. Ps. lxxii. 15, according to the right translation); and such faith as would stand the test, would endure in the furnace of affliction, in the πύρωσις (1 Pet. iv. 12); Vitringa: ' Vera et solida fides, quæ sustinere possit afflictiones.' Then should he be rich indeed; this is the true πλουτίζειν (1 Cor. i. 5), better than that spoken of in the book of Job (xxii. 23, 24); though that, as God's gift, might be good; then should he be indeed one εἰς Θεὸν πλουτῶν (Luke xii. 21), rich toward God, not walking, as now, in a vain imagina-

tion of wealth which he had not.—Πεπυρωμένον ἐκ πυρός
=δοκιμαζόμενον διὰ πυρός, 1 Pet. i. 7 (cf. Zech. xiii. 9;
Ps. lxv. 10; Prov. x. 20; LXX); for, in the words of the
Latin poet (Ovid, *Fast.* iv. 785):

> ' Omnia purgat edax ignis vitiumque metallis
> Excoquit.'

The Latin language, which has dropped the noun substantive corresponding to the Greek πῦρ and to our ' fire,'
taking ' ignis' instead, has yet ' purus,' closely connected
with these, and attesting to a sense of the cleansing,
purifying energy of fire. Compare Pott, *Etym. Forsch.*
vol. ii. pt. ii. p. 1102.

But secondly, as he is ' *naked*,' ' *Buy of Me*,' says the
Lord, ' *white raiment, that thou mayest be clothed, and that
the shame of thy nakedness do not appear*.' Instead of
the αἰσχύνη here, we have in the parallel passage, xvi. 15,
ἀσχημοσύνη (cf. Ezek. xvi. 8, LXX), translated also
' shame,' but better, ' unseemliness' or ' uncomeliness;'
cf. τὰ ἀσχήμονα, 1 Cor. xii. 23. ' *Do not appear*' is too
weak a rendering of μὴ φανερωθῇ, which translate rather,
' *be not made manifest*;' so the R.V., φανεροῦσθαι expressing constantly the manifestations or revelations which
God makes of the hidden things of men (John iii. 21;
1 Cor. iv. 5; 2 Cor. v. 11; Eph. v. 13); either now, or at
that last day when every guest that has not on a wedding
garment is at the same instant discovered and cast out
(Matt. xxii. 11–13; cf. Isai. xlvii. 3; ἀνακαλυφθήσεται ἡ
αἰσχύνη σου; Lam. i. 8). As stripping, and laying bare
the nakedness, is a frequent method of putting to open
shame (cf. 2 Sam. x. 4; Isai. xx. 4; Ezek. xvi. 37, 39;
xxiii. 26, 29; Hos. ii. 3, 9; iii. 5; Mic. i. 8, 11; Nah. iii.
5; Rev. xvi. 15; xvii. 16), so the clothing with comely
apparel those unclothed or ill-clothed before, of imparting
honour; cf. Gen. xli. 42; Esth. vi. 7–11; Dan. v. 29;

Luke xv. 22; Zech. iii. 3-5; Ezek. xvi. 10-13; and above
all, Gen. iii. 7, 21, where it is shown that God, and not
himself, is the true coverer and concealer of the nakedness
of man; for while he can discover his own shame, it is
God only who can cover it. This, *the shame of the nakedness* of him who, professing Christ, has not put on Christ,
may be, and often is, revealed in the present time; it *must
be* revealed in the last day (Matt. xxii. 11-13; Dan. xii.
2; 2 Cor. v. 10); looking on to which revelation, and
that 'everlasting contempt' which shall then be the portion
of so many, the Psalmist exclaims, 'Blessed is the man
whose sin *is covered*' (Ps. xxxii. 1); and those interpreters
seem to me to give too narrow a range of meaning to this
'*white raiment*,' who limit it to the graces of the Christian life, and the putting on, in this sense, of the Lord
Jesus Christ (Col. iii. 10-14). We should understand by
it not merely the righteousness of Christ *imparted*, but also
that righteousness *imputed*; for both are needful, the one
as needful as the other, if the shame of our nakedness is
not to appear; nor can they be separated the one from
the other (Ezek. xxxvi. 25-27); it is the being 'found in
Him' (Phil. iii. 9), with all which this implies and in-
volves' (cf. Job xxix. 14; Isai. lxi. 10). So Vitringa:
'Vestimenta alba, h.e. justitiam Christi, verâ fide acceptam,
quæ nos obtegat quâ parte nudi, id est, expositi sumus
ardenti iræ Dei; tum quoque habitus Christianarum virtutum, quæ faciunt ut quis cum fiduciâ absque pudore coram
Deo et sanctis ausit comparere, inter quas eminent caritas,
simplicitas, humilitas et zelus.'

And then lastly—'*anoint thine eyes with eyesalve, that
thou mayest see.*' The eye for which this salve is needed
is, of course, the spiritual eye, that eye of the conscience
by which spiritual things are discerned and appreciated;

which eye may be sound or single (ἁπλοῦς, Matt. vi. 22),
or contrariwise may be evil (πονηρός, Matt. vi. 23; cf. 1
John ii. 11); and according as it is one or the other, as it
is enlightened (Ephes. i. 18) or darkened (Zech. xi. 17),
the man will see himself as he truly is, or see nothing as
he ought to see it. The beginning of all true amendment
is to see ourselves as indeed we are, in our misery, our
guilt, our shame; and the ability to do this is the first
consequence of the anointing with that eyesalve which the
Lord here invites this Angel to purchase of Him. The
Spirit convinces of sin, and by this 'eyesalve' we must understand the illuminating grace of the Holy Ghost, which
at once shows to us God, and in God and in his light
ourselves. And if the eyesalves of antiquity commonly
caused the eye to smart on their first application (Tob. xi.
8, 12), 'mordacia collyria,' 'acre collyrium,' as Augustine
therefore calls them (In Joh. Tract. xviii. § 11 · Conf.
vii. 8), δριμὺ κολλύριον, as the Apostolic Constitutions,
β 41, this will only set forth the more fitly to us the
wholesome pain and medicinal smart which belong to the
spiritual eyesalve as well; making for us discoveries so
painful as it does, causing us to see in ourselves a nakedness and poverty which had been wholly concealed from
us before; while yet only through the seeing and confessing of this can that poverty be ever exchanged for riches,
or that nakedness for 'durable clothing.'

It has been already remarked, and assuredly it is very
well worthy of notice, that the two Churches which
spiritually have sunk the lowest, that, namely, of Sardis
and this of Laodicea, are also the only two in which there
are no traces either of adversaries from without, or of
hinderers to the truth from within. Of the absence of
heathen adversaries there was occasion to speak there;

but more noticeable still is the fact that neither there nor
here are there Nicolaitans, as at Ephesus, nor Balaamites,
as at Pergamum, nor Jezebelites, as at Thyatira, nor those
who say they are Jews and are not, as at Smyrna and
Philadelphia.　We have notice of none of these seeking to
seduce Christ's servants, and giving them no choice but
earnestly to contend for the truth, if they would not be
robbed of it altogether.　From the lukewarmness and
faintness of these Churches, from the indifference and
lethargy into which they, who had no truth to secure or
defend from gainsayers, were sunk, we may gather a pregnant hint of all which the Church owes to the heresies
and heretics that, one after another, have disturbed her
repose.　Owing to them no thanks for what she has
gained by them, the gains themselves have not the less
been immense; even as St. Paul long before declared that
she could not do without them (1 Cor. x. 19).　There are
remarkable acknowledgments to this same effect made in
the heat of the great conflicts of early times by more than
one of the Fathers; as by Augustine, *De Gen. con.
Manich.* i. 1, and often.　Tertullian, indeed, had anticipated him here (see *De Præsc. Hæret.* i. 4); and Origen
(*Hom.* 9 *in Num.*).　Contending against these gainsayers,
she has learned not merely to define more precisely, but to
grasp more firmly, and to prize more dearly, that truth of
which they would fain have deprived her.　What would
the Church of the second century have been, if she had
never learned her strength, and the treasures of wisdom
and knowledge which she had in Christ Jesus, in the
course of that tremendous conflict with the Gnostics
which through all that century she sustained?　Would
the Church herself have ever been the *true* Gnostic, except
for these *false* ones?　Again, what an education and disci-

pline for her were the fast-succeeding conflicts, Sabellian, Arian, Nestorian, Monophysite, Monothelite, of the centuries which followed; and not an intellectual education only, but ' as iron sharpeneth iron,' so the zeal of the adversaries of the truth served often to excite the zeal and love, which might else have abated, of her friends. Of Augustine himself Luther, though with some exaggeration, has said, that his controversy with the Pelagians 'first made a man of him' (*Table Talk*, c. 29). Assuredly it was not good for the Sardian and Laodicean Churches to be without this necessity of doing earnest battle for the truth. Perhaps they gloried in their freedom from conflicts which were agitating, disquieting, and shaking it may have been Churches around them. But we may be bold to say that in a world of imperfections like ours, it argued no healthy spiritual life that there were none there to call the truth into question and debate. Misgrowths are at any rate *growths*; and if there is a spiritual condition which is *above* errors (though hardly to be found in this present world), so also there is one which is *beneath* them; when all in a Church is dead 'as the fat weed that rots on Lethe's wharf,' when there is not interest enough in theology, not care enough to know anything certain about God, or about man's relation to God, even to generate a heresy. As we read the history of the Church, we may perhaps find some consolation in considerations such as these. Assuredly in reading many a page in that history we need the strongest consolations which anywhere we can find.

Ver. 19. '*As many as I love I rebuke and chasten; be zealous therefore, and repent.*'—Observe the use of φιλεῖν here, a tenderer word than ἀγαπᾶν would have been, which He employs in his address to Philadelphia (iii. 9). He has wounded sharply, even as He meant to do; but will fain before He has done pour some soothing oil into the wounds which He has inflicted. Bengel says well: 'Philadelphiensem ἠγάπητε, Laodicensem φιλεῖ. Illud judicio, hoc gratiâ;' and compare my *Synonyms of the New Testament*, § 12. He, the great Master-builder, squares and polishes with many strokes of the chisel and the hammer the stones which shall find a place at last in the walls of the heavenly Jerusalem (cf. Prov. iii. 12; xiii. 24; xxvii. 6; Ezek. xx. 37; Job v. 17; Acts xiv. 22; 1 Cor. xi. 32; Heb. xii. 6; 2 Chron. xxxiii. 11-13; Ps. xciv. 12; Ecclus. xxx. 1; Wisd. iii. 4-6); on which Gregory the Great, with allusion to 1 Kin. vi. 7, has very beautifully said (*Reg. Past.* iii. 12): 'Hinc est enim quod lapides extra tunsi sunt, ut in constructione templi Domini absque mallei sonitu ponerentur; quia videlicet nunc foris per flagella tundimur, ut intus in templum Dei postmodum sine disciplinæ percussione disponamur, quatenus quidquid in nobis est superfluum modo percussio resecet, et tunc sola nos in ædificio concordia caritatis liget.' And this is a rule which endures no exception. In that ' *as many* ' (ὅσους) here lies the same emphasis as in the ' *every* son ' of Heb. xii. 6. *All* whom He loves are included in the same discipline of correction, are made sooner or later to be able to say, ' Thy loving correction shall make me great ' (Ps. xviii. 35). Of *all* it is true that, if not scourged, they are not sons (Heb. xii. 8; 2 Macc. vi. 12-16); if not rebuked and chastened, they are not loved. Others may be let alone (Ps. lxxiii. 5, 12; Isai. i. 5); but not they. Not a few, if their prosperity lasts a little longer than that of others, fancy that they shall be exceptions to this rule. But it never proves so. They can only be excepted from the discipline through being excepted from the sonship; as

Augustine excellently well (*Serm.* xlvi. § 11); 'Flagellat, inquit, omnem filium quem recipit. Et tu forte exceptus eris? Si exceptus a passione flagellorum, exceptus a numero filiorum;' and again (*Enarr. in Ps.* xxxii. 11): ' Vis audire quam omnem? Etiam Unicus sine peccato, non tamen sine flagello.' Many other beautiful passages to the same effect may be found in his writings; thus, *Enarr. in Ps.* xxxi. 11; xciii. 14; cxiv. 5. Jerome, too, very profoundly says (*in Ezek.* 9): ' Magnæ interdum felicitatis est, ad præsens misericordiam non mereri.' It is the crushed grape, and not the untouched, from which the costly liquor distils.

Ἐλέγχειν and παιδεύειν are often found together, as here; thus Ecclus. xviii. 13; Ps. cxl. 5; so too παιδεία and ἔλεγχος, Prov. vi. 23; cf. Heb. vii. 5; but they are very capable of being distinguished. Ἐλέγχειν is more than ἐπιτιμᾶν, with which it is often joined (see my *Synonyms of the New Testament*, § 4; and J. H. H. Schmidt, *Synonymik d. Griech. Sprache*, p. 136 sqq.). It is so to rebuke that the person rebuked is brought to the acknowledgment of his fault, is *convinced*, as David was when rebuked by Nathan (2 Sam. xii. 13); for, in the words of Aristotle (*Rhet. ad Alex.* 13), ἔλεγχός ἐστι μὲν ὃ μὴ δυνατὸν ἄλλως ἔχειν, ἀλλ' οὕτως ὡς ἡμεῖς λέγομεν: and this rebuking, or convincing of sin, is eminently the work and office of the Holy Ghost (John xvi. 8; cf. iii. 20; Ephes. v. 13). See upon this subject an admirable note by Archdeacon Hare, *Mission of the Comforter*, vol. ii. p. 528. Παιδεύειν, being in classical Greek to instruct, to educate, is in sacred Greek to instruct or educate *by means of correction*, through the severe discipline of love (παιδεύειν and μαστιγοῦν are joined together, Heb. xii. 6), 'per molestias erudire' (Lev. xxvi. 18; 1 Kin. xii. 11 :

Ps. xxxvii. 1); as Augustine (*Enarr. in Ps.* cxviii. 66), tracing the difference between its sacred and profane uses, explains it. As David had found his ἔλεγχος when he exclaimed, 'I have sinned against the Lord' (2 Sam. xii. 13), so his παιδεία was announced to him in the words which followed: 'The child also that is born unto thee shall surely die' (ver. 14)—which passage is alone sufficient to refute those who affirm that we have in this ἐλέγχω καὶ παιδεύω here a ὕστερον πρότερον. Not so. It will indeed continually happen that the same dealing of God with men is at once ἔλεγχος and παιδεία, but only παιδεία through having been ἔλεγχος first; which therefore rightly precedes. Brightman: 'Observandum est illum *arguere* et *castigare*; id est, convincere et plectere. Simul enim sunt hæc duo conjungenda. Inutilis est animadversio, ubi verba silent, verbera sæviunt. Unde recte vocatur castigatio, disciplina quâ delinquens una dolet et discit.'—For ζήλωσον of the received text, read rather ζήλευε, from ζηλεύω, another form of ζηλόω. This word, through ζῆλος connected with ζέω and thus with ζεστός (ver. 15), is chosen as the word of exhortation, with special reference to the *lukewarmness* which the Lord so indignantly saw in the Laodicean Church. It was *warmth, heat, fervency,* which He required there. St. Paul uses ζηλοῦν in a good sense, Gal. iv. 18; 1 Cor. xii. 31; xiv. 1; which passages are the best parallels to its employment here.

Ver. 20. '*Behold I stand at the door and knock.*'— The Hellenistic κρούειν is here, as always in the New Testament, the word used to describe this knocking at the door (Luke xii. 36; xiii. 25; Acts xii. 13, 16). The Greek purists preferred κόπτειν; yet see Lobeck, *Phrynichus,* p. 177. These gracious words declare the long-suffering of Christ, as He waits for the conversion of sinners (1 Pet. iii. 20); and not alone the long-suffering which waits, but the love which seeks to bring that conversion about, which ' *knocks.*' He at whose door we ought to stand, for He *is* the Door (John x. 7), who, as such, has bidden *us* to knock (Matt. vii. 7 ; Luke xi. 9), is content that the whole relation between Him and us should be reversed, and instead of our standing at his door, condescends Himself to stand at ours,—θυραυλεῖν, as the Greeks called this waiting and watching at the door of the beloved.

Very beautiful on the matter of this infinite condescension on his part are the words of Nicolaus Cabasilas, a Greek mystic of the fourteenth century : ὁ περὶ τοὺς ἀνθρώπους ἔρως τὸν Θεὸν ἐκένωσεν. οὐ γὰρ κατὰ χώραν μένων καλεῖ πρὸς ἑαυτόν, ὃν ἐφίλησε δοῦλον, ἀλλ᾽ αὐτὸς ζητεῖ κατ-ελθών, καὶ πρὸς τὴν καταγωγὴν ἀφικνεῖται τοῦ πένητος ὁ πλουτῶν, καὶ προσελθὼν δι᾽ ἑαυτοῦ μηνύει τὸν πόθον, καὶ ζητεῖ τὸ ἴσον, καὶ ἀπαξιοῦντος οὐκ ἀφίσταται, καὶ πρὸς τὴν ὕβριν οὐ δυσχεραίνει, καὶ διωκόμενος προσεδρεύει ταῖς θύραις, καὶ ἵνα τὸν ἐρῶντα δείξῃ, πάντα ποιεῖ, καὶ ὀδυνώμενος φέρει καὶ ἀποθνήσκει.

' *If any man hear my voice, and open the door, I will come in to him, and will sup with him, and he with Me.*' —Christ does not knock only ; He also speaks ; makes his ' *voice*' to be heard—a more precious benefit still ! It is true, indeed, that we cannot in our interpretation draw any strict line of distinction between Christ knocking and Christ speaking. Both represent his dealings of infinite love with souls, for the winning them to receive Him ; yet at the same time, considering that in this natural world a knock may be any one's, and on any errand, while the voice accompanying that knock would at once designate who it was that stood without, and with what intention

(Acts xii. 13, 14), we have a right, so far as we may venture to distinguish between the two, to see in the voice the more inward appeal, the closer dealing of Christ with the soul, speaking directly by his Spirit to the spirit of the man ; in the knocking those more outward gracious dealings, of sorrow and joy, of sickness and health, and the like, which He sends, and sending uses for the bringing of his elect, in one way or another, by smooth paths or by rough, to Himself. The '*voice*' very often will interpret and make intelligible the purpose of the '*knock.*'

It is true that the one and the other may alike remain unheard and unheeded. It is in the power of every man to close his ear to them; therefore the hypothetical form which this gracious promise takes : '*if any man hear my voice, and open the door.*' There is no *gratia irresistibilis* here. It is the man himself who must open the door. Christ indeed knocks, claims admittance as to his own ; so lifts up his voice that it may be heard, in one sense *must* be heard, by him ; but He does not break open the door, or force an entrance by violence. There is a sense in which every man is lord of the house of his own heart ; it is his fortress ; he must open the gates of it, and unless he does so, Christ cannot enter. And, as a necessary complement of this power to open, there belongs also to man the mournful prerogative and privilege of refusing to open : he may keep the door shut, even to the end. He may thus continue to the last blindly at strife with his own blessedness ; a miserable conqueror, who conquers to his own everlasting loss and defeat.

At the same time, these words of Christ, decisive testimony as they yield against that scheme of irresistible grace which would turn men into mere machines, and take away all moral value from the victories which Christ obtains

Q

over the sullenness, the pride, the obstinacy, the rebellion
of men, must not be pushed, as some have pushed them,
in the other direction, into Pelagian error and excess.
This is done when the words are taken to affirm that men
can open the door of their heart when they will, as though
repentance was not itself a gift of the exalted Saviour
(Acts v. 31); when it is forgotten that the words of the
Holy Ghost, Acts xvi. 14, 'whose heart the Lord opened,'
must stand true as well as these. Men can only open
when Christ knocks; and they would have no desire at all
to open unless He knocked, and unless, together with the
external knocking of the Word, or of sorrow, or of pain,
or whatever other shape it might assume, there went also
the inward voice of the Spirit. All which one would
affirm is that this is a *drawing*, not a *dragging*—a knocking at the door, not a breaking open of the door. Hilary
has some words very much to the point here (*In Ps.*
cxviii. 89): 'Vult ergo semper introire; sed a nobis ne
introeat excluditur. Ipse quidem semper ut illuminet
promptus est; sed lumen sibi domus ipsa obseratis aditibus
excludit. Quæ si cœperit patere, illico introibit, modo
solis, qui clausis fenestræ valvis introire prohibetur, paten-
tibus vero totus immittitur. Est enim Verbum Dei Sol
justitiæ, adsistens unicuique ut introeat, nec moratur
lucem suam repertis aditibus infundere.'

Some, wishing to deprive the *Song of Songs* of its
honourable place in the Canon, and to reduce it to the
level of a mere human love-poem, the idyl of an earthly
love, have affirmed that there is no single allusion to it in
the New Testament. This assertion is wholly without
warrant. In the words we have been just considering
there is an undoubted allusion to Cant. v. 2-6; where, indeed, the very language which Christ uses here, the κρούειν

ἐπὶ τὴν θύραν, the summons ἀνοίγειν recurs. Nor is the
relation between the one passage and the other merely
superficial and verbal. On the contrary, it lies very deep.
The spiritual condition of the Bride there is in fact precisely similar to that of the Laodicean Angel here. Between sleeping and waking she has been so slow to open
the door, that when at length she does so, the Bridegroom
has withdrawn, and she has need to seek for and to follow
Him (ver. 5, 6). This exactly corresponds to the lukewarmness of the Angel here. See the two passages brought
into closest connexion in this sense by Jerome, *Ep.* xviii.
ad Eustochium. Another proof of the connexion between them is this,—that although there has been no
mention of anything but a knocking here, Christ goes on
to say, ' *If any man hear my voice.*' What can this be
but an allusion to the words in the *Canticle* which have
just gone before, ' It is the *voice* of my beloved that knock-
eth, saying, *Open* to me, my sister '? In the face of this,
and much more of the same kind which might be adduced,
Ewald asserts, ' Cantico *nunquam* utuntur scriptores Novi
Testamenti ; ' and rather than look there for this ' *Behold,
I stand at the door and knock,*' he prefers to find allusion here to Peter's standing and knocking at the door of
Mary's house after he was released from prison by the
Angel (Acts xii. 13, 14) ! We need not go far before we
find further evidence of the intimate relation between
these words of Christ and those of the Bridegroom in that
Book. We trace it in the words which almost immediately
follow : ' *and will sup with him, and he with Me.*' There
may possibly be in these a more immediate reference to
Luke xii. 36 ; but that to the *Song of Songs,* because it
lies deeper, must not therefore be overlooked. There too
the mutual feasting of Christ with the soul which opens

to Him, and of the soul with Him, is all set forth. There too the bride prepares a feast for her Beloved: 'Let my Beloved come into his garden, and eat his pleasant fruits' (iv. 16); but He had first prepared one for her: 'I sat down under his shadow with great delight, and his fruit was sweet to my taste' (ii. 3). Few, I suppose, would be disposed to deny a mystical significance to that meal after the Resurrection on the shores of the Sea of Tiberias, recorded with so much emphasis by the beloved disciple (John xxi. 9-13); which wonderfully fulfils the same conditions, being made up of what the disciples bring and what Christ brings. This mutual feasting of Christ with his people, and of his people with Him, finds in this present life its culminating fulfilment in the Holy Eucharist; which yet is but an initial fulfilment; it will only find its exhaustive accomplishment in the marriage supper of the Lamb (Rev. xix. 7-9; Mark xiv. 25).

Ver. 21. '*To him that overcometh will I grant to sit with Me in my throne.*'—A magnificent variation of Christ's words spoken in the days of his flesh: 'The glory which Thou gavest Me, I have given them. . . . Father, I will that they also whom Thou hast given Me, be with Me where I am' (John xvii. 22, 24); as also of the words of St. Paul, 'If we suffer with Him, we shall also reign with Him' (2 Tim. ii. 12). Wonderful indeed is this promise, which, being the last and the crowning, is also the highest and most glorious of all. Step by step they have advanced, till a height is reached than which no higher can be conceived. It seemed much to promise the Apostles themselves that they should sit on thrones, judging the twelve tribes of Israel (Matt. xix. 28); but here is promised to every believer something more than was there promised to the elect Twelve. And more wonderful still, if we con-

sider to whom this promise is here addressed. He whom
Christ threatened just now to reject with loathing out
of his mouth, is offered a place with Him on his throne.
But indeed so it is; the highest place is within reach of
the lowest; the faintest spark of grace may be fanned into
the mightiest flame of divine love. It will be observed
that the image here is not that of sitting upon seats on
the right hand or on the left of Christ's throne (1 Kin. ii.
19), but of sharing that throne itself. To understand this,
we must keep in mind the fact, that the Eastern throne is
much ampler and broader than ours; rather a sofa than
a chair; so that there would be room upon it for other
persons, besides him who occupied as of right the central
position there (Matt. xx. 21). Witsius : 'Erudite obser-
vavit Ludovicus de Dieu thronum regis apud orientales
amplum et latum esse, lecticæ instar, fulcris aliquantulum
supra terram evectum, ac tapetibus ornatum, adeo ut
præter sedem regi propriam, alii quoque quos honore
afficere cupit rex, in eodem throno sedes habere queant.'

'*Even as I also overcame, and am set down with my
Father in his throne.*'—The Son is σύνθρονος with the
Father (Wisd. ix. 4; cf. Rev. xxii. 1, 'the throne of God and
the Lamb'); as the early Church writers loved to express
it, with a word employed already in the heathen mythology, perhaps borrowed from it (see Suicer, *Thes.* s. v.);
his faithful people shall be πάρεδροι with Him. These
words, '*I overcame*,' remind us of other words spoken by
the Lord while as yet He had not so visibly overcome as
now: 'Be of good cheer, I have overcome the world'
(John xvi. 33); and the manner in which the overcoming
of the world and the sitting down with his Father in his
throne are brought together here, puts this passage in
close connexion with Phil. ii. 9: '*Wherefore* God also

hath highly exalted Him, and given Him a name which is above every name;' cf. Heb. i. 3.—On this ' *my throne*,' and ' *my Father's throne*,' Mede says well (*Works*, p. 905): ' Here are two thrones mentioned. *My throne*, saith Christ; this is the condition of glorified saints who sit with Christ in his throne; but *my Father's* (*i.e.* God's) *throne* is the power of Divine majesty; on this throne none may sit but God, and the God-man Jesus Christ. To be installed in God's throne, to sit at God's right hand, is to have a god-like royalty, such as his Father hath, a royalty altogether incommunicable, whereof no creature is capable.'

Ver. 22. ' *He that hath an ear, let him hear what the Spirit saith unto the Churches.*'—Compare ii. 7.

A few words in conclusion upon the order in which the promises of the seven Epistles succeed one another. It is impossible not to acknowledge such an order here,—an order parallel to that of the unfolding of the kingdom of God from its first beginnings on earth to its glorious consummation in heaven. Thus the promise of Christ to the faithful at Ephesus is, ' *To him that overcometh will I give to eat of the tree of life which is in the Paradise of my God* ' (ii. 7) ; thus taking us back to Genesis i. ii. But sin presently entered into Paradise, and death, the seal and witness of sin (Gen. iii. 19); while yet for the faithful at Smyrna,—and the promise that is good for them is good for the faithful everywhere,—this curse of death is lightened. It shall be to them but the gate of immortality, for ' *he that overcometh shall not be hurt of the second death* ' (ii. 11). The next promise, that to the faithful at Pergamum, brings us to the Mosaic period, to the Church in the wilderness: ' *To him that overcometh will I give to eat of the hidden manna'* (ii. 17); and if the interpretation of the '*white stone*' which has been ventured here is the right one, that promise will also fall in perfectly with the wilderness period and the institution of the high-priesthood, which at that period found place. In the fourth, that namely to Thyatira, we have reached the full and final consummation, in type and prophetic outline, of the kingdom, the period of David and Solomon,—the triumph over the nations, the Church sharing in the royalties of her King (ii. 26, 27). Every reader will recognize this as a characteristic feature of those reigns (2 Sam. viii. 1-13; x. 19; xii. 29, 30; 1 Chron. xvii. 1-13).

Here there is a pause; and with this consummation reached, than which in type and prophecy there can be nothing higher, a new series begins; the heptad falling, as is so constantly the case, into two groups; either of three and four, as in the Lord's Prayer, or of four and three, as in the parables of Mt. xiii., and as here. And now the scenery, if I may use the word, shifts and changes; it is not any longer of earth, but of heaven. The kingdom, not of David, but of David's greater Son, has come; all his foes are under his feet; his Church is not any longer contemplated as militant, but triumphant; and in the succession of the three concluding promises we learn that even for the Church triumphant there are steps and advances from glory to glory. Thus, in the promise addressed to the Angel of Sardis, we have the blessings of the judgment-day, the name found written in the book of life, Christ's confession of his own before his Father, the vesture of light and immortality, in other words, the glorified body which it shall be then given to the saints to wear (iii. 5). This, however, is a personal, a solitary benefit, belonging to each of them alone; not so the next. In the promise

made to the faithful at Philadelphia, it is declared that as
many as overcome shall have right to enter by the gates
into the heavenly City, where City and Temple are one,
shall be themselves avouched members of that heavenly
πολιτεία, and shall have their place in it for evermore
(iii. 12). And then, it having thus been declared what
they have in themselves, namely, the glorified body, and
what they have in and with the company of the redeemed,
the citizenship of the heavenly Jerusalem, it is, last of all,
in the concluding words to the Angel of Laodicea, declared
what they possess with God and with Christ; that it shall
be granted to them to sit down with Christ on his throne,
as He has sat down with his Father in his Father's throne
(iii. 21). There can be nothing behind and beyond this;
and with this therefore is the close; in Herder's words,
' Die Kränze werden immer höher und schöner ; hier *hängt*
der höchste und schönste.' It is here, to compare divine
things with human, as in the *Paradiso* of Dante. There,
too, there are different circles of light around the throne,
each, as it is nearer to the throne, of an intenser brightness than that beyond it and more remote, till at last,
when all the others have been passed, the throne itself is
reached, and the very Presence of Him who sits upon the
throne, and from whom all this light and all this glory
flows.[1]

---

[1] Tertullian gathers up the promises in a few pregnant words
(*Scorp.* 12) : ' Victori cuique promittit nunc arborem vitæ, et mortis
veniam secundæ ; nunc latens manna cum calculo candido et nomine
ignoto ; nunc ferreæ virgæ potestatem et stellæ matutinæ claritatem ;
nunc albam vestiri, nec deleri de libro vitæ, et columnam fieri in
Dei templo in nomine Dei et Domini. et Jerusalem cælestis inscripta,
nunc residere cum Domino in throno ejus, quod aliquando Zebedæi
filiis negabatur ' (Mt. xx. 23).

EXCURSUS

'Mali moris est sensum in S. Scripturam inferre, non efferre.'

THE large space which any adequate treatment of the
historico-prophetical interpretation of these Epistles would
demand has made it necessary to withdraw the consideration of this subject from the Exposition itself; and I have
therefore reserved this for an *Excursus* at the end of the
volume, which I proceed to devote to it alone.

It is, doubtless, familiar to as many as have at all
studied the history of the exposition of these seven
Epistles, that a large body of interpreters, several of these
distinguished for their piety and their learning, have not
been content to take them merely for what they seem to
announce themselves to be, namely, seven 'words' of
instruction, warning, consolation, addressed by the great
ascended Shepherd and Bishop of souls to seven Churches
of Asia; but have loudly proclaimed that these Epistles
have a much wider outlook than this, that they contain
far deeper mysteries than any which such an estimate
of them as this would imply. Those who affirm this, have
doubtless a full right to be heard. In the Scripture are
such depths of meaning, so much remains to be discovered
in them, in addition to all which has already been discovered, their wealth is so inexhaustible, that any one,

whose incapacity is not patent, may rightly claim from us a patient and attentive hearing, when he offers to lead us into these depths, to show us that, where *we* thought there were but golden harvests, the food of all, waving upon the surface, there are also veins of richest metal below, the wealth of those who will be at the pains to dig for and search out these hid treasures. And yet, at the same time, before we admit any such discoveries of treasures hid in the field of Scripture, it will be good always to remember, that there is a temptation to make Scripture mean *more* than in the intention of the Author of it, the Holy Ghost, it does mean, as well as a temptation to make it mean *less*; and that we are bound by equally solemn obligations not to thrust on it something of ours, as not to subtract from it anything of its own (Rev. xxii. 18, 19); the interpretation *in excess* proving often nearly, or quite, as mischievous as that *in defect*; while yet the temptations to it are not few, though it would lead us too far from our immediate theme, if we attempted to trace them here.

But what, it may be asked, is this wider horizon, which, if we would meet the Divine intention, it is declared to us we should ascribe to these Epistles, and what the deeper mysteries which they contain? Before I attempt to answer this, let me first, by way of clearing the ground, set down those points on which *all* are agreed, upon which there is no dispute; and then secondly, that which, if not all, yet the greater number of competent judges would admit; that so, this done, and these matters of universal or general agreement separated off, we may more clearly present to ourselves what are the precise points on which the controversy turns.

All, then, are agreed that these seven Epistles, however primarily addressed to these seven Churches of Asia, were also written for the edification of the Universal Church; in the same way, that is, as St. Paul's Epistle to the Romans, or to Timothy, or St. James' to the Dispersion, were written with this intention. The warnings, the incentives, the promises, the consolations, and, generally, the whole instruction in righteousness in these contained, are for every one in all times, so far as they may meet the several cases and conditions of men; what Christ says to those here addressed He says to all in similar conditions. Thus far there can be no question. 'All Scripture,' and therefore this Scripture, was 'written for our learning.'

It may fail to meet with acceptance as universal, yet will, I suppose, be further admitted by many thoughtful students of God's Word, probably by most who have entered into the mystery of the heptad in Scripture (see p. 59), that these seven Churches of Asia are not an accidental aggregation, which might just as fitly have been eight, or six, or any other number. They will acknowledge, on the contrary, a fitness in this number, and that these seven do in some sort represent the Universal Church; that we have a right to contemplate them as offering to us the leading aspects, moral and spiritual, which Churches gathered in the name of Christ out of the world will assume. No one, of course, affirming this, would mean that they could be contemplated as exhaustive of these aspects; for the infinite depth and richness of that new life which Christ brought into the world testifies itself in nothing more than in this, the rich variety of forms which this new life of his, embodying itself in the lives of men, will assume, the very malformations themselves witnessing in their own way for the fulness of this life. But

though not exhaustive (for what could be this ?), they give
us on a smaller scale, ὡς ἐν τύπῳ, the grander and more
recurring features of that life; are not fragmentary, for-
tuitously strung together; but have a completeness, a
many-sidedness; being, as we may well believe, selected
on this very account; here, perhaps, being the reason why
Philadelphia is included and Miletus passed by; Thyatira, outwardly so insignificant, chosen, when one might
have beforehand far sooner expected Magnesia or Tralles.
Thus what notable contrasts do these seven offer,—a Church
face to face with danger and death (Smyrna), and a Church
at ease, settling down upon its lees (Sardis); a Church
with abundant means and loud profession, yet doing little
or nothing for the furtherance of the truth (Laodicea),
and a Church with little strength and small opportunities,
yet accomplishing a mighty work for Christ (Philadelphia);
a Church intolerant of doctrinal error, yet too much
lacking that love towards its Lord for which nothing else
is a substitute (Ephesus); and over against this a Church
not careful nor zealous, as it ought to be, for doctrinal
purity, but diligent in works and ministries of love
(Thyatira); or, to review these same Churches from
another point of view, a Church in conflict with heathen
libertinism, the sinful freedom of the flesh (Ephesus), and
a Church or Churches in conflict with Jewish superstition,
the sinful bondage of the spirit (Pergamum, Philadelphia);
or, for the indolence of man a more perilous case than
either, Churches with no vigorous forms of opposition to
the truth in the midst of them, to brace their energies and
to cause them, in the act of defending the imperilled
truth, to know it better and to love it more (Sardis,
Laodicea).   That these Churches are more or less *representative* Churches, having been selected because they are

so ; that they form a complex within and among themselves, mutually fulfilling and completing one another;
that the great Head of the Church contemplates them for
the time being as symbolic of his Universal Church,
implying as much in that mystic seven, and giving many
other indications of the same,—this also will be accepted,
if not by all, yet by many.

But the Periodists, as they have been called, the upholders of what may be fitly termed the historico-prophetical scheme of interpretation, are by no means satisfied with these admissions.   They demand that we should
recognize in these Epistles very much more than this.
They affirm that we have in them, besides counsels to the
Churches named in each, a prophetic outline of seven successive *periods* of the Church's history ; dividing, as they
do, into those seven portions the whole time intervening
between Christ's Ascension and his return in glory.   As
in making a statement for others, above all for those from
whom one is about to dissent, it is always fairest, or, at
all events, most satisfactory, to cite their own words, I
will here quote two passages, one from Joseph Mede, another from Vitringa, in which these severally set forth that
historico-prophetical scheme ; which they both favoured
and upheld ; and certainly the statement of the case could
scarcely be in discreeter or in abler hands.   The modesty
with which the former propounds it is in striking contrast with the arrogant confidence of some others, who
were well nigh disposed to make here a new article of
faith, and the acceptance or rejection of this interpretation
a test of orthodoxy.   These are Mede's words ; they occur
in one of his sermons (*Works,* 1672, p. 296) : ' It belongs
not much to our purpose to inquire whether those seven
Epistles concern historically and literally only the Churches

here named, or whether they were intended for types or
ages of the Church afterwards to come. It shall be
sufficient to say, that if we consider their number, being
seven (which is a number of revolution of times, and
therefore in this Book the seals, trumpets, and vials also
are seven); or if we consider the choice of the Holy
Ghost, in that He taketh neither all, no, nor the most
famous Churches then in the world, as Antioch, Alexandria, Rome, and many other, and such, no doubt, as
had need of instruction as well as those here named; if
these things be well considered, it will seem that these
seven Churches, besides their literal respect, were intended
(and it may be chiefly) to be as patterns and types of the
several ages of the Catholic Church from the beginning
thereof unto the end of the world; that so these seven
Churches should prophetically sample unto us a sevenfold
temper and constitution of the whole Church according
to the several ages thereof, answering the pattern of the
Churches named here;' compare some other words of his
to the same effect, p. 905. Vitringa (*Anacrisis Apoca-
lypsios*, p. 32), moving on the same lines, expresses himself thus: 'Omnino igitur existimo Spiritum S. sub typo
et emblemate septem Ecclesiarum Asiæ nobis mystice
et prophetice voluisse depingere septem variantes status
Ecclesiæ Christianæ, quibus successive conspiceretur usque
ad adventum Domini et omnium rerum finem, phrasibus
desumptis a nominibus, conditione et attributis ipsarum
illarum Ecclesiarum Asiæ nobiliorum, quæ ad hunc usum
et scopum sapienter adhibuit; sic tamen ut ipsæ illæ
Ecclesiæ Asianæ simul in hoc speculo se ipsas videre,
suasque tam virtutes quam vitia ex illis epistolis cogno-
scere, et quæ in iis sunt admonitiones et exhortationes ad
se ipsas quoque referre et applicare possent: quippe quod

summa suadet jubetque ratio. Quod enim alterius rei typum et figuram sustinebit symbolicam, ita affectum esse oportet ut attributa subjecti analogi in ipsâ illâ re figurante omnium primo demonstrari possint.'

I have cited these two writers of a later age; but the scheme itself, in one shape or another, may be traced to a much earlier date; though, indeed, it is very far from being as old as some of its favourers would have us to believe, claiming, as not seldom they do, several of the early Fathers, as early at least as Augustine and Chrysostom, for the first authors and upholders of it. There is no warrant for this. No passage has been quoted, and I am convinced none could be quoted, bearing out this claim of theirs. In an eager debate carried on for the larger part of a century, the opponents of this interpretation repeatedly challenged the advocates to bring forward a single quotation from one Father, Greek or Latin, in its support. None such was ever produced; so that Witsius has perfect right when he affirms, 'Nullibi id dicunt [antiqui] quod viri isti eruditi volunt, quibuscum hæc nobis instituta disputatio est; nimirum proprie, literaliter atque ex intentione Spiritûs Sancti verbis harum Epistolarum delineari, non quod Johannis tempore in Asiæ Ecclesiis agebatur, sed quod in universali Ecclesiâ septem temporum periodis ordine succedentibus futurum erat. Id non liquet antiquorum ulli vel in mentem venisse.' This quotation is from his essay, *De Septem Eccles. Apocalyp. Sensu Historico an Prophetico* (*Opp.* vol. i. pp. 640–741), remarkable for the moderation of its tone and the fairness with which all that can be said on the other side is weighed. It is quite true that Augustine, with others before and after him, acknowledged that symbolic representative character of these Epistles, whereof I just now spoke. Thus Andreas, the earliest commentator on the Apocalypse whose work has reached us, gives this as the reason why the Lord, through St. John, addressed Himself exactly to seven Churches; διὰ τοῦ ἑβδοματικοῦ ἀριθμοῦ τὸ μυστικὸν τῶν ἀπανταχῆ ἐκκλησιῶν σημαίνων. Augustine (De Civ. Dei, xvii. 4), explaining the Canticle of Hannah, in which it is said, 'The barren hath born seven' (1 Sam. ii. 5), goes on to say, 'Hîc totum quod prophetabatur eluxit agnoscentibus numerum septenarium quo est universa Ecclesiæ significata perfectio. Propter quod et Johannes Apostolus ad septem scribit Ecclesias, eo modo se ostendens ad unius plenitudinem scribere;' or, as the last clause of a similar statement reads elsewhere (Exp. in Gal. ii. 7): 'quæ [Ecclesiæ] utique universalis Ecclesiæ personam gerunt;' cf. Ep. xlix. § 2. And Gregory the Great almost word for word (Moral. xvii. 27): 'Unde et septem Ecclesiis scribit Johannes Apostolus, ut unam Catholicam, septiformis gratiæ plenam Spiritu designaret;' cf. Præf. c. 8. But to accept them as historico-prophetical is quite a different matter, and of any allowance of this there is no vestige among them; no evidence that it had ever so much as come into their minds.

Still the notion itself undoubtedly dates back to a period anterior to the Reformation. The Fratres Spiri-tuales, or more rigid Franciscans, who refused the mitiga-tions of the severity of St. Francis' rule, in which the majority of his followers allowed themselves, and who on this account separated themselves from their laxer brethren, and from the Church which sanctioned such relaxations, are the first among whom this scheme of interpretation assumed any prominence. It is familiar to as many as are at all acquainted with this wonderful body of men, what an important part the distribution of the

Church's history into seven ages played in their theology, and what weapons they contrived to find in this armoury for the assault of the dominant Church and hierarchy of Rome. Looking everywhere in Scripture for traces of these seven times, it is not strange that they should have found such in these seven Epistles. At the time of the first rise of these, one but recently dead, high in reputation for sanctity throughout the Church, himself regarded as little less of an apocalyptic seer, I mean the Abbot Joachim of Floris (he died in 1202), had already shown the way in this interpretation;[1] and the Spiritualist Brethren did not fail to adjust the seven ages of the Church and the seven Epistles prophetic of them, so that these should prophesy all good of themselves, and all evil of Rome.

It is evident that when the scheme was adopted two or three centuries later by theologians of the Reformed Church, it would require readjustment and redistribution throughout, and this at once chronological and dogmatic. Such readjustment it was not difficult to effect. The whole thing was a subjective fancy of men's minds, not an objective truth of God's Word, and would therefore oppose no serious resistance. It was easy to give it whatever new shape was required by the new conditions under which it should now appear. After the Reformation, the first in whom I meet this interpretation of the Epistles to the seven Churches as predictive of the seven ages of the Church and foreshadowing their condition, is an English divine, Thomas Brightman (b. 1557, d. 1607). I feel quite sure that it had earlier advocates, but I have not traced it

---

[1] For an account of Joachim of Floris' seven ages, see Hahn, *Gesch. d. Ketzer im Mittelalter*, vol. iii. p. 112; Engelhardt, *Kirch. Gesch. Abhandlungen*, p. 107. For English readers there is an excellent summary of what they taught and did in Elliot's *Apocalypse*.

higher up. Brightman belonged to the Puritan school of divines, as they existed within the bosom of the Anglican Church, and though in opposition to its spirit, not as yet visibly separated from it. At the same time his work, *Apocalypsis Apocalypseos*, 1612, avouches him a man of no ordinary gifts, and of warm and earnest piety; so that Marckius has perfect right when he says of it, 'eruditionem et pietatem non vulgarem spirat.' But although he, and Joseph Mede, as we have seen (he died in 1638), and Henry More,[1] lent to this suggestion the authority of their names, it never seems to have struck any vigorous root in England, nor to have awakened interest enough to make men very earnest either in its assertion or its denial. It was in the Reformed Churches of Holland and Germany, but predominantly in the former, that this periodic interpretation first assumed any prominence or importance. There indeed, during the middle and latter part of the seventeenth century and beginning of the eighteenth, it was debated with animation, and often with something more than animation. The very able *Præfatio de Septem Novi Testamenti Periodis*, which Marckius has prefixed to his *Commentary on the Apocalypse*, 1699, shows how angry the disputants could be on one side and the other.

The theologian who by his adoption of the historico-prophetical interpretation gave an importance to it, and procured for it an acceptance, which in any other way it would scarcely have obtained, was Cocceius (b. 1603, d. 1669). It is indeed with him only part of a larger whole—one among many testimonies for a divinely-

---

[1] *Prophetical Exposition of the Seven Epistles sent to the Seven Churches in Asia from Him that is, and was, and is to come,—Theological Works*, London, 1708, pp. 719-764; first published in 1669.

intended division into seven periods of the whole history of
the Church. This division found favour with many ; but
in no one does it recur with so great a frequency, exercise
so powerful an influence on his interpretation of Scripture,
constitute so vital a portion of his theology, as in him.   I
am not aware whether Cocceius at any time made himself
at all felt in England ; his reputation, if it ever reached us
here, has now quite passed away ; but his influence for good
on the Protestant communities of Holland and also of Germany, as a promoter of a Biblical in place of a scholastical
theology, leading as he did those Churches from the arid
wastes of a new scholasticism to the living fountains of
the Word of God, was immense, and survives to the present hour.   But this distribution of the Church's history
into periods of seven, seven before Christ's coming, and
seven after, is a sort of ' fixed idea' with him.   It is indeed his desire to make Scripture the rule in everything,
and to find all that concerns the spiritual life and development of man cast in a scriptural framework, this desire
' in season and out of season,' which has led him astray.
And thus it is that he finds, or where he does not find he
makes, everywhere in Scripture a prophecy of these periods ;
in the seven days of creation, in the seven beatitudes, in
the seven petitions of the Lord's Prayer, in the seven
parables of Matthew xiii. ; not seldom forcing into artificial
arrangement by sevens, Scriptures which yield themselves
not naturally and of their own accord, but only under
violent pressure and constraint, to any articulation of the
kind, as Hannah's Prayer, the Song of Moses, of Deborah,
the Song of Songs, not a few of the Psalms, and, I dare
say, much else in Scripture besides.[1]

---

[1] Let me rescue from vast unread folios of his, as not very alien
to the matter we have in hand, one noble passage, and he abounds

But despite of all the excesses of his interpretation, Cocceius never refused to these Epistles a true historical foundation. The historico-prophetic meaning was no doubt far the most precious in his eyes; and it had good right so to be, if only it had been designed by the Spirit; but he did not deny that there had been actual Churches at Ephesus, Smyrna, and the rest, to which these several Epistles were primarily addressed, and to whose moral and spiritual condition they, at the time they were written, fitted. Others, however, have proceeded to far more serious lengths. They have refused to see any reference whatever to Churches actually, at the time when this vision was seen, subsisting in these cities of Asia, and to their spiritual condition. These they regard merely as the vehicles for the conveyance of the prophecy; the seven Epistles not in the least expressing, except, it might be, here and there by accidental and undesigned coincidence, the actual condition of these seven Churches. Despite of anything which these Epistles may seem to affirm to the contrary, the Church of Ephesus, according to their view, may at this time have been tolerant of false teachers, and Thyatira intolerant; Philadelphia may have been slack in

---

in such, on the analogy of faith, and the help which the different portions of Scripture mutually afford to the right understanding of one another. It is from the *Præfatio ad Comm. in Proph. Min.*, *Opp.* tom. v., without pagination: 'Habet enim divina institutio Scripturæ instar augusti palatii, in quo ordine consideant innumeri seniores, qui viritim admissum novum discipulum erudiant, a collegis suis dicta confirment, roborent, explicent, illustrent, nunc fusius dicta contrahant, nunc contractiora diffundant et diducant, generalius dicta distinguant, distincta generatim innuant, regulas exemplis fulciant, exempla in regulis judicent, ita ut omnium de eâdem re agentium dictorum is sensus accipi debeat, qui est ullius, et qui nulli refragetur, et plena institutio ea demum censeri quæ omnium virorum Dei sit vox, συμφωνία, et ὁμόνοια.'

deeds of faith and love, and Laodicea fervent in spirit, and
Sardis with not a few only, but many names, that had not
defiled their garments. No Antipas need have actually
resisted to blood at Pergamum; there may have been no
tribulation of ten days imminent upon Smyrna.[1]

This extravagance may be dismissed in a few words.
Origen is justly condemned, that, advancing a step beyond
other allegorists, who *slighted* the facts of the Old Testament history for the sake of mystical meanings which they
believed to lie behind them, he denied, concerning many
events recorded there as historical, that they actually hap-
pened at all; rearing the superstructure of his mystical
meaning, not on the establishment of the literal sense, but
on its ruins. Every reverent student of the Word of God
must feel that so he often lets go a substance in snatching
at a shadow, that shadow itself really eluding his grasp
after all. He who in this sense assails the strong historic
substructures of Scripture, may not know all which he is
doing; but he is indeed doing his best, or his worst rather,
to turn the glorious superstructure built on these, which,
though resting on earth, pierces heaven, into a mere sky-
pageant painted on the air, a cloud palace waiting to be
shifted and changed by every breath of the caprice of man,
and at length fading and melting into common air. It
was not without reason that Augustine, himself not wholly
to be acquitted of excesses in this direction, did yet urge
so strongly the necessity of maintaining, before and above
all, the historic letter of the Scripture, whatever else to
this might be superadded (*Serm.* ii. 6): 'Ante omnia,
fratres, hoc in nomine Domini et admonemus quantum

---

[1] Floerke, in an able work on the Millennium, *Lehre vom tausend-
jährigen Reiche*, Marburg, 1859, is the latest denier *in toto* of an
historical element in these Epistles; see p. 59, sqq.

possumus et præcipimus, ut quando auditis exponi sacramentum Scripturæ narrantis quæ gesta sunt, prius illud quod lectum est credatur sic gestum quomodo lectum est, ne subtracto fundamento rei gestæ, quasi in aëre quæratis ædificare.' Similar warnings in his writings continually recur. Who indeed could remain confident that anything presented in Scripture as history, with all apparent notes of history about it, was yet history at all, and not something wholly different,—parable, or allegory, or prophecy, —if these Epistles, which St. John is bidden to send to the seven Churches in Asia, which profess to enter minutely into their spiritual condition, were yet never sent to them at all, had no relation whatever to them, no more, I mean, than to any other portion of the universal Church?

But leaving these, and addressing ourselves only to the more moderate upholders of the periodic scheme of interpretation, to those, namely, who admit a literal and present sense, while they superinduce upon it a prophetical and future, we ask, what slightest hint or intimation does the Spirit of God give that we have here to do with the great successive acts and epochs of the kingdom of God in the course of its gradual evolution here upon earth? Where are the finger-posts pointing this way? What is there, for instance, of chronological succession? Does not everything, on the contrary, indicate *simultaneity*, and not *succession*? The seven candlesticks are seen at the same instant; the seven Churches named in the same breath. How different is it where succession *in time* is really intended; how impossible then not to perceive it; see, for instance, Dan. ii. 32, 33, 39, 40; vii. 6, 7, 9. On this matter Marckius says very well (*Præf.* § 52): ' Attamen ut Ecclesias has agnoscamus pro typicis, sive significantibus ex Dei intentione alias Ecclesias aliorum locorum et temporum, oportet nos a Deo doceri. Typos enim, non magis quam allegorias, pro lubitu nostro in Scripturam inferre licet, cum non sit ἰδίας ἐπιλύσεως, propriæ inter-pretationis, 2 Pet. i. 20. Non sufficit ad typum consti-tuendum nuda convenientia, quæ inter res, personas, et eventus plurimos a nobis observari potest, sed oportet nobis amplius constet de divino consilio quo rem similem servire voluerit alteri præsignificandæ, cogitationibusque nostris illuc ducendis.'

But all such objections, with all those others which it would only be too easy to make, might indeed be set aside or overborne, if any marvellous coincidence between these Epistles and the after course of the Church's development could be made out; if history set its seal to these, and attested that they were prophecy indeed; for when a key fits perfectly well the wards of a very complicated lock, and opens it without an effort, it is difficult not to believe that they were made for one another. But there is no such accurate correspondence here; as is abundantly tes-tified by the fact that the interpreters of the historico-prophetical school, besides their controversy with those who deny *in toto* what they affirm, have also an intestine strife among themselves. Each one has his own solution of the enigma, his own distribution of the several epochs; or, if this is too much to affirm, there is, at any rate, nothing approaching to a general *consensus* among them. Take, for instance, the distribution of Vitringa. For him Ephesus represents the condition of the Church from the day of Pentecost to the outbreak of the Decian persecu-tion; Smyrna, from the Decian persecution to that of Diocletian, both inclusive; Pergamum, from the time of Constantine until the close of the seventh century; Thya-tira, the Church in its mission to the nations during the

first half of the Middle Ages; Sardis, from the close of
the twelfth century to the Reformation ; Philadelphia, the
first century of the Reformation ; Laodicea, the Reformed
Church at the time when he was writing. Lange, *Das
apostolische Zeitalter*, vol. ii. p. 472, has a nearly similar
distribution.

There are two or three fortunate coincidences here between the assumed prophecy and the fact; without such
indeed the whole notion must have been abandoned long
ago as hopeless; such coincidences could scarcely have
been avoided. Smyrna, for instance, represents excellently well the *Ecclesia pressa* in its two last and most
terrible struggles with heathen Rome ; so too for such
Protestant expositors as see the Papacy in the scarlet
woman of Babylon, the Jezebel of Thyatira appears exactly
at the right time, coincides with the Papacy at its height,
yet at the same time with judgment at the door in the
great revolt which was even then preparing. But I would
ask any one fairly grounded in the subject whether there
is any true *articulation* of Church history in the distribution above made ? any general felicity of correspondence
between what are averred to be the prophetic outlines and
the historic realities adduced as fulfilling them ? Take,
for instance, Philadelphia, as representing the Reformation
period. The praise bestowed on the Philadelphian Angel
may be said to culminate in these words, ' *Behold, I have
set before thee an open door, and no man can shut it* '
(iii. 8). Was this the fact? Can anything, on the contrary, have been more mournful than the way in which,
when '*an open door*' was set before the Reformers, they
suffered it to so great an extent to be closed on them
again ? There was a time, some five and twenty or thirty
years after Luther had begun to preach, when Austria

and Bavaria and Styria and Poland, and, in good part, France, had all been won for the Reformation. Thirty years more had not elapsed when they all were lost again; and it was confined within the far narrower limits which it occupies at the present day (see Ranke, *History of the Popes in the Sixteenth and Seventeenth Centuries*)—this door, once open, having been closed mainly through the guilt of those contests, very far from *Philadelphian* (for the names too have been pressed into service), among the Reformers themselves.

Then, again, other interpreters, as I have already observed, distribute the epochs according to schemes altogether diverse from this. Thus it is far more common among the Protestant theologians of the seventeenth century to apportion, not five Churches, but only the first four, to the pre-Reformation period; to claim as Brightman does, Philadelphia, with all its graces, for themselves, and, as must necessarily follow, to contemplate Sardis as representing the Church of the actual Reformation. Certainly the Reformation had blots and blemishes enough; but its faults were those of zeal and passion; they had nothing in common with that hypocritical form of godliness, that death under shows of life, imputed to Sardis; and any dutiful child of the Reformation, who at all felt the immense debt of gratitude which he and the whole Church owed to it, notwithstanding all its excesses and all its shortcomings, might reasonably hesitate long as to the accuracy of a scheme which should brand it with this dishonour. See Marckius, *Præf.* § 55; and on the other hand as saying, and saying well, whatever there is to be said in support of the historico-prophetical school in this particular aspect, see Henry More, at p. 756 sqq., in his treatise already referred to.

S

Much more might be urged on the arbitrary artificial character of all the attempted adaptations of Church history to these Epistles; but this Essay has already run to a greater length than I intended; and indeed it is not needful to say more. Where there were no preëstablished harmonies in the Divine intention between the one and the other, as I am persuaded that here there were none, it could not have been otherwise. The multitude of dissertations, essays, books, which have been, and are still being written, in support of this scheme of interpretation, must remain a singular monument of wasted ingenuity and misapplied toil; and, in their entire failure to prove their point, of the disappointment which must result from a futile looking into Scripture for that which is not to be found there,— from an attempt to draw out from it that which he who draws out must first himself have put in. Men will never in this way make Scripture richer. They will have made it much poorer for themselves, if they nourish themselves from it with the fancies of men, their own fancies or those of others, instead of with the truths of God.

PRINTED BY
SPOTTISWOODE AND CO., NEW-STREET SQUARE
LONDON

OTHER FINE VOLUMES AVAILABLE

1978 SPRING TITLES

Author	Title	Retail
Schilder, Klass	THE TRILOGY (three volumes)	39.95
Kellogg, Samuel H.	THE BOOK OF LEVITICUS	15.50
Pusey, Edward B.	DANIEL THE PROPHET	16.50
Blaikie, William G.	THE BOOK OF JOSHUA	11.50
Liddon, Henry P.	THE FIRST EPISTLE TO TIMOTHY	4.95
Mayor, Joseph B.	THE EPISTLE OF ST. JUDE & THE SECOND EPISTLE OF PETER	12.50
Blaikie, William G.	THE FIRST BOOK OF SAMUEL	10.95
Blaikie, William G.	THE SECOND BOOK OF SAMUEL	10.95
Liddon, Henry P.	THE DIVINITY OF OUR LORD	16.95
Gibson, Edgar	THE BOOK OF JOB	7.95

1978 SUMMER TITLES

Author	Title	Retail
Delitzsch, Franz	COMMENTARY ON THE EPISTLE TO THE HEBREWS (two volumes)	24.95
Trench, Richard C.	COMMENTARY ON THE EPISTLES TO THE SEVEN CHURCHES	6.95
Oehler, Gustave	THEOLOGY OF THE OLD TESTAMENT	16.50
Ramsay, William M.	HISTORICAL COMMENTARY ON THE EPISTLE TO THE GALATIANS	12.95
Lillie, John	LECTURES ON THE FIRST AND SECOND EPISTLES OF PETER	14.95

1978 FALL TITLES

Author	Title	Retail
Shedd, William G.T.	HISTORY OF CHRISTIAN DOCTRINE (two volumes)	24.95
Manton, Thomas	AN EXPOSITION OF THE EPISTLE OF JUDE	9.50
Westcott, Brooke F.	ST. PAUL'S EPISTLE TO THE EPHESIANS	7.95
Bernard, Thomas	THE PROGRESS OF DOCTRINE IN THE NEW TESTAMENT	7.50
Rackham, Richard B.	THE ACTS OF THE APOSTLES	16.95
Brown, John	THE INTERCESSORY PRAYER OF OUR LORD JESUS CHRIST	8.95
Brown, John	THE RESURRECTION OF LIFE	10.95
Delitzsch, Franz	A NEW COMMENTARY ON GENESIS (two volumes)	21.95

1977 FALL TITLES

Author	Title	Retail
Armitage, Thomas	A HISTORY OF THE BAPTISTS (two volumes)	24.95
Fairweather, William	BACKGROUND OF THE GOSPELS	12.50
Fairweather, William	BACKGROUND OF THE EPISTLES	11.50
Green, William H.	THE ARGUMENT OF THE BOOK OF JOB UNFOLDED	8.95
Johnstone, Robert	LECTURES ON THE EPISTLE OF JAMES	11.50
Johnstone, Robert	LECTURES ON THE BOOK OF PHILIPPIANS	13.50
Lindsay, Thomas M.	THE CHURCH AND THE MINISTRY IN THE EARLY CENTURIES	9.95
Mayor, Joseph B.	THE EPISTLE OF ST. JAMES	15.95
Murphy, James	A CRITICAL & EXEGETICAL COMMENTARY ON PSALMS	17.95
Orelli, Hans C. von	THE TWELVE MINOR PROPHETS	10.95
Orelli, Hans C. von	THE PROPHECIES OF JEREMIAH	10.95
Zahn, Theodor	INTRODUCTION TO THE NEW TESTAMENT (three volumes)	39.95

FEATURE TITLES

Author	Title	Retail
Barber, Cyril J.	THE MINISTER'S LIBRARY (expanded edition)	12.95
Barber, Cyril J.	SUPPLEMENT NO. 1 to THE MINISTER'S LIBRARY	2.95

Klock & Klock Christian Publishers
2527 GIRARD AVE. N.
MINNEAPOLIS, MINNESOTA 55411